CAV WITH SMARTPHONE$

how evolution shaped history and finance.

CAVEMEN WITH SMARTPHONE$

how evolution shaped history and finance.

RICHARD AMADOR

Published by Inktelligence

Second edition

ISBN: 978-1-9160088-0-9

Cover design & interior formatting:

Mark Thomas / Coverness.com

Get exclusive, never-before-published content when you sign up for my reader's group (**www.richardamador.com/cwssubscribe**)

TABLE OF CONTENTS

PREFACE

Before we begin our tale, I would like you to pick up the nearest pencil lying haphazardly on your desk and look at it. For the vast majority in my audience, a pencil would seem to be a fairly innocuous object. Yet, the truth is, it's a remarkable item.

To borrow from a Leonard Read analogy[01] [1], there is not a person alive today, or at any period in world history, that could have single-handedly produced it. The wood from which it's made likely came from a cedar tree in North America. To cut down said tree, you would need a saw, which would require steel to produce; said steel would require iron ore, and said iron ore might only be found on a completely different side of the world, perhaps the Kiruna mine in Sweden is a good candidate. Further adding difficulties, you would need to be gifted in metallurgy and mining to even stand a chance of creating a saw. This is only a small component within the process of pencil-making and, by itself, would more than likely require a lifetime to accomplish.

Even building something as seemingly ordinary as a pencil, requires the work of thousands. Chances are that these people shared no common tongue, and might have even disliked each other had they met in person. Yet they all worked in unison, despite their alien cultures and different views on life, to

01 Which was then popularised by Milton Friedman in the book and television series *Free to Choose*.

create that pencil. By having purchased it, and now holding it in your hand, you have inadvertently changed all their destinies by a marginal amount. Money makes the world go around and it has thus had a deep connection with our behaviour throughout history.

To talk about finance is to talk about trade; to talk about trade, is to talk about history; to talk about history is to talk about people; and to talk about people is to talk about biology. You cannot separate any of these factors and ever hope to understand the whole picture.

Perhaps that is the malady of the modern age, the rise of specialization has made us blind to adjacent fields. The modern economist is a mixture of pseudo-mathematician, prophet, gambler, and charlatan, all with equal parts hubris. This is not a book where I attempt to abstract the human condition to an arcane equation where I vaguely gesture at utility maximisation graphs or determine the value of algebraic notation through exhaustive quantitative economics. I have neither the inclination, spirit nor ability to do so.

Instead, this is a book that seeks to understand the origins and effects of the human condition. It is by comprehending these primal motivations, that we can make predictions more knowledgeably about the likely development of society and, by extension, our investments. Much too often, economics forgets the intrinsic role that human beings play in market economics, substituting instead the Übermensch that are the actors in economic models.

By understanding what drives a human being to behave the way in which he does and how these behaviours aggregate to form complex systems, one is inordinately more well-suited to invest wisely than the arrogant investor who believes that history does not repeat itself.

Our circumstances in the modern age, far from being unique, are merely an echo of the patterns that were established over 100,000 years ago, and continue to influence human behaviour today. Over the course of this book, we will seek to show that by knowing evolutionary science, one can better understand humanity in whichever circumstances it may find itself in; regardless of whether they happen to be in a cave or on the moon.

PART I: DAMN DIRTY APES – PSYCHOLOGY AND EVOLUTION

In this section, we shall be discussing how human psychology is an adaptive mechanism suited for our ancestral environment. We'll discuss why it is that humans, despite great technological feats, are more or less identical to their progenitors, and see why it is that humans have built the existing environments, such as social constructs, organizational systems, and financial methods, given their biological predispositions.

1 - The Blind Watchmaker

"But we are not here concerned with hopes or fears, only with the truth as far as our reason allows us to discover it. I have given the evidence to the best of my ability; and we must acknowledge, as it seems to me, that man with all his noble qualities, with sympathy which feels for the most debased, with benevolence which extends not only to other men but to the humblest living creature, with his god-like intellect which has penetrated into the movements and constitution of the solar system — with all these exalted powers — Man still bears in his bodily frame the indelible stamp of his lowly origin."

- Charles Darwin

It seems an odd choice to begin a book on investing four billion years ago, long before the first investment banker crawled out of the primordial ooze. Nevertheless, our biology and psychology first began to take shape in these times. At the time of writing, nobody truly knows what exactly it was that gave rise to the first self-replicating organism, shortly after the planet was formed. However, it is a commonly held assumption that molecules bonded with each other and used the resources in their environment to replicate themselves, giving rise to cells that became the building blocks for life.

The great, great, great, great [x a couple of billion times] grandparents of every living thing today were among those original organisms and cells. In a very real way, we are related to every plant and creature out there, that we know of. When looked at it from a certain lens, it can become quite disconcerting. For example, technically I'm writing this chapter on furniture made from the corpse of a very distant cousin of mine: an oak tree. This goes to show how the very simple rule of "create more copies of yourself" can give rise to immense complexity through an unconscious and adaptive system. Further along the book, we'll see that this complexity is not solely a characteristic of the natural world, but an emergent property of large interconnected systems when given enough time.

In either case, these new organisms, which originated from the molecules bonding with each other, suffered small, random mutations from generation to generation in trying to replicate themselves. Slowly, these mutations aggregated, and changed the organisms, which allowed them to fill different environmental niches. These changes, weathered by countless generations, are what we call "evolution" [2]. However, some of these alterations were more beneficial than others; the less-adapted organisms died out and were outcompeted by more efficient ones, which were better at filling a particular environment.

An error that people often make when talking about evolution is assigning it morality or personality[02]. Organisms aren't evolving to an optimum state of being. There are no "higher evolved" life forms. If it's well-suited for its current environment, succeeding at passing on its genes to the next generation, and can adapt to change, then it has succeeded in its purpose. Evolution is an unconscious mechanism, and, like any such system, it works by harnessing randomness. The evolutionary process tries many different combinations and, intrinsically, only allows models that function in the long run to survive; after which, it keeps fine-tuning the elements that had previously worked.

An organism is never designed from scratch, without concern for previous

---

02 Partially this is an issue of language, as it necessarily assigns agency by allowing statements such as "evolution prefers x factor." Thus, by using verbs in many languages, we're having to assign personhood to intangible concepts.

iterations. Instead, only gradual changes are made from one generation to the next, giving rise to a seemingly infinite array of variety. Critics would naturally argue that such a thing is akin to monkeys typing the complete works of Shakespeare on a typewriter. It is partially true, but imagine that every time a monkey wrote a word in the right order by accident, that newly-achieved progress became its new starting point. Eventually, you'd have the completed works of Shakespeare, given that you wouldn't have to start from scratch with every new successive attempt. Instead, you'd keep what worked and discard what didn't. Unconscious mechanisms work in the same way, allowing simplicity to give rise to complexity when given the right platform and time.

Furthermore, the victors in this randomly selective process are often quite surprising. Truth be told, from an evolutionary perspective, human beings are far from being a success story. That honour depends on what your parameters are. If you define success by raw numbers, surface area covered, species longevity, and ability to wipe out the competition, then microbes are ahead of any of the likely competition. Perhaps making one think twice about having gone through all the effort of evolving, when the winners are those that remained virtually unchanged.

As biologist Richard Dawkins put it, ultimately evolution is an unconscious mechanism - a blind watchmaker [3]. It may be capable of creating an unquantifiable number of fantastic creatures, but it does so blindly. A useful adaptation in one circumstance may become a liability in another one. The opposite may be true as well, a liability may become an asset in a different set of circumstances.

"Good Enough," in an evolutionary sense, means just that – that you are good enough. Meaning that if you fall within a certain variance within a range of acceptable behaviour for your species, you too can be an evolutionary success by passing on your genes to the next generation. In other words, if the circumstances remain the same, any random mutation you might have gotten by accident will be averaged out over the eons, as no further minute adaptation actually makes any difference. Or put in economics lingo, over time your random walk behaviour will regress to the mean.

It stands to reason that for there to be an actual permanent change there has to be a strong incentive to do so - certain characteristics must be selected for via natural selection. If circumstances remain the same as they've been for millennia, there's no reason to change at all. *Why fix what's not broken?* So, a species remains locked in stasis, unchanged as time goes by.

Let us now assume that the environment quickly changed somehow (it can do so for any number of reasons: the weather changed, there are new predators, there's no more of a type of food, etc). Suddenly, there is a very strong selective pressure for creatures adapted to the new environment. If a random mutation proved marginally more beneficial than the average in the species, instantly this mutation has a competitive advantage over other similar creatures. As a result, the organism will have an easier time surviving and will find it simpler to pass on its genes, making it even likelier for the next generation to resemble the mutant.

This process is called Punctuated Equilibrium; which, contrary to what one might have learned in school, is evolutionary change that can occur abnormally fast [4]. In the natural world, one has to adapt rapidly to the whims of mother nature, or face extinction. The peppered moth is a perfect example of this phenomenon. Normally, this insect is white-bodied, so as to better camouflage with the lightly coloured flora; but in the first few decades of the Industrial Revolution, soot covered the forests of Manchester and the environment darkened. As such, the lightly-coloured moths stuck out like a stripper at church, and were quickly gobbled up by predators. This created an inherent advantage for being dark- coloured in urban areas [insert racist joke here], and thus the ratio of light-to-dark pigment in peppered moths rapidly shifted to favour the darker-coloured moths. Nevertheless, since the environment is less polluted nowadays than it was during the Industrial Revolution, this effect is being reversed [5].

Interestingly enough, species can develop in different ways when far apart from other members of its own species, given that they have different circumstances to adapt to. Their environment will shape their behaviours, and over time this has the potential to completely alter every aspect of themselves. Eventually, if the creatures are geographically separate enough from each other, and can't share beneficial mutations with each other, there can be speciation[03]. Over time they will become different types of creature altogether, and at one point will be unable to reproduce with each other, even if they were to mate by chance again.

Furthermore, not every ability gained from said adaptations was actually the purpose of the adaptation in the first place. Humans, for example, did not develop hand-eye coordination to be able to paint, play sports or perform surgery. Instead, it was a happy by-product of evolution that an adaptation just so happened to help us be able to do that. These happy accidents of unintentional utility are termed as "spandrels"[04] [6].

Amidst all this dramatic outward change, we must remember that evolution also goes deeper than skin deep. Despite having an essentially infinite range of possible behaviours available, humans tend to cluster on certain behavioural tendencies. The reason for that is that for most of the 150,000-200,000 years of human existence, we were hunter-gatherers, and hence had to work within a certain range or risk a speedy death.

History, and civilization as we know it, is around 12,000 years old, and thus represents less than 1% of humanity's time on Earth[05]. Consequently, it makes perfect sense to understand the environment in which humans evolved in, as it undoubtedly left marks on our psychological development.

---

03 It's the evolutionary process by which populations evolve to become distinct species. Typically, it counts as a new species when the creatures can't produce a fertile offspring when they happen to mate with each other.

04 So called after the flat space that unites the dome and the arches of a cathedral. This is a space that naturally occurs when wanting to have the two architectural designs within the same space. Over the centuries they evolved to be artistic wonders in their own right, as evidenced by the world renowned "Spandrels of San Marco" in Venice, despite them originally having no other purpose but a utilitarian one to connect the two architectural elements.

05 This is if we include all hominids within the timeline, if we only include modern Homo sapiens into the calculations then it's closer to 10%.

Modern Homo sapiens are a far cry from the rational automata, known as *Homo economicus* that economists invoke to make their models work. As we'll see, despite all our flaws, it may be for the best that we don't adhere to their, frankly, sociopathic behavioural models.

2 - The Red Queen and Game Theory

> *"Now, here, you see, it takes all the running you can do, to keep in the same place. If you want to get somewhere else, you must run at least twice as fast as that!"*
>
> \- *The Red Queen, Through the Looking-Glass*

When I first started learning about evolution and biology, I was struck by the utter ruthlessness of the system. Ultimately, an organism is an integrated collection of problem-solving devices - adaptations - that were shaped by natural selection over evolutionary time to promote, in some specific way, the survival of the genes that directed their construction [7]. These adaptations are not concerned with the human concept of right and wrong, if they don't happen to help procreation or survival in some way. The potential genetic legacy is far more important than any other consideration.

In the natural order of things, harmony is non-existent. Life is a Sisyphean struggle for every living creature out there. Go to a placid lake with a nearby forest, where the birds are chirping and the flowers are blooming, and you might disagree with this notion. Nevertheless, when you look at it from a different angle, you'll be able to see the epic struggle.

The trees in forests are tall because they're in a struggle to the death with all other trees in the contest for sunlight. The smaller a tree is, the less likely it is to get sunshine, and thus survive. The male birds are chirping because they're essentially desperately screaming to all females in earshot, to come and have sex with them. However, as all other males are also following this attention-grabbing strategy, only the most melodious ones stand a chance at winning. The flowers are blooming because they need to be pollinated by fauna, thus they need to grab animals' attention - one of the detriments of wanting to have sex, but being unable to move.

It's a very curious thing that such beauty can stem from such struggle. There might not be harmony, but there are order and rules. If one of your opponents (be they hunter, prey, or competition) reacts in a certain way, you must react accordingly or be left behind. As such, by always having to adapt to new situations, and your opponents as well, you're all never better or worse off than when you started. No matter how much you run, you always end up in the exact same position you started in as everything else is moving with you.

Imagine running a race, wherein the prize is merely your continued survival - there is no end in sight - but you must keep pace with your competition. If you fall too far behind, then you're wiped from the face of the Earth and the race goes on without you. Not wanting such a grizzly fate for yourself, you throw your whole being into it with blood, toil[06], tears and sweat, but so does everyone else in the race. In the end, no matter how much spirit goes into it, given that everyone else is also doing the same, you never actually gain an advantage. This phenomenon is called *the Red Queen* - where no matter how much things change, they still remain the same.

The Red Queen is a name given to the arms race that is life. In a way, you could compare it to the Cold War, a period of military tension that occurred directly after World War II between the United States of America and the Soviet Union. The more military advances that one side developed, the more the other side had to invest in and expand their own military. When a "missile

06 When quoting the famous Winston Churchill quote everyone seems to forget about the toil - perhaps it's indicative of people's priorities wherein they're fine with the bleeding, the crying and the sweating as long as there's no strenuous labour involved.

gap"[07], a perceived deficiency of offensive and defensive ballistic missiles, was said to have occurred, the United States had no choice but to increase its own military capabilities. In turn, the Soviets had to respond by doing the same, and tensions grew. In other words, their capabilities for damage increased, but proportionally they were still at the exact point where they started at in terms of ability to defeat their foe.

The Cold War created an environment where one small mistake could lead to Armageddon, otherwise known Mutually Assured Destruction (or MAD). The most publicised of these events was the Cuban Missile crisis, which most people believe is the closest humanity has gotten to nuclear war. Unfortunately, this was far from the only time, or the closest time, where we got one button push away from ending life on the planet as we know it[08]. It's unsurprising that in such an environment of necessity, a means of understanding the patterns, rules and behaviours of the game was developed - a "Game Theory" so to speak. Whilst some of the concepts central to the idea were then centuries old, it was only during the Cold War that it came to its own.

Game Theory is "the study of mathematical models of conflict and

07 The Missile gap was a completely fictional concept, of the perceived asymmetry between US and the Soviet Union's defence capabilities. Kennedy used it as a platform to increase military spending, as supposedly the United States was lagging. As the Soviets knew the fictional nature of this imbalance, they began to believe that Kennedy was dangerous and war mongering, and thus had to raise their own capabilities in response, hence the Cuban Missile Crisis [8].

08 There have been several incidents over the decades on both sides, most of which occurred due to some unforeseen harmless circumstance which accidentally seemed like an attack from the other side. Had protocols been followed strictly to the letter, the world would've been blown several times over - so many times even that Wikipedia has a whole listing on it called "List of nuclear close calls" and those are just the ones the public is aware of. Fortunately, there were always people at the helm that were hesitant to press the button in the end. Unfortunately, there are automatic systems in place even today, like Russia's "Dead Hand" computer system, which can be activated in an emergency, under the assumption that the command systems have been blown up. In other words, even if one side managed to annihilate the other side completely, they'd still be able to retaliate fully. [10]

cooperation between intelligent rational decision-makers." [9] Its applications are far-reaching in fields as diverse as economics, politics, business mergers, military strategies, divorces, poker games and biology. This system allows us to determine the optimal decision based on what other agents are likely to do and on our own likely behaviour.

As such, this collection of mathematical models and logical reasoning allow us to understand how evolution will develop, given that the ultimate goals of an organism are to reproduce as widely as possible and to give its offspring the best chance of survival by either giving it the best genes, the best attention or, in the rare exception, both. Once we understand this intrinsic and essential motivation, everything else falls into place, and hundreds upon millions of strategies are developed as corollaries to this prime goal.

In the 1970s, a political scientist by the name of Robert Axelrod sought to determine the optimal strategy for a successive Prisoner's Dilemma problem. The Prisoner's Dilemma is a thought experiment where two complicit criminals are put into separate interrogation chambers, and whosoever rats the other one out first gets a reduced sentence. The catch is that if they collude, then neither person gets punished and both go free; however, the problem is that they don't fully know if the other person is trustworthy enough to protect their interest, and they can't coordinate with each other due to their separation. Axelrod decided that the best way to predict the optimal solution for the problem was to pit all possible strategies against each other in a computer simulation. In order to come up with all the different strategies to analyse, he tried to get the full spectrum of human decision making - so he asked game theorists in economics, sociology, political science and mathematics how they would behave in a certain situation [11].

He analysed all of their answers, proceeded to quantify them and then entered them into a computer program. Afterwards, he organised a round-robin tournament; all strategies would be paired off with every other strategy, and the winner would be the one with the most points. Out of the maelstrom of all the different tactics, came a very simple and effective strategy, which is nowadays called "Tit for Tat." The strategy, in essence, is to start off cooperating with the other agent. If the other agent responds in kind in the first round, you also do not betray him. If, however, the other person betrays you, then you respond offensively the next round until the other agent makes an overture of peace by playing in kind once more; at which point, you forgive him and respond in kind as well - though it bears saying that the "forgiving" component in the algorithm was a later addition.

Tit for Tat, over the many generations, drove the other strategies into extinction. The strength of this strategy was that it wasn't blind to its environment, and it reacted proportionally to the circumstances. It "won, not by doing better than the other player, but by eliciting cooperation [and] by promoting the mutual interest rather than by exploiting the other's weakness." [12] As such, this strategy developed its environmental niche by understanding the environment it found itself in. As none of the agents had full information and thus can only necessarily work with partial information, it did so via two means - signalling and screening [13]:

- **Signalling** is a technique which gives reason for the other person to believe in the honesty of your intentions and goals, and hence have them be more willing to cooperate with you. In the earlier game, the Tit for Tat strategy "signals" its cooperative mindset by initially playing in kind and not trying to take more than it has contributed. As such, other strategies that aren't solely out there to take advantage of others will want to cooperate with it, as they see a mutual benefit. However, in the real world, where there's far more complexity than within a mathematical model, there are both cheap and expensive signals to consider. Not all signals have the same worth when considering the optimal strategy.

  Cheap signals are any and all ways which can be used to attempt to make one party believe in the honesty of the other, but with few costs. If I were to simply ask you to trust me, there's little consequence for me not keeping my word; as such "talk is cheap" and not that useful for determining whether someone's telling the truth. I could just as well be a liar or an honest person when I don't have skin in the game. If, on the other hand, I'm attempting to get a job and I point to my degree as a signal, that is an *expensive signal.* It doesn't guarantee that I will be a perfect candidate, but the fact that I went out of my way to get a degree is a means by which I can signal my intentions and commitment to the cause of my potential employer. Reason being that for me to fake that sort of signal, it would be very costly and inefficient.

In biology, a peacock's tail is a perfect example of an expensive signal. By having and maintaining such a tail, he is showing off his health and ability to procure resources. Not only that, but by having it you become a target to predators [14]. Ideally, the most efficient peacocks would not have this, as it puts their lives in danger, which implicitly means that peacocks are handicapping themselves. Nevertheless, given that all other males are willing to pay the increased mortality rate as a means to show their mating and survival capabilities, even despite the handicap of the tail, every other peacock has to adopt the strategy to maintain a competitive advantage. If one were to deviate, and de-escalate by foregoing the gaudy tail, the peahens would likely associate the differentiation as negative, assuming that he is unable to have one due to poor health or ability (even if that were to be far from the case).

- **Screening** is the other side of the signalling strategy. In other words, it's the decoding of the message that is being sent via a signal. The Tit for Tat strategy screens for potential allies by looking for other agents who seem to show signs of willingness to cooperate; they signal this by foregoing the maximum payoff and thus be willing to share the payoff with the other player. By correctly identifying these strategies, they can form an alliance that is symbiotic in the long run.

Nevertheless, the strategy also fully admits that there may be dishonest agents who masquerade as honest ones. As such, this strategy relies on the willingness to punish the other party if they show signs of treachery.

> The key to successfully screening to your benefit is seeing what the other party stands to lose from treating you poorly. If the punishment is greater than the benefit of cheating, one can be reasonably certain that their interests are aligned.

This Tit for Tat strategy could very well be said to be the first stepping stone towards life and intelligence, as it contains the foundational blueprint to complex emotions and actions, like altruism and revenge. This is how you can have kindness and caring in a chaotic universe. In the long run, nice guys might finish first. Evolution merely makes you a more adept player at utilizing the Tit for Tat strategy, by honing your psychology and anatomy to fit the needs of your environment. Simple rules over countless generations can lead to unfathomable complexity, give or take a couple billion years. Soon enough, by following such adaptive rules, you may one day even find Homo sapiens roving in the savannah with all their fascinating complexity.

3 - A Day in the Life of a Hunter-Gatherer

"Violence, naked force, has settled more issues in history than has any other factor."

Robert A. Heinlein, Starship Troopers

Depending on whom you ask, life in prehistoric times was either short, brutish and violent or a Paradise of Eden. As with everything in life, the truth is likely to have been somewhere in the middle. If you ask cognitive psychologists like Steven Pinker, they will say that archaeological and statistical inference points to the fact that in the hunter-gatherer societies about 15% of human beings died of violence - or at least that's what the injuries on the skeletal remains would imply [15]. This death rate by violence is above the casualty rate that most countries faced during WWII (Ukraine, Poland and Belarus being the exceptions and above this threshold) [16].

In other words, even if you had been front and centre in the largest and most deadly battlefield the world has ever seen, you would still have a smaller chance of dying violently than had you been a hunter-gatherer over your lifetime. Worse still, the case has been made that other hominid species did not make it to the modern age because our ancestors began a genocidal warpath against them over the course of millennia [17]. This evidence hardly paints an appealing picture, yet we must also remember that all societies are not the same and that these genocidal explanations for hominid extinction are somewhat outdated. Even today, we are aware of how environment shapes culture. When you live a life of plenty in every respect, there's hardly a reason to fight.

Such rose-tinted views of life may seem quaint, but it's been proposed that some hunter-gatherers lived in such a life of abundance. Anthropologists have even gone the whole nine yards and dubbed them "the original affluent society" [18]. At most, these societies worked three-to-five hours per day, while the rest of the time was spent in leisure. Life abundantly supplied them with anything their heart desired and they lived content. Whilst this reeks of Rousseau-tinged "Noble Savage"[09] wishful thinking, there does seem to be some evidence backing this claim.

Yet for all its beauty, nature can be a cruel mistress where any benefit you might derive from it can be quickly snatched away when you make a false move. Hence why we humans generally developed a risk-averse personality, we prefer not to take risks and conserve what few endowments we've gotten. Studies point to the fact that the pain of loss is felt twice as much as the elation of acquisition [19] and thus we'll take great pains to avoid loss - often far in excess to what is mathematically sensible to do. When it's uncertain that you'll be able to live long term, it hardly makes sense to plan for the future or to develop the mental capacity for it. Even today, we have problems thinking in the long term, and over the course of a lifetime, this accidental hedonism might cost us a fortune. An oft-quoted experiment by Stanford University showed that children capable of planning for the future, by withholding instant gratification, make for better investors when they reach adulthood. Sadly, most children do not innately possess that trait, and researchers are unsure whether teaching children to delay gratification would make any long-term difference in their behaviour [20].

We're not programmed for a life where patience pays off, and compound interest, as well as dividend reinvestments, can be our path to fortune. We are

---

09 The belief that humans are inherently good and it was the complexity of civilization which proved to be their moral downfall. The political theorist Jean-Jacques Rousseau is closely associated with the idea, given that he postulated a similar premise in his writings, yet he never actually used the phrase "Noble Savage."

trying to operate cutting edge software (ideas) with 40,000-year-old hardware that hasn't been updated (our brains). Obviously, some glitches are to be expected when running civilization.exe; yet despite this fact, our underlying biology is under no real motivation to upgrade the system – good enough is good enough, after all. Consequently, we're likely stuck with our human idiosyncrasies.

As a species, humans err on the side of conservatism and hedonism. In fact, it takes conscious mental effort to disregard the pull of these behaviours as it might've otherwise spelled our doom to not follow them. In primal times, it made sense to throw caution to the wind, eat and be merry for tomorrow all your food might rot and be inedible.

Hence, if we were to ignore the desire to be risk-averse hedonists, it should very well be for a good reason. Enter the Savanna-IQ Interaction Hypothesis, which suggests that dumber individuals have greater difficulty than more intelligent people with comprehending and dealing with evolutionarily novel entities and situations that did not exist in the ancestral environment [21]. Or, in plain English, the smarter you are the likelier you are to try something that a caveman would've never done due to the inherent restrictions in their lifestyle. This list can include everything from programming a computer, to staying up late or developing a drug habit.

Part of the curse of intelligence is that you realise that a lot of the traditions and beliefs that society develops for its correct functioning lack nuance, or even sense at the individual level. In time, you learn to ignore the brunt of social conditioning as you see the flaws in its logic. However, because of this wilful disconnect with social convention, you may at times forget that society might've developed its rules for a good reason. Hence, smart people may be likelier to do objectively dumb things (like developing a drug habit) because they are far more willing to try out novel behaviours, which might not have been properly thought out.

Culture does not develop randomly, it is usually shaped at a glacial pace and it often has logical reasons for developing as such. In Part I, Chapter 10 (PI - Ch10, from now on), I will discuss how environment shapes the development of culture in detail. For now, I shall simply come back to the topic at hand, and hammer home that our lives were uncertain in prehistoric times and it was best to follow the tried-and-true method rather than experimenting with random and untested ideas, unless absolutely necessary.

Humans were often at the mercy of nature, which we were also subtly and accidentally changing as a result of our emergence as the dominant species. A perfect example of this is the sudden, but catastrophic extinction of megafauna[10] throughout the world, most likely because of overhunting [22].

As humans spread throughout the planet, they perfected their hunting techniques. There were many, but among the more interesting one of these is the idea of persistence hunting. Any animal worth hunting is, in all likelihood, faster than a human. Yet, much as the tortoise and the hare fable, persistence pays off. The idea behind persistence hunting is to use our natural predisposition towards endurance to overcome a huge disadvantage in speed. By using this method, even early hominids could exhaust speedier prey to such an extent that, by the end of it, we just put it out of its misery. Take the cheetah, the fastest land animal alive, it can run at speeds well over 100 km per hour, and nothing can hope to catch it - for a handful of seconds. After that period, it has to rest, before it attempts such a feat again, or it risks dying from overheating [23]. Now, take the modern human distance runner. Modern humans all around the world take part in gruelling 42 km marathons - for fun.

Now, imagine what human beings that exercise for a living are capable of doing when their lives depend on it, and they have adrenaline to fall back on. This is why you will not often see wild animals or hunter-gatherers with ulcers, as all chemicals their bodies secrete tend to have a direct life-or-death function, and as such rarely have long-term imbalances. Wild animals and hunter-gatherers, don't tend to suffer under chronic stress unless they happen to be at the bottom of their hierarchy. Instead, they suffer under episodic stress,

---

10 Exceedingly large animals that roamed the Earth. Anything from mammoths, to sabre tooth tigers, to giant koala bears, kangaroos, turtles and enormous birds used to roam the Earth.

e.g. a snake has just made its presence known and they have to flee the scene [24]. Stress, as we experience it in the modern age, is a luxury that is only affordable in a life of plenty.

Perhaps it was our exceptional hunting skills or maybe it was the sudden shift in climate once the ice age ended, but in a very short timeframe, a good percentage of the large creatures in the world disappeared. Many of these could've been domesticable over time, and been useful for civilization if given the chance. Instead, this mass extinction would reverberate over the millennia, as many future civilizations would be unable to use animal labour, given that there were no domesticable animals in their area, and thus were left behind, technologically speaking. They would be unable to develop agriculture, beyond hand ploughs, trade would be severely limited as they would depend on raw human muscle to lug goods around, and infrastructure projects would become that much more difficult to build, for this exact reason. Put succinctly, some areas of the world might just have been primed for early success from a civilizational standpoint; if domesticable animals had survived in the New World, history might have been very different as the societies around the globe might've been on more equal footing, for example.

To add even more injustice into the mix, many of the crops that would one day feed empires were unequally distributed in some areas of the world. This phenomenon about how geography affects development will be covered in more depth in Part II. Suffice it to say that life was not easy in this changeable environment. Many people perished, but as a species, we endured. We always found a way around our difficulties. Homo sapiens are not the biggest, meanest or most physically-adept animal out there. Yet over the course of a relatively short amount of time, we managed to take over the world, despite ice ages, other hominids, hazardous environments, etc.

4 - Why Gossiping Got Us to the Moon

"There is only one thing in life worse than being talked about, and that is not being talked about."

- Oscar Wilde

We, as humans, have three main advantages at our disposal when pitted against most other animals:

- Cooperative mindset
- Ability to model the world through thought alone
- Perseverance

By themselves, none of these advantages is truly capable of handing us the keys to the world. A cooperative mindset alone just means you get to be part of a group of well-meaning idiots. An ability to model the world is useful, but if you can't use other people to make your ideas a reality, or to pass on your ideas once you're dead, then any brilliant idea you might have had is useless in the long run. Perseverance is a fine trait to have as well, but if that's the only thing you have, then you are little better than a salmon swimming upstream. In other words, you need an interplay of all these factors to help you thrive.

It might initially seem that I am painting humanity in broad strokes and forgetting the nuance. To a great extent, this is true and I make little apology for it. To uncover all nuances in human behaviour, history and biology and relate them to modern economics, all in a couple hundred pages, is almost assuredly impossible. Instead of focusing on the details, I would like to see the whole canvas to acknowledge what the painting is, and so appreciate the interplay of the colours and details without fully mentioning the encyclopaedic levels of the particulars. If one is enjoying an Impressionist painting, focusing on the brushwork is somewhat missing the point.

Even worse, to most people reading this book, it might more or less be an appalling waste of time to venture forth into the yawning chasm of deep scientific analysis. Humans have a horrifying track record when it comes to understanding, much less appreciating, nuance. Out in the wild, where we fine-tuned our modes of thinking for millions of years, things are more or less black and white: *What to do when a tiger is trying to eat you? Should you run or should you hide? Can you trust the person you just met, or are they a threat?* These are all matters that have little room for subtlety and require quick decisions.

On the other hand, there are matters that are not as evident. *Is your friend slacking off, hoping that you pick up his work? Does your partner love you? What is the meaning of life? Should you save more grains for next year's harvest or have a banquet tonight?* These are all worthy questions as well, but they're not as easily answerable. They require further, slower analysis.

It would almost seem that the brain has two types of thinking. One that is fast, which requires immediate impressions to make decisions. The other one is slow, which uses the information available and considers nuance more thoroughly. This idea was first suggested by psychologist Daniel Kahneman, and it has caused quite a stir in economics. At the core of the idea, it states that there are two ways by which the brain operates and decides on matters: System 1 and System 2; fast and slow, respectively [25].

System 1 (Fast) is the intuitive side of our reasoning. It analyses information quickly based on past impressions and it uses contextual information to make decisions. Despite its efficacy, this mental framework is predisposed to cut corners and not consider all possible information, as it uses our preconceptions to arrive at conclusions. These cognitive shortcuts are called "heuristic judgments." Heuristics and oversimplifications are an excellent tool when your life is in peril, as it allows you to act quickly and efficiently. Yet in a world of statistical uncertainty, much the opposite is true and following our biases can be disastrous. Disappointingly, this is the cognition process we're most likely to engage in, even when making important financial decisions.

On the other hand, we have System 2 (Slow) which is the side of our reasoning that we most identify with. It analyses matters based on available information and tries to come up with what we presume to be the soundest reasoning. It takes time and effort to will it into action; as such, our bodies, which are primarily designed for efficiency, tend not to make use of this cognition process unless absolutely necessary. Whilst this slow process may be the one which we think we embody the most, studies suggest that it isn't so.

Humans are bad at analysing more complicated matters because they were mostly non-existent or unimportant for our survival for most of our psychological development as a species. This is of little consolation when you have a big report to present by Friday at 17:30 modelling the nuance of foreign exchange markets to your boss.

Yet, there was a time when there was no such thing as a paycheque or a boss. A hunter-gatherer would surely have laughed at the fact that you're trying to precisely predict the whims of nature through mathematical means, for they barely had any use for numbers at all. To such an extent, that what few hunter-gatherers still exist today may even have difficulty wrapping their heads around such bizarre concepts as "numbers" [26].

Far from being able to tame nature, we were often at its mercy. The only thing that could save us from it was each other, since if we worked together, we might just survive, and perhaps even thrive. We're liable to group consensus and not calling attention to ourselves. If the group does not believe in something, it's best we don't believe it just as well. This is incidentally why bubbles (when assets are massively overvalued when compared to their function) are so easily blown in world markets, and why it's so difficult not to fall for them.

There have even been studies where 200 strangers were told to randomly walk in a large room; yet after enough time had passed, they started walking in counter-directional concentric ring patterns [27]. As if agreed on beforehand, everyone started moving in an elegant swirling ballet. Meaning that group mentality is so powerful that even if we have nothing to lose from exercising our own free will, and we don't know our peer group, we might still prefer to defer responsibility to the crowd.

The same studies were even more striking when they included confederates, which were planted by the researchers amidst the crowds to subtly try to manipulate the direction of the people through confident striding. Turns out that to affect the default directional path of the people they needed a 5% proportion of the group to be confederates, and the effect grows symmetrically with further conspirators. Below that number and they couldn't affect the crowd strongly enough for the group to be controllable.

Yet even without a de facto leader, a certain harmony emerged from the initial chaos. The wisdom of the crowds averaged out the mass of humanity and established order in a chaotic system. It's in exercises such as these when we can see the power of the group.

Being ostracised in prehistoric times was akin to being sentenced to death. Worse even, as being sentenced to death would be quick. Instead, you would probably starve for a couple of weeks, eventually get wounded, get an infection, and ultimately be mauled to death by some wild beast in the end. Your name and reputation are consequently sacrosanct, and must be protected at all costs when you are a hunter-gatherer, or inhabit a more primitive society.

Whilst perhaps somewhat alien to more modern sensibilities, honour and maintaining your standing in society was quintessential for most of our existence. Hence there were (and still are in more backwards societies) generations-long blood feuds, honour killings and duels all in the name of saving face. Nevertheless, while chivalric virtues of honour, duty and piety have taken a backseat in modern times, the motivations that birthed their necessity are still with us. Obviously, this still has unforeseen consequences in the modern age. Public speaking, for example, is an act where you risk making an ass out of yourself and being subjected to social ostracization. We deeply care for our standing in society and are painfully aware that any *faux pas* can downgrade us on the social totem pole. Hence, many people put the fear of public speaking in the same league of importance as their fear of death [28]. Worse still, this is why you can't talk to that cute girl at the office without feeling like your organs are going through the wash cycle in a washing machine. It feels like you're about to die because it could have very well happened. Back in the day, there was the very real risk of Chad McCaveman bashing your brains in for looking at her funny.

It's been said that the main reason we developed big brains in the first place was mainly for socialising, this is commonly known as "the social brain" hypothesis [29]. A surprising amount of our time spent communicating is actually devoted to gossiping and keeping track of the movements within our social network [30]. The reason for this is simple, knowledge is power and knowing the shifting power dynamics in the tribe might well mean the difference between life and death. Yet people will not simply tell you this information point-blank. It's in the best interests of the powerless to seem powerful (so that people treat them with more standing than they deserve) and of the powerful to seem powerless (so that people do not immediately view them as a threat). Furthermore, being able to outwit the competition can allow one to rise up the ranks, and vastly outperform everyone else in furthering our genetic lineage. As such, we intuitively know that most important information is left unsaid. Hence, we evolved highly-complex biological machinery to be able to sift through bullshit, and it had the added side effect of being able to model the world so well that it allowed us to eventually reach the moon.

Noticing and interpreting exformation (information which is deliberately kept out of a message) soon became a highly sought-after skill, from an evolutionary standpoint. With a more robust Theory of Mind[11], one could more easily navigate social situations without getting one's heads bashed in. Not only that, but one might even charm one's way up the hierarchy if one were to model other people's behaviour correctly. Naturally, we developed

---

11 The ability to understand that other people have ideas of their own, and have different wants/needs/information than you possess.

a thirst for any gossip, which might give our knowledge and thus models of people, an edge over the others who were doing the same. This is why we can remember information much easier, and find it more engaging, if it's organised as a narrative (which is essentially just pseudo-gossip). Slick businessmen and Wolf of Wall Street types are hardly immune to this effect either. When you read books like *Beating the Street* by mutual fund managing legend Peter Lynch, he repeatedly refers to investment prospects as "stories." Stories are the lifeblood of our species, they're what binds us together. Hence, the ability to tell a good story is the easiest way in which you can win the hearts and minds of people.

Even with the dawn of the modern age and social networks where we have millions of "friends," we still very much maintain a tribal attitude in our socialising. Our brains have a bias towards tight-knit communities. On Facebook, for example, we still only maintain regular contact with 150 people [31]. This is even despite the fact that you may very well have hundreds of people attached to your account. Curiously, 150 is the approximate population size that hunter-gatherer communities were supposed to have been back in the day. It's such a noteworthy number, that it has been studied extensively, and has its own name - "Dunbar's Number."

Worse still, your moods, thoughts and feelings are linked to these 150 people. By this point, it's a cliché to say that you are the average of the people you spend the most time with. Yet, as the controversial Facebook emotion manipulation study would attest to, this cliché is true. In 2012, Facebook took 689,000 unwilling participants and altered the updates that they saw from their friends in their Facebook feed. Those that were presented with positive stimuli, tended to post happy posts; however, those who were presented with negative stimuli suffered through a brief depression. Emotions are contagious [32]!

We depend on our social network to build a consensus about the state of the world, the quality of our lives and even what topics we should or should not care about. Collectively, as a species, we dread having to be pariahs, and thus seek like-minded individuals to decrease the chance that we, and our ideas and behaviours, will have to stand alone against the tide. Is it any wonder that stock market bubbles and crashes can occur on mere gossip?

5 - Animal Instincts

"It is impossible to overlook the extent to which civilization is built up upon a renunciation of instinct...."
- Sigmund Freud, Civilization and Its Discontents

People in the financial world often like to boast about having an "animal instinct" in regards to markets, and their potential developments. Business magnate George Soros, for example, has claimed that he gets a back pain whenever he needs to make changes in his portfolio, well before he has had time to look at the facts.

This statement seems odd, not least because it bears a striking resemblance to people throughout history who allegedly received divine signals. The list of prophets receiving signs to follow a certain life path, is long and has often had a profound effect on history. Most of the time, the communication purportedly happened through innocuous telepathy. To explain this, it's been suggested that some schizophrenic people's temporal lobes are susceptible to common electromagnetic waves[12]. Some people even go as far as to indicate that they

12 Electromagnetic waves are photons. These are massless 'groups' of energy which oscillate at a given frequency. While oscillating, they produce electric and magnetic fields. An electron, the subatomic particle orbiting the atomic nucleus, can emit a photon by dropping its energy level to a lower orbit. Everything from visible light, to x-rays to radio waves, are stray photons oscillating at different frequencies. In other words, these are all different forms of radiation, which when grouped together, form the electromagnetic spectrum.

are feeling presences in a room, when under the influence of these waves [33]. This is incidentally, a proposed theory as to why people experience ghostly presences in old houses with faulty wiring.

Nevertheless, judging by his career and general demeanour, Soros seems like a rational person without a history of psychotic episodes. As such, it has to be a psychosomatic symptom - his body is essentially willing the back pain into existence after processing certain information. This "mind over body" paradigm is hardly novel, in fact, it's a well-known phenomenon. The "placebo effect" is the tendency of the body to self-correct a health issue when provided by an ineffectual, but seemingly convincing treatment. This happens with such regularity that in many countries to be able to sell a medicine, it has to be tested to be more effective than a placebo.

There is also the opposite effect, that is the "nocebo effect." If a person believes something has been done to them, which warrants making them sick, then the body will often be all too happy to oblige to that request. The effect is also the offered scientific explanation for voodoo curses, black magic and similar circumstances where someone who is perfectly healthy can suddenly take ill - even to the point of dropping dead.

Yet, the interesting element that these noxious triggers have in common is that they have little in common with each other outside that the person affected by them strongly believes in their efficacy. Sure, there are Jungian archetypes of what humans universally have an aberration or love for, but by and large, the triggers and the importance that we assign to them is personal. You may, for example, be a missionary in the jungle; at which point a shaman performs a ritual and curses you for your meddling. Your belief in God and his protection remains steadfast though, and you all but ignore and forget about the whole affair, whilst people who believed in the shaman might've taken ill in similar circumstances. Some years pass, and you've raised the ire of the Pope for your unorthodox beliefs, and as punishment, you get excommunicated.

On the face of it, the shaman's ritual is not all that different from the Pope's excommunication. But this time, you take violently ill; you feel as if you've had your heart ripped out of you and you grow desperate, suicidal even because the pain becomes too great. This time, what is happening, is that your body perceives this event as a real threat. As a response, your body produces cortisol, which completely unbalances your system when it's produced in such constant and vast quantities [34]. So naturally, you take ill.

In other words, what happened in that thought experiment is that you have been classically conditioned to interpret reality via a certain lens. Much like Pavlov's dog being trained to salivate at the sound of the bell, you would have pegged your wellbeing to that of the word of the Pope. In that light, George Soros' back pain takes a much different meaning. If people fall ill at the sign of divine ill will to one's life decisions, why should they not also be able to fall ill at the sign that the free market's invisible hand is displeased with their choices?

In the first half of the twentieth century, in the early days of modern science, when psychological studies were part of the unregulated Wild West, and scientists didn't have to contend with pesky ethics boards, there was a very curious study in 1919. John B. Watson and his graduate student, Rosalie Rayner, at Johns Hopkins University decided to see whether it was possible to wilfully classically condition a phobia into an emotionally stable human being. As such, they went to a hospital and essentially kidnapped a child, referred to as "Albert," for a while to carry their experiment [35].

They quickly determined that a child's fear of loud noises was intrinsic in a human being; besides that, they determined that the child presented no natural fear to other stimuli, like burning newspapers, rats, rabbits, monkey masks, etc. In the next stage of their experiment, they tried to make the child afraid of rats by making a loud noise whenever he got near it. Soon the child became distressed, to the point of crying and trying to flee, at the mere sight of the rat, even without the sound. Interestingly enough, the phobia became more generalised to anything that remotely presented the general look and feel of a rat, like a furry dog, a rabbit, or even inanimate objects like coats.

Whilst unusually cruel, even possibly scarring a child for life, the Little Albert experiment might've accidentally pointed us to a far greater truth about the nature of aversion in a human being. When perceiving a threat, humans will create rules of thumb, by generalising the identifying elements of the source of stress. The underlying assumption is that the objects and creatures that possess a certain common trait are likely to be similarly dangerous as the thing that sparked the phobia in the first place. Poisonous animals in the jungle, for example, often colour code themselves to signal their potential danger [36]. Other animals thus learn not to go near them[13]. It's not that much of a stretch that someone could inadvertently classically condition themselves against bad investments - as, by their very nature, big losses are bad experiences that we'd all prefer not to struggle through.

Soros' reaction is likely psychosomatic, a nocebo which came about as the result of the mind being programmed to react in a certain way to a stimulus - but that does not mean that it is not useful. We would all like to have multibillion-dollar generating back pains. So how do they work? Not every back pain is likely to land you on the Forbes 100 list. How does one develop such an acutely specific thing? Or better yet, how does one develop the skills to understand the market?

A common answer to that sort of question by a layman or a successful and boastful investor would be "you're either born with it, or you're not," but that's a deeply unsatisfying answer. It's very much the same sort of answer you would get when talking about developing social skills, or public speaking. Yet the fact remains that people do learn social skills and improve their ability to speak in public. Same with value investing, for instance, an unusual cluster of the stratospherically-successful investors seem to be associated with the teachings of Benjamin Graham, as Warren Buffett puts it in the endnote's commentary of *The Intelligent Investor*, whilst making reference to a coin-flipping analogy:

---

13 Some animals even "piggyback" on this natural aversion by copying the colour scheme of a more dangerous, yet similar, animal. Hence in a way, they're able to be free-riders, given that they have the protection that comes from being poisonous, without having to incur the metabolic cost of actually being able to make good on the threat.

> *"...the children who left the house of this intellectual patriarch [Graham] have called their "flips" in very different ways. They have gone to different places and bought and sold different stocks and companies, yet they have had a combined record that simply couldn't be explained by random chance. It certainly cannot be explained by the fact that they are all calling flips identically because a leader is signalling the calls to make. The patriarch has merely set forth the intellectual theory for making coin-calling decisions, but each student has decided on his own manner of applying the theory."*

The evidence would suggest that value investing is an acquired skill! Furthermore, science doesn't really back up the idea of innate skills. Especially something as obscure and unconnected to survival as stock-picking. At absolute best, value investing is a spandrel, a skill that happens to piggyback on abilities that would've actually been useful in our primeval lives in the savannah.

As you read this, you will naturally have thought about the greats, with seemingly natural talents in different fields of human achievement. You might think about the Mozarts, the Da Vincis and the Einsteins, and possibly think I'm making this up as I go along. Nevertheless, there have been sterling defences arguing that human beings are blank slates, where effort and conscious specialisation lead to genius. One such example is Malcolm Gladwell's book *Outliers*, where he puts forth the idea that the main component one needs to achieve genius and mastery over a given topic is 10,000 hours of practice and betterment.

But I'm sceptical of such claims as well, not least because I don't think I had the same chance as Mozart to become a musical genius, even had I had his training and opportunities - and overwhelming amounts of the scientific research support this view. Don't get me wrong, it's important to practice, but one cannot fully do away with one's natural predispositions. Or as a meta-analysis studying how much deliberate practice affected your abilities in a skill put it:

> *"We conclude that amount of deliberate practice - although unquestionably important as a predictor of individual differences in performance from both a statistical and a practical perspective - is not as important ... Moderator analyses revealed that the strength of the relationship between deliberate practice and performance varied by domain. In terms of percentage of variance in performance explained, the effect of deliberate practice was strong for games (26%), music (21%), and sports (18%), and much weaker for education (4%) and professions (< 1% and not statistically significant)... the effect of deliberate practice on performance tended to be larger for activities that are highly predictable (e.g., running) than for activities that are less predictable (e.g., handling an aviation emergency)."[37]*

In other words, in a lot of respects we cannot change our starting positions. We might be able to improve our lot in life, but not wholly change our core traits. It's unreasonable to assume that you will achieve the same outcome, even if you put the same amount of deliberate effort, than someone who exited the womb in the right time, place and with the best genes.

For good or ill, we are born with predispositions and these will affect how our life takes shape, despite having very little power to alter them. For example, your chances of developing a psychological or physiological illness are increased not only by your parent's genes, but how your direct ancestors lived their own lives. As a result, it's easy to grow downright pessimistic of being on equal footing with others.

Welcome to the wonderful world of epigenetics, where your current obesity and heart disease might have been caused by the Nazis over half a century ago. You might think this is a joke, and it is, but it would be way less funny if your Dutch mother had been pregnant with you between late 1944 and early 1945. This is the period where the Dutch famine happened, where the Nazis punished the Dutch population for civil disobedience by withholding food. Most of the population starved, and when the pregnant women within this timeframe gave birth, their babies developed certain unique traits. Not only were they smaller than average, and stayed so throughout their lives, but they also had a much higher rate of heart disease, diabetes and obesity.

Researchers postulate that the stress hormones and malnourishment of the pregnant mothers "programmed" the children to develop in such a way [38]. In essence, their bodies learnt that the outside world was dangerous and often prone to scarcity, thus they had to keep as much food as possible and take any potential threat very seriously. To add insult to injury, if you're temporarily separated from your mother at an early developmental stage, as war is prone to do, this could provoke permanent character traits as well. It can, for example, make one more prone to stress [39]. Sadly, stress has been proven to inhibit learning as well [40]. As such, you might not be a world-renowned figure, despite potentially having the genes, the means, the luck and the upbringing, because your ancestors lived a stressful life and passed on the side effects to you.

All is not doom and gloom though, at the end of the day, the reason for why epigenetic changes are passed on to you, is to give you a better fighting chance in the real world, to be adapted to novel circumstances. Irrespective of all that, our everyday decisions have more bearing of where we end up in than whether your grandpa got stressed one afternoon. This is one of the reasons I have my doubts when people somehow assume that stock picking abilities can be passed down. It's such a specific skill, that it just seems bizarre.

Surely, if it was a genetic adaptation of some sort, you'd see clans of people who had the trait. Yet, as books like *The Millionaire Next Door* suggest, where there aren't artificial safety nets, most millionaires' wealth is made in a single generation and then the fortune is usually lost within one or two generations[14].

Furthermore, in terms of inheriting skillsets, this is not at all how evolution operates. Yes, it is true that there are skills that are passed on. Often this happens by tradition, through apprenticeships and the like. That doesn't quite fit our bill

---

14 That is unless the fortune is such a comically huge amount, where even when mismanaged by the heirs it survives, or is tied to autonomous investment vehicles, which cannot be meddled with by the heirs. Some examples that come to mind are the Rothschilds and the Fugger line.

though, we're looking for a skill that comes naturally and with little coaxing. At which point, we'd probably turn up empty-handed. What evolution does, when it somehow comes across a skillset it wishes to preserve because they're useful in aiding survival and/or reproduction is to pass on the facility for developing it. This is otherwise known as the "Baldwin effect." [41]

In other words, evolution does not pass on a skill per se, but passes on the ability to learn and develop it easier. If, for example, knowing algebra was a useful skill to have in one's survival and/or reproduction, evolution would pass on the facility to understand numbers and think in a numerate way, given that individuals with that facility would have an advantage. At the end of the day, one would still have to develop the skill through practice and repetition, but would have a greater desire and ease to do so. As such, genetics and biology are determining the boundaries of what the potential abilities are going to be throughout our lives.

Nevertheless, a lot of what we consider as set in stone in terms of human behaviour, is actually, at best, set in mud. Potentially, someone could have everything going for them in terms of initial starting position (imagine that they've been bred in a laboratory with the sole purpose of stock picking), but if they do not exercise those capacities, then the average person, if he worked hard enough, could do better. Raw instinct has nothing on actually knowing what you're doing.

6 - The Flintstones and the Modern Stone Age Family

"I may not have gone where I intended to go, but I think I have ended up where I needed to be."
- Douglas Adams, The Long Dark Tea-Time of the Soul

About 30,000 to 40,000 years ago something very curious happened. Humanity started to behave less like animals, and began to develop the first vestiges of culture. For the first time ever, we began to develop abstract thinking and symbolic behaviour, and culture was born. This was the time wherein humans started acting for less than utilitarian reasons. We started representing nature through art, using ornamentation and creating burial rituals for the dead. This is such a huge leap, that it is often called "The Creative Explosion," but other competing hominids, like the Neanderthals, did not join in with these advances [42].

It's unclear what exactly happened which shifted our behaviour in such a radical way. Some have suggested that our voice boxes changed enough for us to develop proper speech, others suggest that a random genetic change allowed our brains to finally mature enough for us to be able to think abstractly, but overall it is still unclear. To further add to the difficulties, we're not exactly sure how the hypothetical change was propagated - as either a handful of people ate from the tree of knowledge and used this advantage to take over the world, or a large portion of Homo sapiens developed the adaptation in parallel.

These two possible interpretations are dubbed as the Multiregional Continuity Theory (MRC), which attests that modern humans developed this adaptation in parallel, all over the world, at roughly the same time; and the Out of Africa Theory (OOA), which supports that a small subset of modern Homo sapiens developed in Africa and rapidly supplanted every other hominid variation out there [43].

Whatever it was, we owe all that we eventually became to this random change. If we put this change within the dual-process theory, we can say that human thought up to this point was governed by direct impressions (System 1) but, for the first time ever, we started developing nuance (System 2). This was, and still is, a tricky adaptation. For where there is nuance, and abstraction, there is room for error and misinterpretation.

Before we move on to the subject of abstraction, we must first explain how we come to have the impressions that we use to abstract. System 1 is a cognitive process that collates contextual information to determine which information is relevant for a given situation. It does so with the use of heuristic judgements - algorithms that determine the hierarchy of information based on clues within the environment. Heuristic judgements are permanently running in the back of our mind, helping us to make sense of things both simple and complex. In everyday situations, they typically work adequately, which is why it is difficult to acknowledge our cognitive failings in more complex matters.

Whilst the mind is a universe unto itself, there are patterns that our brain follows to categorise our thoughts. In his book *Thinking Fast and Slow*, Daniel Kahneman identified six main heuristic judgements, which create the bulk of our cognitive biases:

1. **Anchoring** - A process by which you inadvertently peg your expectations on the first piece of information that could theoretically fit within the parameters of the matter at hand. This "anchor" will be the Platonic standard by which you assess any further pieces of information. If a high number is initially quoted, humans have a propensity to overestimate, and if a lower number is initially mentioned, humans tend to underestimate numbers.

   In financial analysis, this could be triggered in reports or stock pitches, wherein forecasts could be put in the medium, and regardless of whether they have any merit or not, we take them at face value and any further information we receive will be analysed against that artificial gold standard.

2. **Availability** - Humans, possessing a reduced perspective and understanding of the world, have a tendency to make sense of complex systems through their own experiences. In other words, this heuristic gives a hierarchical value to the likelihood of scenarios by how easy it is to think of examples of similar situations.

   The underlying assumption in this cognitive process is that the user possesses knowledge of a representative sample of all available scenarios, and failing that, that the user lives in a static environment with no unpredictable and random events. For most of human history, this much was true, humans have existed for around 160,000 years and it was only in the last 40,000 where behavioural modernity[15] started. Additionally, it was only in the last 11,500 years or so that agriculture allowed for sedentary tribes to exist, and with it civilization. Once society was established, humans designed institutions and cultural norms that created unconscious mechanisms (such as the free market) that often have unforeseen consequences that may not be self-evident until many generations later. Change became the norm.

15 A set of behaviours that distinguishes Homo sapiens from other animals. Among the list of behavioural traits are abstract thinking, culture creation and planning depth.

In statistics, the greatest variance can occur with the smallest sample sizes, as one might have inadvertently chosen a random data string that contains a lot of circumstantial outliers. In the same way, minuscule moments in time may seem to be the norm to contemporaries, but they may just be an anomaly in the system. Sooner or later, there is a regression to the mean of the system, and this often requires radical change. An investor, failing to see the forest for the trees, may accidentally be caught in the crossfire of such a regressionary force, and inadvertently put his wealth in jeopardy.

3. **Substitution** - Answers are often unavailable without further information, time or analysis. Yet, it still remains that our everyday lives require decisions on difficult matters. As such, a heuristic judgement by which we efficiently answer questions, is via subconsciously substituting the question altogether for one where the answer is more readily available.

In an interesting study, Kahneman and Tversky analysed this heuristic with the "Linda Problem," wherein they offered the following conundrum to a group of participants [44]:

Linda is 31-years-old, single, outspoken and very bright. She majored in philosophy. As a student, she was deeply concerned with issues of discrimination and social justice, and also participated in anti-nuclear demonstrations.

Which is more probable?

1. Linda is a bank teller.

2. Linda is a bank teller and is active in the feminist movement.

85% of the participants responded that Option 2 is more likely, even though Option 2 is, by definition, only a fraction of the possibilities in Option 1. It's possible to be a bank teller and a feminist, but it's also possible to be a host of other traits. Nevertheless, Option 2 is far more appealing, even though it's far more restrictive as well, as it fits within the narrative that we have established. System 1 is hence artificially limiting our possible interpretations of these events, to create a better story; if it helps to tell a good fib, our brains tend to favour that result.

Economic analysis tends to use a narrative approach, it seeks to predict scenarios by following an allegorical style. It creates a coherent narration with a clear beginning, middle and end, often both with a villain and a plausible resolution. It stands to reason that because of this heuristic, one should be sceptical of analysis that focuses on explaining results with fanciful, convoluted stories, as offering a cause for an effect is an effective way of convincing people, even if the story is untrue upon further inspection. The more complex the story, the more we should be careful. We thought we knew Linda as a person, and what she would do with her life because of a brief blip of information, and much in the same way we think we understand businesses because we saw a brief blip on a quarterly report.

4. **Optimism and Loss Aversion** - Traditional economic theory asserts that Homo economicus[16] is risk-neutral, meaning that he would take a fair bet, like a coin toss. A Homo sapiens, on the contrary, is loss averse, as he loses more utility by losses than he gains by earning. Having said this, humans possess such a capacity for doublethink that they underestimate the likelihood of risks. In particular, when the risks are not as evident one way or the other, humans tend to believe that they're in a unique situation, and thus the traditional risk ratio doesn't apply to them, while simultaneously believing that their results will be far beyond the norm.

   We're horrible judges of our own conditions and abilities, as by definition we have our ego tied into the mix. Add to it a healthy dosage of magical thinking and the narrative fallacy, and any unbiased self-assessment we could have had flies straight out the window. Hence, even in simple things we are unfoundedly optimistic. For example, 93% of American drivers and 69% of Swedish drivers claim to be above average in their driving abilities - a claim of dubious statistical probability, to say the least [45].

---

16 A concept making a distinction between humans and the creatures that rational choice theory implies that humans are.

Consequently, even though people's emotional wellbeing is tied to them not incurring losses, they will often take wild gambles, as they underestimate the risk and overestimate the potential payoff - case in point, people who play the lottery. In other words, in investing, one should not expect supernormal profits as a given, and consider historical averages of the industry as a whole.

5. **Framing** - Raw data and information would seem to be nonpartisan, for a number isn't supposed to conceal the truth if it was arrived at through honest and respectable methods. Nevertheless, the underlying interpretation of the data is always partisan. The backdrop before which an idea is placed will be the strongest contributor to the interpretation the idea is given; as humans have Platonic predispositions to what is considered "good" and "bad," yet the filters we use to identify them are extremely contextual. It would stand to reason that a party interested in achieving an outcome might frame the issue in a way that would suit them.

A collection of researchers in the *New England Journal of Medicine* explored such an idea by asking medical advice from physicians on treating cancer [46]. The two options were surgery and radiation. The five-year survival rates clearly favour surgery over radiation, yet there is the caveat of an initial surge in mortality when choosing surgery. The statistics regarding surgery were presented as follows to two different groups of doctors:

1. The one-month survival rate is 90%.

2. There is a 10% mortality rate in the first month after surgery.

In the first group, 84% of physicians chose surgery over radiation. In the second group, only 50% chose it. In other words, lives may be decided by how an idea is framed, even if done unintentionally. The first option, by emphasising survival, biases the person to think about the possibility of life; whereas the second option makes the listener think about death and how they might be directly responsible for ordering a man to die. The exact same information, but presented in a different light, can have dramatically different interpretations.

In regards to investing, this raises some interesting concerns. Firstly, as is pointed out in *The Intelligent Investor* by Benjamin Graham, balance sheets and income statements can be manipulated to show non-existent growth or trends due to how they treat certain line items [47]. These are meddled with to such an extent that in the book's commentary it's advocated to read company reports backwards to forwards, as they have to explain their methodology in the notes, which are often hidden away in the back and written in nigh incomprehensible language. Secondly, if something damaging manages to come through this first line of defence in a company, and the investing population catches wind of it, companies have teams of people that function as personal Public Relations consultants, and go by the name of Investor Relations. These people, unlike the scientifically-minded physicians who may subconsciously frame the argument in a certain way, do have a vested interest in the wellbeing of the company, and thus reframing information is one of their primary job occupations. *Caveat Emptor* should apply when dealing with companies, and businesses should have a good and proven track record of management, honesty and profitability before attempting to invest in them.

6. **Sunk-Cost** - This heuristic judgement refers to a progressive escalation of commitment in a certain area solely because there's been commitment in the past, and not because it's beneficial in the short- or long-term to continue to do so. Cumulative decision-making, wherein one considers all the assets that have been utilised to achieve a certain scenario, is liable to lead to this fallacy. Reason being that one may frame the argument in such a way that it could be possible to earn a benefit proportional to the cost incurred, rather than accepting the failure of one's decision and writing off unpayable liabilities. Instead, one tries to dig oneself out of a hole, by digging an even deeper one.

A perfect example is former presidential candidate John Kerry's testimony before subcommittees of the U.S. Senate in April 1971 where he rhetorically asked "How do you ask a man to be the last man to die in

> Vietnam? How do you ask a man to be the last man to die for a mistake?" whilst criticising the then ongoing violence in Vietnam. Meaning that because people have died in the past for an error in judgement (the Vietnam War) it became policy of the United States to continue to send people to die simply because the deaths of all soldiers beforehand would somehow be rendered pointless by accepting the fact that circumstances were different than originally imagined.
>
> In investing, this heuristic judgement may allow one to rationalise one's losses in such a way as to make them momentarily palatable. For example, a business may have failed, but a business owner may decide to pump liquidity into the enterprise, to great expense, rather than write off the investment as a failure. As such, one ends up losing more money than would have otherwise been lost by trying to mitigate one's losses.

It is with these heuristic judgements that we build stories and abstract narratives, where we inadvertently lie to ourselves, as they aggregate on each other, and create an unseemly mess of our understanding. The more we believe that we understand the world, the less we actually know. Psychologists have termed this as the *Dunning-Kruger Effect* wherein people first starting to learn a skill suffer from illusory superiority. Few people are aware that they have not seen the full complexity of a skill, and hence assume that they know a good portion of what there is to know [48]. The uneducated and the ill-informed tend to believe they're knowledgeable and behave accordingly, gaining status and respect for their unwavering confidence. Field experts, on the other hand, tend to have a diminished confidence in their belief that they understand all worth knowing, as they've been exposed to all that they do not know. Accordingly, they develop a humility in their field of study and rarely adopt extremist attitudes.

By definition, we know less about any given topic than the experts, as such we usually take them at their word. The problem is that we don't know who the experts are, and often can't tell them apart from the charlatans, as they both use similar nigh incomprehensible jargon. Back in the day, we used to know all people in our tribe personally, and thus we knew who was actually worth listening to, as the results spoke for themselves. Nowadays, people publish their successes, but rarely their failures. Thus, there's a survivor bias[17] towards kooks that happen to try something extremely risky and come out unscathed. Truth is, we don't really know anyone, unless they are in our immediate social circle or there's a large and transparent enough sample size to be able to make accurate estimations about their abilities.

We may only truly be able to maintain cohesive structures of about 150 people in our day-to-day lives. Yet, we somehow managed to create cities of millions of people. How is that possible? In short, it was the power of stories and fiction, which allowed us to bridge the gap between cultural necessity and biological constraints.

Humans have an "ingroup" and "outgroup" bias, meaning that we are kinder, more caring and understanding to anyone within a group to which we believe we belong [49]. Conversely, we are hostile, more prejudiced, less generous and less understanding to anyone we believe falls outside those perceived groups. This is why millionaires give proportionally less of their income to charity than poor people. Poorer people see themselves as part of the flock, and feel more empathy toward those in need [50]. For most of human history, the "ingroup" has mainly been comprised of people with whom we shared blood relation.

It made evolutionary sense to treat those in our ingroup with care and compassion. By helping the community, you inadvertently helped yourself - or more precisely, your genes. For example, if you happened to save the life of multiple family members, at the cost of your own, your genes still have a chance of being widely propagated through your blood ties. This is how you can find altruism within a selfish system. Ultimately, a chicken is an egg's way of creating more eggs. The same idea applies to humans. We are somewhat servile to our biological programming.

---

17 It's the tendency to overestimate the chances of success by simple virtue that examples of success are readily available, rarely do examples of failure come to mind. It's an example of the availability heuristic, which we mentioned earlier.

Civilization came about with the invention of a social mechanism that co-opted a natural impulse, and used it for its own purposes. We expanded the familial bond by fudging the definition of what it means to be a family. All of a sudden, all people of a certain ethnicity were birthed by some spirit, god or some such mythical creature. We were all brothers now, under the watchful eye of a paternalistic figure. Eventually, these ethnic alliances would come to share a culture and thus all of a sudden, the "ingroup" would expand to be the size of a nation.

We invented a fictional reality through pure consent, which allowed us to achieve an outcome we found useful. Our small hunter-gatherer bands expanded into larger entities, but soon we reached a new hurdle. Small groups are, more or less, self-policing. Nobody can truly get away with any crime and consequently any detrimental deviance is stamped out quickly and effectively.

The larger a community, the more difficult the maintenance of the community becomes. You must thus expand on the fiction which unified them in the first place, and create a behavioural framework. Which means that the mythical beings which birthed us are no longer pleased to see their progeny roam free. Now they wished for order - as such, rules and traditions are crafted to keep the divine beings happy.

Tradition becomes the framework by which we understand reality. The earlier analogy of a computer might make this clearer: Imagine your brain as the hardware on a computer. No matter what program you try to run on it, it has to be operable within the limitations of the hardware, or it won't work at all. Tradition hence becomes the operating system by which ideas function. Tradition, and all its rules and taboos, is what allows the interaction between ideas and our biology. By definition, a culture that has existed for a long time must necessarily have characteristics which allow their culture to thrive, unless it somehow managed to exist with few to no adverse selective pressures. As such, if an idea happens to radically alter the fabric of society, it will usually be dismissed because it may well disrupt that which allowed them to survive in the first place. This is why the older generations usually fret for the changes brought about by the younger ones.

In either case, with these restrictions and modes of thinking, we have the first semblance of laws and a common heritage. Granted, the authority rests in the priests, shamans and magic men but, over time, the authority would eventually trickle down to the everyman. For millennia, only the oracle, priest or perhaps the king could interpret the will of the gods. Their judgement was absolute. Yet one day, far off in the future, all it would take to interpret the will of the gods was a law degree and the ability to recite obscure magic spells in Latin (laws) on command. *Ipso facto*, the modern lawyer is the closest thing we have to real magicians in the twenty-first century, as by quoting an arcane document he can imbue special properties onto something, where there used to be none.

Eventually though, our rules and traditions seem to take a life of their own. Nobody seemed to be truly in control of them. What happened is that the system became far too complex, and much like the weather, became subject to trillions of input points. As a result of this, not a single actor could know and understand the system by themselves. At one point, far into the future, we invented the fiction of efficient markets and rational agents, and this took a life of its own as well.

7 - The Meme Doctor

"Behind this mask there is more than just flesh. Beneath this mask there is an idea. and ideas are bulletproof."
- Alan Moore, V for Vendetta

A gene, in its purest form, is a piece of information whose sole purpose is to be transferred *ad infinitum* to successive generations. In the process of doing so, it adapts to its current environment by mutating and working alongside other genes to develop its potential to the fullest. Memes, which are otherwise known as a unit of culture and thought, work much in the same way and with similar selective pressures. They suffer random changes from being transferred from one person to the next, and they work symbiotically with other memes to generate the most adaptable and transferable idea possible. Note that this does not necessarily mean the best memes are passed on, just ideas that momentarily have an emotional response on the host and are adaptable in many circumstances. For a viral disease to be truly deadly, it can't kill off the host before it's passed itself onto other people, as then it won't have an opportunity to spread. The same concept applies to ideas, especially bad ones.

A bad idea may appear spectacular in the short term. This is because of the survivor bias or, put briefly, because we only see the stories of people who succeeded, not the ones who failed whilst following the wrong idea. As such, bad ideas may seem alluring and possess an aura of invincibility, because of the availability heuristic, as we can't readily think of counterexamples of the meme. The more people follow the meme, the more examples you can think of that favour this erroneous mindset. For this reason, we fall into a false sense of security with wrong ideas, and readily admit them into our lives, thus being infected by them as well.

An idea, by its own design, can only be truly successful by being passed on to another host. Otherwise, it might unceremoniously go extinct. The new host will only pass the idea on to another generation, of potentially infectible hosts, if he or she has a positive or negative reaction to it. For example, when someone tells you a joke, you will only "infect" others with the thought germ if it provoked some reaction: you will only ever tell a joke if it happens to excel in being amazing, terrible (so bad it's good), or if it's offensive (so bad, it invokes the need for shared outrage). Ironically, by doing so you're applying selective pressures to jokes to fit into one of the three criteria, and naturally there will be more of that type. Otherwise they won't be told, and die out by being forgotten.

Facing apathy is the worst thing that can happen to an idea. Love and hate are not opposites to each other - indifference is. The complete absence of response is the antithesis of either of those two powerful emotions, and hence it's the kiss of death to any idea as it simply won't be passed on. If, however, it manages to infect you and make you care enough to pass it on, then you become the latest generation in the pandemic. It also faces adaptive pressures and random mutations, as any game of Chinese Whispers will attest to.

In other words, with each new host, the idea adapts to suit its environment. At times, these random mutations can develop a spandrel, or a completely new use for a by-product of another element within the idea, just as organisms do. A good case study of this occurring is the adoption of Dr.Seuss' children book *Horton Hears a Who!* by the pro-life movement in the United States. Within the book, the following phrase was written in reference to the microscopic *Who* people, whose home was about to be demolished without them having a say in the matter: "A person's a person, no matter how small." Theodor Geisel, who penned many children's books as Dr.Seuss, had no intention whatsoever to ever allude to abortion in that sentence, so much so that he tried to sue the protesters for perverting his words in such a manner [50]. What he failed to realise is that ideas have a life of their own, his original meme had branched off into multiple species that could no longer coexist when put within the same environment.

A successful meme, much like a successful organism, is one that adapts to circumstances and spreads like wildfire. The environment, in this case, being cultures and the minds therein. Ideas can form symbiotic bonds with each other and help perpetuate themselves. This can even happen when on the surface the ideas might be violently opposed to each other. For example, the Roman persecution of Christians did little but bolster their faith and radicalize them. Even when Emperor Nero made living candles out of Christians for his parties, they still failed to see the light that was literally burning over their heads. A few hundred years later and Christianity came to dominate the Roman Empire's inner workings [51]. Surprisingly, had they been left to their own devices, they might not have developed martyrs and thereby publicity, thus likely remaining an even more obscure sect than the one which birthed them in the backwaters of the empire. On the internet, this is known as the *Streisand Effect*, named after the scandal created when Barbra Streisand wanted to get photos of her villa taken off the web. What followed was a media blitz where everyone was discussing the photos, and showing them; precisely because of the drama she herself had created [52]. A fire burns best when obstacles are thrown into its way, not when it's starved for nourishment.

As long as a meme does not wipe the other one out of existence, it may well create an ecology that spreads farther and wider than it could have on its own by pitting the two against each other. Eventually, there might be a tipping point where only one of the two shall survive, thus creating a new status quo. In the meantime, "there's no such thing as bad publicity" after all.

We're getting ahead of ourselves though. Let us momentarily turn back to the Dr.Seuss story and discuss how he accidentally created a monster by having his words twisted to mean something completely different.

Once Dr.Seuss wrote those words in 1955, he ceased to own them. Obviously, he still owned the copyright, but where it truly mattered, in the hearts and minds of the people, they were interpreted in a very different way and became their own product. Much in the same way that when I say the word "house" you have a different image in your mind than I do, we do this for every concept we hear. Much to the chagrin of Plato, there doesn't seem to be a Platonic ideal which we draw on when conversing. Everyone has a slightly different take on reality.

Having said this, we're also not the special unique little snowflakes that our mother tells us that we are. Broadly speaking, we're taught how to think by society – we develop a value system, moral code and an ideal to strive for based on those that our peers already have.

I must stress that this does not necessarily happen voluntarily, nor is it necessarily malicious. This phenomenon occurs whenever you have communication with another human being in any shape or form. Whether you wish it to be so or not one is subtly telegraphing one's value system in the very act of communicating and transferring memes. To quote Oscar Wilde's *The Picture of Dorian Gray* on the matter:

> *"There is no such thing as a good influence, Mr. Gray. All influence is immoral - immoral from the scientific point of view.'*
>
> *'Why?'*
>
> *'Because to influence a person is to give him one's own soul. He does not think his natural thoughts, or burn with his natural passions. His virtues are not real to him. His sins, if there are such things as sins, are borrowed. He becomes an echo of some one [sic] else's music, an actor of a part that has not been written for him. The aim of life is self-development. To realize one's nature perfectly - that is what each of us is here for. People are afraid of themselves, nowadays."*

For the less artistic, and more scientifically-minded readers in my audience, this could partially be called part of the *Sapir-Whorf Hypothesis*. This theory of linguistic relativity states that languages determine thought by providing a framework from which to understand the world. In other words, the language we're using changes how we understand the world itself - our peer groups alter reality.

This phenomenon produces some curious results, on the weirder side of the spectrum, there's the fact that even objective reality seems to be liable to misinterpretation or subject to debate. Russians, for example, can recognize more hues of blue than the average person because their language allows them to make the distinction [53]. Given that their language and culture allow them to make the distinction, it is a detail that people pay attention to, and thus they develop the skill to do it effortlessly.

Changing how we interpret reality itself, can make one develop seemingly supernatural skillsets as well. Certain Australian Aboriginals have the ability to determine the cardinal points of whichever location you put them in, as their language does not have the concept of "right" or "left" and they have to determine everything via cardinal direction "the pot is to the west of the table" [54].

As such, by having to think within a certain framework, you develop a mode of thinking to the detriment of other areas. At the risk of speculating a bit, I suspect that there are optimal ways in which to think about investing. Initial evidence seems encouraging, as Keith Chen found out in 2013 when he discovered that countries with languages featuring terminology to discuss the future in present tense tend to save an average of 6% more of their Gross Domestic Product (GDP) per year [55]. This result is unaffected by the addition of life-cycle-savings controls, holds in every major region of the world, and appears stable across time. The proposed explanation behind it is that by having sentences - which in English sound bizarre - such as "Tomorrow it rains," be grammatically-correct and commonplace, the speakers don't disassociate the future from the present and thus they don't forego saving in exchange of momentary indulgences as readily, given that they subconsciously understand that they're harming their future selves by doing so.

Correlation is not causation, but it definitely gives one food for thought. If this is true then, among many other factors, an accident of language might have helped seal the fate of entire civilizations. For example, if your culture views history as being cyclical, where any advancement will be eventually eroded by the passage of time, does it really make any sense to try to change your surroundings with advancement and innovation? Perhaps a lone individual would buck the trend, but traditionalists of future generations would regress back to the historical mean out of simple inertia and ignore the advancement. Some societies didn't even bother keeping a record of the chronology and succession of their leaders and history, as they saw little point in doing so. Oftentimes they would take past historical events, update the characters to be more contemporary, and tell it as if it had just happened, merely to tell a moralising fable [56].

It's a relatively new notion to think that "history marches on" rather than it being cyclical, which may explain the comparatively lacklustre technological advancement of the last few millennia when compared with the last few centuries (arguably even the last decade). The framework by which we understand our society will undoubtedly mark the limits of that which we think is possible, or worthwhile doing.

A situation that highlights this perfectly is the four-minute mile phenomenon. Several decades ago, it was believed that humans had reached the limits of physical exertion and efficiency. The records that had been recorded were seemingly set in stone and would never be broken, but one day the unthinkable happened - somebody broke them. Almost immediately, when it became known that an Oxford student by the name of Roger Bannister had finally done it, other people began to do it as well. He held the record as the sole verified human being who had done it for only 46 days. Just knowing that it had been done before made people more adept at achieving this previously unbeatable record [57].

This event is usually quoted as a triumph of will and the human spirit, whilst it may be so, it is also a testament to our failure to differentiate objective reality from our collective reality. An obstacle might seem unassailable when viewed from a specific viewpoint, but when viewed from another angle, it might appear trivial. This is why there have been studies hinting at the fact that people who speak more than one language are more creative [58].

By learning and understanding a new framework by which to decode the world, it's easier to solve problems from an unorthodox point of view that most might not have even considered. One should always try to play devil's advocate and try to prove oneself wrong. If an idea that has a large effect on our lives does not survive further examination, it should be discarded. Because of this, at times, communicating with people whom you vehemently disagree with, and trying to understand their reasoning, will inoculate you from becoming too biased, as you may well see a flaw in your line of thinking and amend it. This is of course assuming that the people with whom you're talking are worthwhile hearing, and you are not so dead set in your reasoning that you will offhandedly dismiss any and all evidence.

More often than we care to admit though, we become fanatics to our own particular brand of understanding the world. Hence, we're far more likely to agree with things we are already predisposed toward, and deny anything that does not conform with our pre-established notions. We live in our own little solipsistic universe and aggressively scorn any reminder of the outside world. This paradoxically means that we often present the staunchest defence when presented with more robust and authoritative evidence against our own interpretation.

In psychology, this is called "Reactance Theory," and it affects our relationship with authority. It's even been observed in health matters, where there are objective answers to what the most rational course of action to take is. However, we will often dig into our preconceived biases all the more when faced with something that limits our choices. Hence, it's been suggested that health campaigns ought to be less prescriptive and emphasise more choice - as such you can exert influence over someone without having them be resentful. But this still leaves the door open for dissent and political upheaval. Regardless of what one does, one might not be fully able to make everyone happy or convince them of something objective, despite one's best efforts [59].

Ultimately, Dr.Seuss didn't stand a chance when convincing people that their interpretation was the wrong one, or shouldn't be used to support antiabortion views. Much like parents can't control how their children will end up, a thinker cannot control the final fate of his or her ideas. One day, they will have to venture off into the cold unknown by themselves, and likely won't come out the same as they went in.

8 - On Fake Boobs and Happiness

"I'd far rather be happy than right any day."
- Douglas Adams, The Hitchhiker's Guide to the Galaxy

Natural selection processes are incalculably cruel and ultimately unknowable (two adjectives which incidentally happen to describe a surprising number of my exes). The unconscious forces within a complex system will quickly topple down any sacred cows, as their sole purpose is to perpetuate the system itself. The reason for this ruthless effectiveness is that the impersonal system and rules themselves are judge, jury and executioner - they're self-enforcing.

As long as a human being produces offspring at a steady rate, natural selection as a system does not care whether they're happy and content with their lives. At best, we're Sisyphean animals who roll our emotional boulder up and down the Psyche hills. Just as we think we have it all to be happy and we're up high, something will happen and the boulder will come rolling down. It's not in the best interests of evolution to have happy people. Permanently satisfied people will rarely have the necessary drive to improve their social standing, have copious amounts of sex, have numerous children and be an evolutionary success. It's much better to have them mostly unsatisfied with their current circumstances, but with just enough optimism to think that their big payday is just around the corner.

Evolutionary forces will programme into you the desire to do beneficial actions from a survival and reproduction standpoint by giving you a dopamine rush when you perform them. Exercise, sex and a hearty meal are all things which will put a smile on one's face. The intensity of the feelings will have been carefully calibrated over the eons to help one prioritise what is best for passing on genes to the next generations. Kind of as if you were a junkie and your drug dealer only supplied drugs if you're an upstanding member of society.

Evolution's approach of the kind-hearted drug dealer, who supplies his wares only in proportion to the good that the drug addict does, might work in the long term ... that is until the junkie learns where the drug dealer's stash is and abuses the reward mechanism safeguarding them. Initially, the junkie might keep the pretences and convince himself that he's still performing a good deed, but he will pay himself in a disproportionate amount to what the incentives are worth now that he has full control of his situation and its reward. In biological terms, these are called "Supernormal Stimuli."

As we've shown over the course of this book, the initial circumstances of humanity often involved periods of scarcity or life-threatening circumstances. Yet, over the millennia we've slowly managed to domesticate our environment and utilise it to our whims. We started being able to actively affect the development of various species by helping breed only the organisms that benefit us. We make a mockery of the apparent original intentions of nature, and instead use it for our amusement and benefit. The list is innumerable, but a few of the types of change we have wrought, alongside with some of their effects, include:

- Plants that were previously poisonous are now enjoyed by millions and custom bred for their rich flavour - Wild almonds are mostly inedible, and they contain the poison cyanide, for instance. Vegetation in the wild often has defence mechanisms so as to not be consumed at the wrong moment, or by the wrong species, which wouldn't spread the seeds in the most efficient manner. With the plants we eat, we've mostly managed to sidestep those problems almost entirely [60].

- Animals are bred, which could not exist except in captivity, because their characteristics make them unable to live in the wild - The bulldog mastiff is but an abomination of nature. They should mercifully be put out of their misery by not breeding them. Their head, for the most part, is far too big to be born via anything but caesarean section [61]. Besides that, they have congenital breathing problems, which is why they sound like a sputtering engine, even when at rest.
- Human behaviour alters the ecology of vast regions – Humans are inconvenienced by dense foliage, hence ever since we mastered fire, we've been using it to make the environment suitable to us. Therefore the development of "slash-and-burn" tactics, which destroyed entire forests to make room for arable plains. Classical authors, for example, often mentioned large forests in the Mediterranean, which are mostly non-existent in this day and age [62].

Point is, that at the first sign of dominion over nature, we seem to alter it in our favour. Now, in reference to our dopamine-led incentive systems, since we started to control a lot of the aspects of nature, we could create abundance where there was once scarcity. Sugar, for example, is a resource we naturally crave because it was very hard to come by. If you managed to find it in any sizeable quantity (fruits, berries, etc) it was in your best interests to gorge yourself on as many as you could.

Modern life hijacks these natural impulses and cranks them up to 11. The sweetest meal you might've been able to have 12,000 years ago was perhaps a peach. Now, you can walk into any convenience store and get the sugar intake dozens of times that, with little to no effort. That said, our reward system is still calibrated for prehistoric stimuli. These supernormal stimuli would've been all but impossible to get in the wild, and hence why our mind rewards us so highly for consuming it. It's thoroughly unsurprising that obesity rates skyrocket once a society has enough material wealth and technical know-how to build a McDonald's or to produce pizza in industrial quantities.

Speaking as a formerly obese person, the syren call of a cheesecake is all but irresistible. In comparison though, what might've counted as a succulent treat in the past is now considered a poor substitute for dessert. We've gone so far down the rabbit hole that the stratospheric heights of the supernormal stimuli are all we crave. To a modern audience, past behaviour in regards to a "normal stimuli" seems downright bizarre and ludicrously eccentric - In the Winter of 1742, Frederick the Great famously paid the equivalent of over three years' salary of his court physicians for the pleasure of eating cherries out of season [63].

Food is not the only realm of the supernormal stimuli. It can also go the more cerebral route – for what is a magazine's gossip column but a super-efficient means to convey information regarding the movers and shakers in the community? These insatiable cravings are not things that we were ever meant to actually satiate, they were deliberately designed to be a thirst all but impossible to quench, so that we kept looking for more.

Instead of understanding that there are diminishing returns for doing anything to excess, we reacted like a drug addict by exponentially increasing the dosages and hoping that the reward would increase with it. At some point, it starts being comical the lengths to which we'll go to satisfy our increasingly desensitised minds. Take a look at the glitzy bar in your town where trophy wives hang out. You'll soon realise that these are the first silicone-based life forms on our planet. Humans, in their childish approach in thinking that more of anything is necessarily good, will implant such gigantic fake boobs on themselves, that one has to wonder when it starts counting as a person attached to two globs to silicon, instead of the other way around.

We're far from the only animal to fall for supernormal stimuli. You can substitute some bird's eggs for increasingly larger egg-shaped objects, sometimes even volleyballs; and if they still have a similarity to the original product they will ever more excitedly try to hatch them as their own [64]. Yet, we're the only creatures on the planet that are aware of the sleight of hand, and don't seem to particularly care about it. As long as a woman has great tits, a part of our brain doesn't really care where she got them from. Sex is like pizza after all – even when it's bad, it's still pretty good.

9 - Sex: Need I Say More?

> "Everything is about sex, except sex itself. Sex is about power."
>
> - *Robert Michaels*

I'll grant you that a chapter on sex in a quasi-economic history book seems odd and out of place. A cynical reader might even come to the idea that I have only included a chronology of the evolution of sex and courtship throughout this book to sell more copies. After all - sex sells.

Yet, is that not proof enough that if one wants to understand the development of economics thoroughly, one has to acknowledge the fact that sex sells, and interpret how and why that happens? Considering the amount of time, effort and money that is expended in its pursuit, it would be remiss to ignore its effects on our behaviour simply out of prudishness. So I shall talk about it, warts and all ... *(perhaps that wasn't the most appropriate wording, come to think about it)*. Regardless, throughout this book I will analyse how courtship and sexuality develops, as a response, and as a cause of social and technological developments.

I will spare you the birds and the bees talk, as I assume that you are well acquainted with such platitudes already. If not, your parents owe you an awkward conversation where they haphazardly shove a pack of condoms in your hands before they push you off into one of life's strangest and most paradoxical areas.

In either case, contrary to what your parents, teachers and general fear-mongering might have taught you, it's difficult to get someone pregnant. Most women are not fertile most of the time. If you're particularly unlucky it can take several hundred unprotected attempts to sire even a single child. Think of Henry VIII who essentially took close to a lifetime to sire a paltry number of heirs, despite his enthusiastic efforts to the contrary. Though, the average is a pregnancy every 1 in 20 times when there's unprotected sex [65].

This initially seems like a terrible waste of time and energy, from a biological standpoint. After all, we've established that, from the point of view of genetics, the only purpose of a human being is to create more human beings. It gets even stranger, humans engage in sex even when there are no chances whatsoever that there is a chance for pregnancy.

A good proportion of animals only go through the trouble of showing any signs of possessing a libido when the female is in heat, i.e., when she can get pregnant. Humans, and a few of our other evolutionary cousins, hide their ovulation cycles and have sex at random and frequent intervals [66]. To further add to the mystery, anatomically speaking, human beings possess gigantic sexual organs, in proportion to their body size. Reports, which I'm frankly unwilling to double-check personally and thus I'll take them at their word, point to the fact that the massive silverback gorillas have a whopping 2.54 cm (1 inch) penis [67] - which must surely put a smile on all my male readers' faces.

We seem to be the sexual deviants of the animal kingdom. We are one of the few animals that have sex recreationally and as a bonding exercise. Yet here as well, the Rousseauian myth of the noble savage is pervasive. Books such as *Sex at Dawn* point to the fact that human beings have all these traits to facilitate consensus by widespread sex to all. After all, who can really deny that they would be happier if they were getting laid all the time? Would one really rebel against a status quo that is providing them with food, leisure and sex?

Childcare, it's been argued, in a hunter-gatherer community where collective labour is required for one's survival, would be done by all. In a sense, all adults would be the child's parents. As no man would truly know whether they were the father, they would have no other choice but to treat all of the children as their own, if they feel a sense of loyalty to their kin [68]. This is nice in theory, and there is a fair amount of evidence to support elements of it, but it paints an overly utopian understanding of humans in a finite world.

For one, it ignores the role of jealousy and the desire to monopolise sexual resources. Meaning that there would be multiple cavemen taking the lion share of the bounty and outcompeting all others; leaving the rest to do little else but polishing their spears. Secondly, there's evidence to suggest that with the advent of property rights, and with it the ability to entrench power structures through inheritance, the gender reproduction ratios became extremely skewed. Meaning that, for a period when agriculture started, for every 17 women that reproduced, only one man reproduced [69].

Males, in the grand scheme of life, whether we like to admit it or not, are expendable. Imagine a war that wipes all but 10% of all men, within a generation or two the society could easily recover. The reverse is not true, however. Worse still, if only 10% of women remained, there would likely be deadly violence and increased cultural stratification to restrict access to females. Men receive an endorphin rush when engaged in competition. This chemical, in its raw and unadulterated form, has unironically been likened to cocaine. Add to it the promise of sexual gratification and our testosterone increases, which is a chemical that unsurprisingly controls both the drive for sex and dominance. Even in the modern world, male death rates jump at the dawn of puberty and stay consistently higher thereafter [70]. In essence, we males get more aggressive and risk loving in an attempt to increase our social status, which will ensure more and better quality of partners - or as Tony Montana put it in *Scarface* "In this country, you gotta make the money first. Then when you get the money, you get the power. Then when you get the power, then you get the women."

I can almost hear the howling of the third-wave feminist brigade, and their politically-correct counterparts as I write this. But this is pretty much why men tend to far outnumber women in anything involving deviation from the mean variance. True, we far outnumber women in prisons by orders of magnitude, homelessness, suicides, etc., but we also far outnumber women in top management positions, inventions, and essentially any creative endeavour one would care to mention, despite an ever-fanatical devotion to quotas.

In any room filled with a lot of people, the dumbest and the smartest person to be found there are statistically more likely to be males, yet both genders have about the same average IQ [71]. In other words, men tend to cluster on either extreme of the bell curve, whilst women cluster towards the centre; and hence in aggregate neither sex is more intelligent [72].

Now, please do not misconstrue what I have to say in thinking that men are the superior gender - Lord knows that many people have lost their jobs even alluding to the points I'm making today. There can, and there have been many women out there who have broken these social/biological conventions, and society has been all the richer for it. Truth is, men need women as much as the other way around. Neither gender is superior, we live in a state of symbiosis where our strengths balance out the other's weaknesses. In the algorithm of evolution, women are far more valuable than men are. It makes evolutionary sense to use men as foot soldiers and risk takers to defend and enhance the gene pool, as even if very few men were to succeed in their approach to life, humanity would still march on.

In the masculine world, fortune often favours the bold and novel, as such we have a propensity for more risk taking, and because of this have a broader deviation from the mean in behavioural patterns. Women have a much narrower band in which they can operate successfully from an evolutionary perspective. Reason being that at absolute most they can have one child every nine months during the handful of years they're fertile (even then risking severe birth defects the older they get), whilst men could potentially sire as many children, as the most prolific woman in human history, in a single very fun month from puberty to the end of their natural lives.

As such, from an evolutionary perspective, it pays to be risk loving as a man, given that your success on the social hierarchy often affects the availability of resources which can be used in the essentially limitless pursuit of women.

Whereas women, due to the slower potential pace in reproduction, are more prone to be risk neutral or even risk averse [73].

A good example of the two gender behavioural quirks at work is with the modern phenomena of microfinance. A microloan is a small credit extended to impoverished borrowers who typically lack collateral, steady employment, or a verifiable credit history. They're issued by specialised companies, as traditional banks hardly see the point in bothering with them given the tiny profit margin and high rates of default. It used to be that these microlending companies issued the loans to either gender, but soon they began to put gender-based restrictions on the issuance of loans.

Turns out that not only were women more reliable borrowers overall, but they were willing to accept smaller loans and were likelier to listen to investing advice. Whereas men refused to take smaller amounts, often drank or gambled the money away and more often than not defaulted on the loans due to the risky behaviour they engaged in, whilst ignoring expert advice [74]. The highly erratic behaviour by men leads a small portion of them to hit the jackpot, but the vast majority of them end up as failures. At the risk of repeating myself, I'll restate that in humans, males tend to cluster on either end of the bell curve both for good and for bad, whilst women follow a more conservative pattern of behaviour overall, which admittedly is a far more sensible strategy when it comes to investing. Reason being that by utilising this mindset one may not be able to reliably reach the top tier, but steady and prudent management is far more likely to yield beneficial results over the long run.

It may be the case that this is why males would initially seem to be far more libidinous than their female counterparts. In biological terms, other than STDs, there are few consequences for males to indiscriminately have sex with as many people as possible. Women, on the other hand, when they engage in unprotected sex, essentially play Russian Roulette with their lives. As such, if they take the risk, they will want to do it with a man that has the traits that would warrant such an investment.

Men, for their own part, have other mechanisms in place to guarantee that women have the "right" offspring (in other words, their own). Entire volumes, such as *Sperm Wars*, have been written on the male sexual strategies, but we shall abridge them somewhat:

- **First**, males seem to have a bias for chaste women. As such, the optimal arrangement, from a man's point of view is a harem structure, where the women are monogamous to the patriarch, whilst the men are free to have sex with whomever they please.
- **Secondly**, if a man fails to reach a harem-style option. A man has to stack the odds in his favour. It might seem curious to say, but most ejaculated sperm does not have the capacity to impregnate. There are 3 variants of sperm that are secreted, of which the ratio depends on the subconscious tabulations of a man and how likely he thinks that the women with which he is having sex with have been (or will be) in sexual contact with other males in the recent past (or near future):
    1. *Impregnating Sperm - these do what it says on the tin, and are the ones we collectively dread when having a bit of fun.*
    2. *Attacking Sperm - their sole purpose is to kill off any rival's sperm.*
    3. *Blocking Sperm - these are the rejects and the deformed ones that can barely swim. Their purpose is to act as a living barricade against any competitor sperm.*
- **Thirdly**, the physical structure and size of the penis allows them to create a vacuum, which allows it to pump and scrape out rival sperm out, much in the same way the plunger in a syringe operates.
- **Fourthly**, which is by far the most controversial point on this list, is the threat and use of violence; be it through social rules or outright rape. It may not be the most palatable of solutions in a man's repertoire to secure his lineage, but one cannot argue with its effectiveness for securing a legacy. Just ask Genghis Khan, whose genes are held by 0.5% of the world population [75]. Or ask the Romans, who were initially little more than a band of roving outcasts, criminals and marauders who managed to create a line of succession and ensuing civilization only after kidnapping

> and raping the Sabine women. Or ask traditional Muslim communities that perform clitorectomies, and have women don burqas, even in the gruesome desert heat, to ensure that they are hidden away and do not tempt another man, but the one they've been allotted to.

Depressingly, such cycles of sexual aggression were, and arguably still are, more the norm than what one would hope. This historically happened to such an extent that women evolved coping mechanisms to survive. When your whole village was wiped out - and you were spared because of your perceived value to the raiders - it makes little sense to fight back against physically-superior attackers. Adapting to your new circumstances is key. From a genetic standpoint, you wouldn't be able to pass on your genes if you were killed, and thus there would inadvertently be a selective pressure against your behaviour.

In other words, as a woman in such dangerous circumstances, it makes sense to befriend or mollify your attackers. This is why it's been suggested that women mainly rely on social contacts to face dangers, otherwise known as the "tend and befriend" strategy as opposed to the "fight or flight" instinct [76]. The key is to be able to adapt their behaviour to suit the new circumstances and novel cultures.

Women's sexuality is far more adaptable than men's, which is in many ways a survival technique because of the implicit threat of violence. The concept of Erotic Brain Plasticity highlights this: men, past a certain critical period, are relatively immune to social prescriptions on what to desire - women, on the other hand, have often been known to radically change their stance on turn-ons and turn-offs, even the preferred gender to be intimate with, according to the environment they themselves are currently in [77]. There have even been studies which indicate that a woman's psychology is so malleable that under the right circumstances they can be turned on by viewing sexual acts of different species - whereas males present no such response [78].

Before we assign any morality to any of these behaviours, we must first remember that biological effectiveness is amoral. It's irrelevant what we think ought to happen, the natural mechanisms that drive us are unconcerned with our thoughts about them. One should not get mad at the lion for eating a zebra, because that is what lions do. Yet, it would be foolish to not put a fence between you and the lion simply because the lion is just following its natural compunction.

Morality is a luxury for when our bellies are full and our basic - or psychological - needs are sated. Only then can we sit back and ponder about the world from our ivory towers as we assign labels. Human behaviour did not evolve in such an environment. As such, there are an infinite amount of shades of grey. For example, over 62% of women have had rape fantasies, with a median of four times per year [79]. Among them, you would be hard pressed to find anyone who genuinely wants to experience it in real life.

For every adaptation in one gender there is the other side of the coin. Men have a proclivity towards rape, in fact one study even came to the conclusion that 35% of men had a self-assessed (as such likely underreported) non-zero chance of raping someone, if the chances of discovery were nil [80]. These impulses and desires are simply a fact of life, despite our best attempts of forgetting about them and playing nice, they will still be there.

Yet sometimes the thin veneer of social niceties cracks and the strange and twisted side of our psyche surfaces to the mainstream. It's because of this that we have bestsellers such as *Fifty Shades of Grey*, which is about a very rich and powerful man using said influence to engage a young woman in deviant sexual acts. Far from a book on the fringes of society, this book went on to become one of the most successful pieces of literature in world history. A quick glance at it will dissuade you from any notion that it was the superb prose that transformed this into such a hit. No, in spite of all its flaws, it was able to accidentally tap into a far more primal mechanism. Clearly the dark side of our psyche has a certain allure and profitability - the book alone being worth around $100 million [82], with the first movie of the trilogy earning $571 million [83]. This was a billion-dollar empire birthed in spite of the social taboos in place, as well as despite the actual artistic abilities of the people involved in the project.

Human beings are paradoxical in both their morality and behaviour; and we must accept that human beings naturally play by a much older playbook than modern society allows. We are a far cry from the rational creatures espoused in economic models, who have coherent and non-contradictory thoughts and actions.

Real human beings often want things that are dangerous and taboo, often precisely because they are so. Maximising one's utility, whatever that means, was the central tenet of my lessons in economics at university, but looking at the tangible world, we can see that viewing life in such black and white terms is often dangerous and patently unhelpful.

10 - Culture Vultures

"Nothing in biology makes sense except in the light of evolution."

- Theodosius Dobzhansky

Over the course of this book, we have compared the human brain to a computer that runs an operating system (culture) which processes software (ideas). Now, imagine trying to install the latest operating system on a twenty-year-old computer. You might be able to squeeze out some productivity here and there through careful programming, but eventually you'd hit a wall in what the machine can feasibly do. Under this analogy, it would be difficult, if not impossible, to implement certain ideas without a complete overhaul of the underlying system.

It's been suggested that some mental disorders people have are actually natural adaptations that are outdated in the modern world [83]. They're not malfunctioning mental processes, they might be performing just as they were initially intended. It's just that they haven't been updated in millennia, and thus are ill-suited to function in modernity. For example, psychologists have pointed out that the permanent subordination of men to their bosses in the workplace often makes them lethargic, depressed, substance abusers, or worst of all, tyrants in their homes. By being unable to rise up to their desired heights in the sky-high dominance hierarchy, they seek to compensate for their lack of status by abusing their most defenceless members of the households, which includes their wives and offspring [84]. Reason being that this permanent and relentless character subjugation simply did not exist in the hunter-gatherer era, as people were their own bosses or willingly gave authority to one of their peers. They had to consent to take orders from someone, whereas the modern age just gives you the non-choice of starving if you don't. So, men sense the wrongness of the situation, but when being unable to do anything to change this for their whole lives, they eventually lash out - a cornered animal is always at its most dangerous as it might fight tooth and nail to survive.

There are limits to how much brain power can overcome matter - you can only bend a rigid object so much before it snaps. Humans are not blank slates, despite what the mewling ideologues and hardline philosophers might say. From birth, we have some very real biases, and they tend to come about when said biases would have been useful to have, to quote evolutionary psychologist David Buss [85]:

> *"The specific fears of humans seem to emerge in development at precisely the time when the danger would have been encountered (Marks, 1987). Specialized perceptual templates for spiders suggesting an evolved spider-detection mechanism, for example, have been documented to emerge by five months of age (Rakison & Derringer, 2007). Fears of heights and strangers emerge in infants around six months of age, which coincides with the time when they start to crawl away from their mothers (Scarr &S alapatek, 1970). In a study concerning heights, 80 percent of infants who had been crawling for forty-one or more days avoided crossing over a "visual cliff' (an apparent vertical drop that was in fact covered with sturdy glass) to get to their mothers (Bertenthal, Campos &Caplovitz, 1983). Crawling increases the risk of contact with spiders, dangerous falls, and encounters with strangers without the protective mother in close proximity, and so the emergence of these fears at this time seems to coincide with the onset of the adaptive problems. Human infants' fear of strangers has been documented in*

> *a variety of different cultures, including Guatemalans, Zambians, Kung Bushmen, and Hopi Indians (Smith, 1979). In fact, the risk of infants being killed by strangers appears to be a common "hostile force of nature" in nonhuman primates (Hrdy, 1977; Wrangham & Peterson, 1996), as well as in humans (Daly & Wilson, 1988). Interestingly, human children are considerably more fearful of male strangers than of female strangers-fears that correspond to likelihood that male strangers historically have been more dangerous than female strangers (Heerwagen & Orians, 2002)."*

Our natural behavioural biases have a reason for existing. Honed through millions of years of evolution, they're designed to be *on average* the most effective survival strategy in use. Nevertheless, these biases often have stronger or lesser imperative for existing depending on one's environment. For example, if you live in a colder climate you are much more likely to develop coping strategies for winter, than had you grown up in the savannah.

Over time, these differing selective pressures lead to different lifestyles and traditions. Gather enough of these beliefs, lifestyles and traditions, and you've got yourself a culture. In other words, culture will come into existence as a direct response to the environment and our natural predispositions.

Some people, on first hearing this, will balk at the idea. Stating that we're capable of rational thought, and hence there's an infinite possible variety in which to arrange our desires. "We're not subject to the whims of nature!" they'll cry out. Yet, if there was truly that much of an infinite possible variability, why is it that culture and behaviours tend to fall within a very predictable narrow band? If we were truly as free to choose whatever we wish to do or think, I'm surprised we don't have societies run by children or pets. Those are options after all in a spectrum of infinite possibilities.

Instead, whether you go to the mud huts in the Amazon or the high-rises of New York City, you more or less tend to see the same scenes. There's love, jealousy, anger, warmth, cruelty, etc. Our emotions, hopes and desires work similarly and we tell analogous stories. Read any work of fiction invented in the last 10,000 years and you will recognise the character motivations, even if the stage is different than our own. Research any long-standing society that has existed and you will more or less see the same patterns in hierarchy and social dynamics.

This last point exists to the chagrin of politically-motivated anthropologists, who try to find "noble savages" wherever they go. One of the more notable cases was the research of cultural anthropologist Margaret Mead, who claimed to have found a Samoan society with reversed sex roles, devoid of sexual jealousy, without competition of any sort and peaceful. This was highly publicised and shown as proof of humanity's fall from grace. Subsequent researchers found that many of the original reports of these tropical cultures were simply false. She had either wilfully deceived the scientific community, had been led astray by the locals or had misinterpreted what she observed based on her own biases. One study even found that the murder rates with the Samoan people were higher than the "decadent" United States [86]! So much for free love and Noble Savages.

We were the same creatures 40,000 years ago and now. The fact of the matter is that there seems to be a very compelling case for human universal traits in behaviour [87]. There are no known exceptions for these behaviours. The only thing that changes is the intensity and the form in which we express them because of the environment. Curiously enough, the cultural traits evoked by the environment can be as far-reaching as Mom's cooking. There's a very interesting theory that states that cultures that developed in warmer climates tend to use more spices in their cooking than those that developed in colder climates because of natural selection [88].

Spices often have antimicrobial properties, so you're less likely to develop food poisoning from meals with spices, such as salt, cloves, oregano (sweet marjoram) and cinnamon. Hence in an age without refrigeration, as was most of human history, food preservation, particularly of meat, which will rot quicker in warmer climates, was imperative. People who invented recipes with spices unconsciously created a protective barrier around them from the worst symptoms. Over evolutionary time, those who liked bland cooking in warmer climates were simply bred out of existence. Even in the modern age, diarrheal diseases are the second leading cause of death in children under five, more than AIDS, malaria and measles combined [89]. Imagine being able to reduce this number even by a small percentage. Over the span of several thousand years, this type of minor advantage will compound on itself (the children who would've otherwise died are able to grow and have children of their own, and so on) to exponential levels.

Eventually, you have a pattern: where there's no impetus to use spices, they're used but sparingly, where it can be a life or death matter, they're used generously. Incidentally, this explains why British food is so abhorrently bland, whilst Indian food feels like a nuclear explosion.

Culture cannot, and should not, be viewed outside of the confines of biology. At the end of the day, culture is an expression of biology. If humans start doing something that is not conducive to a stable society, it will quickly be stamped out as the unconscious mechanisms guiding evolution will try to find a new and more stable equilibrium.

This is why we do not find a society run by five-year-olds. Five-year-olds are not known to make rational decisions. If any society actually decided to give five-year-olds ultimate power on a regular basis, it would create instability and it would eventually collapse the whole society through incompetence. The fall would create volatility until more capable rulers came into place:

> "Weak men create hard times.
> Hard times create strong men.
> Strong men create good times.
> Good times create weak men."
> - Anonymous

11 - The Merchant's Collective Brain

> *"The entrepreneur always searches for change, responds to it, and exploits it as an opportunity."*
>
> *- Peter Drucker*

Alright, you knew this was coming. It's mentioned every time someone brings up economics and psychology (I've even mentioned it in passing in earlier chapters) - the Marshmallow Experiment. Sadly, despite its genuinely interesting conclusions, it's become that sort of "*did you know?*" fact that someone breaks out at parties to try to seem smarter than what they are. *(Not that I'm immune from being a pretentious twat, mind you. Talk about the kettle calling the pot black.)*

The Stanford marshmallow experiments were a series of studies that assessed children's ability to delay momentary gratifications for an even greater reward. They did so by putting children into a room, they were given a treat of some sort and then told that if they didn't eat it immediately, and instead waited a short time, they'd get many more of the sweets when the timer ran out. Only a minority of them succeeded in this task, with the older ones usually having the upper hand [90].

Some years later, the participating children were assessed and the ones who had succeeded in the marshmallow experiments showed higher SAT scores, lower BMI (Body Mass Index), higher social competence as well as better ability to handle stress [91][92][93]. We must be careful with associating such conclusions in the interpretation of such studies though. Even the authors of these studies say as much:

> *"We must emphasize the need for caution in the interpretation of the total findings linking preschool delay to adolescent outcomes. This caution applies especially in the interpretation of the associations between preschool delay in the exposed-rewards-spontaneous-ideation condition and SAT scores. On the one hand, our faith in the validity of the links between preschool delay behavior and later relevant competencies is strengthened because the objective test results were consistent with the parental rating data. On the other hand, even the highest correlations account for only about 25% of the variance. In addition, given the smallness of the sample, the obtained coefficients could very well exaggerate the magnitude of the true association "*

Even so, there's still a lesson to be learned from the marshmallow experiment studies. The children who tended to be successful in this experiment are the ones who managed to distract themselves from the task of waiting. If you are constantly waiting for the timer to tick away, you'll drive yourself mad. That might be partially why they're better at stress management than other children.

Same goes for investors, the road to insanity is paved with glances at the Bloomberg ticker. Over the years, it's been suggested by a number of investors that one should only ever look at the stock prices once every couple of months [94]. More to avoid driving yourself insane than any practical consideration. Having stock prices constantly parade before your eyes is much like when the unsuccessful children held the marshmallow, or even went as far as petting it. The key to success is to idiot-proof your investing methodology. As hard as it is to admit, one's not as smart as one thinks.

The vast majority of people are not born with the innate ability to plan for the future. Why else is there the obesity crisis? Why else do less than half of people have savings, even in the wealthiest country on Earth [95]? Why else do a sizeable percentage of gym memberships go unused [96]? Why else do people buy more convertibles on sunny days [97]?

Truth be told, we're a creature that evolved primarily to solve problems of the here and now. There's no reason to think about being fed in the long run when, in the long run, everyone will be dead anyway. Hence, our future planning abilities tend not to be among the best. We often lived in a brutal environment where planning for the future at the detriment of our present wellbeing could've inadvertently marked us for dead.

For this exact reason, we depended on our comrades. Ostracism is often among the worst punishments that a person can undergo, as we discussed in PI-Ch4, because being thrown outside of the community is essentially a death sentence for community-driven creatures.

It might not happen today, it might not happen tomorrow, but someone left without social support would die sooner, rather than later. If a hunter-gatherer in a tribe killed a large animal, it's useful to share both the burden of the hunt and the resulting meat. Not only would unshared food have gone to waste, given that their family can only eat so much, but they would also stack the deck in their favour. As whosoever received their gift would be likely to reciprocate in future, if they happened to have excess meat whilst our hunter-gatherer had been unlucky. Hunting success is highly variable; succeeding in a hunt once does not mean you will succeed in the next, with an average success rate of around 50% [98]. Hence our plans for the future were the development of our social ties. In essence, hunters can "store" surplus meat in the bodies of their friends and neighbours [99].

If I'm allowed to speculate a bit, I'd guess this is one of the reasons why animals engage in "contrafreeloading" behaviour. Animals, when given the choice between getting food without doing anything versus working to get food, will choose the latter rather than the former [100]. Provided, of course, that the task of getting the food is moderately within their abilities[18]. They

18 Or they're not cats. Felines appear to be the exception to these findings. So in a way science has verified that cats are entitled assholes. [101]

may just want to be able to carry their own weight, rather than depend on the charity of others and be a burden.

In a lot of communal animals, evolution has fine-tuned a sense of fairness. Chimpanzees, for example, have been known to retaliate when another chimp appears to have robbed them [102]. They do not do this out of pure maliciousness, but as vengeance for a perceived lack of justice. Our sense of right and wrong, our very morality, might stem from such mechanisms. The psychologist Jon Haidt has proposed that people have "moral emotions" that produce snap judgements on what is ultimately beneficial in the algorithm of evolution [103]. Consider the following situation:

> *"Julie and Mark are brother and sister. They are traveling together in France on summer vacation from college. One night they are staying alone in a cabin near the beach. They decide that it would be interesting and fun if they tried making love. At the very least it would be a new experience for each of them. Julie was already taking birth control pills, but Mark uses a condom too, just to be safe. They both enjoy making love, but they decide not to do it again. They keep that night as a special secret, which makes them feel even closer to each other. What do you think about that? Was it OK for them to make love?"*

If one's is like most people, one is likely to feel minor revulsion at the very thought of incestuous behaviours. Yet, it's a victimless offence. In fact, when looked at it from a purely philosophical standpoint it would fall squarely within the boundaries of John Stuart Mill's *Harm Principle*: "my right to swing my fist ends at the tip of your nose." Even so, it takes some effort to be tolerant of such an act, and our subconscious is still whispering in our ear and giving us a feeling of disgust.

These are Haidt's moral emotions at work. Back in times before reliable birth control, it would indubitably be immoral. After all, they're essentially giving their potential offspring a much higher chance of having severe genetic defects. At best they're negligent, at worst they're being cruel for the sake of getting an orgasm. Yet, this is not the first thought that would course through people's minds when asked why these two shouldn't be allowed to be with each other, they'd just find it somewhat "icky" without quite knowing why. Thereafter, they'd likely backwards rationalise whatever emotions they'd have as being "moral" or "amoral."

For the most part, these moral emotions can allow you to build a good community. Think of them as the human interpretation of the underlying algorithm of evolution. As discussed in the previous chapter, culture (and with it the legal system) develops within a certain variation, but it ultimately serves to create a stable society. Far from being antiquated and cumbersome, these are the foundations which allowed us to interact with each other. Humans sometimes even go the extra mile in punishing wrongdoers and have been known to retaliate at great personal cost in excess to the initial damage done, because they feel satisfaction from doing it, far in excess of the costs they incur from doing so [104]. The classic 1987 movie *The Untouchables* put it best: "You wanna get Capone? Here's how you get him. He pulls a knife, you pull a gun. He sends one of yours to the hospital, you send one of his to the morgue! That's the Chicago way, and that's how you get Capone!" To get Capone one must be willing to sacrifice far more than what Capone is willing or able to put on the line, and from a purely utilitarian standpoint, at the individual level, it's nonsensical.

Escalatory retaliation of this nature might not make sense for a purely rational creature (yet another black mark for "rational" economists). After all, it goes against common sense to wilfully put yourself in a worse situation for an intangible benefit. When all's said and done, you've ended up worse off than had you just taken the initial loss and moved on with your life. Yet, there are people who literally get a high off of punishing wrongdoers, especially when there's an audience to praise their do-gooding [105]. In a purely rational world, if somebody stole your bike, and it took you ten days of labour to repurchase, it would not make sense to lose sleep for anything more than ten days over it. Yet, you would likely love to see the thief punished. If you could, you might even pay money to punish that person, going by the results of the previously cited study. So why would anyone ever take the effort to do so?

This type of "rational" reasoning forgets the meta-game of evolution and social approval. If you have a reputation as an honourable person with little tolerance for injustices, people will likely trust you more, and you have a better chance to climb the social ladder. A perfect example of this was Draco, the Greek lawgiver, who amended the legal system with harsh but fair laws. According to legend, people loved his draconian policies (note the name), so much that he was accidentally killed when a crowd of supporters threw their coats at him in approbation, and he died asphyxiated amidst a pile of clothing [106].

In an evolutionary sense, these overzealous punishers are a check and balance against freeloaders and abusers. These avengers are randomly strewn all across society so they become a permanent and credible threat against asocial behaviour. Hence, it's never really about the success, failure or rationality of a single punishment, but it's about the maintenance of a fair and just social standard [107]. These "self-appointed guardians of the status quo" foster trust and create a better society and get praised in return.

Because of this inherent trust, we're more likely to share food and resources. I've often jokingly said that the one place where communism worked was in smoker communities. Don't have a cigarette? No problem, ask and you shall receive. Don't have a lighter? Not a problem either!

This is done with the implicit understanding that one day the roles will be reversed. Yet, among friends, this can go further. When you invite a friend over to watch a movie you might tell him to bring the beers whilst you will order pizza, or some such arrangement. Food has always been a perfect opportunity to express social unity throughout the ages. Given the topic of social alliances and revenge, I feel compelled to share a quote from one of my favourite novels, *The Count of Monte Cristo*:

> *"Take this peach, then," she said. The count again refused. "What, again?" she exclaimed, in so plaintive an accent that it seemed to stifle a sob; "really, you pain me."*
>
> *A long silence followed; the peach, like the grapes, fell to the ground. "Count," added Mercedes with a supplicating glance, "there is a beautiful Arabian custom, which makes eternal friends of those who have together eaten bread and salt under the same roof."*
>
> *"I know it, madame," replied the count; "but we are in France, and not in Arabia, and in France eternal friendships are as rare as the custom of dividing bread and salt with one another."*
>
> *"But," said the countess, breathlessly, with her eyes fixed on Monte Cristo, whose arm she convulsively pressed with both hands, "we are friends, are we not?"*
>
> *The count became pale as death, the blood rushed to his heart, and then again rising, dyed his cheeks with crimson; his eyes swam like those of a man suddenly dazzled. "Certainly, we are friends," he replied; "why should we not be?"*

In this scene, the Count of Monte Cristo is hesitant to break bread with what he now considers to be a hostile person. Letting his guard down and sharing food, even whilst pretending to be their friend, seems a step too far. Food is an important part of life, and is a mildly intimate, albeit still public, affair. Not without reason, there are meal-oriented social events, such as the "family meal," the "business dinner" or even the "coffee date." Somehow these social interactions would just be weird or far too serious in one way or another without food, given that they require some levity.

Food sets the tone for the affair, and greases the social wheels. Imagine meeting your parents to sit at a table once a week for an hour at a time, or inviting a date to talk rather than for a drink. Whilst doable, it just seems not entirely right. Matt Ridley in his fabulous book *The Rational Optimist* speculates that cooking was one of the main things that developed our desire for barter and trade [108]. Fire has already been linked to important developments in our evolution such as protection, warmth or a high-calorie diet [109].

It also primes humans to share. After all, as the economist Haim Ofek suggested, fire itself is hard to start, but easy to share; likewise, cooked food is hard to make but easy to share [110]. Not only that, but the sheer amount of culinary choices available makes one pause. Imagine bumping into another tribe that had access to a completely different set of ingredients and recipes.

They'd find novelty in whatever you had to offer as well, unless it was verifiably worse. Hence, slowly but surely, communities would benefit from a collective brain. Our grandmother's traditional holiday meal would thus be the brainchild of hundreds of generations of grannies before her, who picked and chose elements that they liked from their neighbours to incorporate into their own unique family recipes. Likewise, their own dishes likely inspired countless other variations. It's a beautiful monument to all those untold stories throughout the millennia of different tastes, environments, resources and exchanges that eventually gave rise to that one particular dish.

Hence our desire to share food communally, alongside with our moral emotions regarding fairness might've primed us to be the species most likely to trade. After all, as the preceding chapters tried to explain, our higher functioning brains primarily evolved as a mechanism to deal with other humans and to gauge reciprocity in social interactions. In Africa, obsidian, shells and ochre were being traded long distances as far back as 100,000 years ago [111]. Trade is prehistoric and ubiquitous.

I'm thoroughly convinced that this is one of the keys as to why civilization was established and grew. A single human without the aid of a collective brain is limited by his own thoughts and resources. The collective brain and the trade networks will bring with them intellectual advancements and wealth. This is the beginning of civilization: when humans finally had more than subsistence-level resources and began to barter with them.

PART II: WE DIDN'T START THE FIRE (IT WAS ALWAYS BURNING SINCE THE WORLD'S BEEN TURNING): HISTORY AND ITS MECHANISMS

Over the last section we have discussed what it entails to be human. Our biases, drives and desires determine how we're likely to behave. Yet, we have also briefly touched upon the emergence of something else entirely - the unconscious mechanisms that drive systems to their point of least resistance. By putting various strategies (be they biological or psychological) in direct competition with each other in different environments, some will begin to dominate each other and bring new points of balance in the system. In Part III we will explain how these strategies have played out over history, and what events and institutions were created in response to them. Nevertheless, before we get to explain the effects of historical change, we must first explain what is history and how it's made.

The statement might initially seem facetious, yet there are various layers of complexity that are often ignored when talking about history. Those few that happen to try to uncoil the mechanisms, often get bogged down in explaining one side of the argument to the detriment of the rest. Some people argue for an environmental determinism, as to what determines the course of history, whilst others prefer a more heroic view of life, where people single-handedly stem the tide. Personally, I think it's much the same as the Nature vs. Nurture debate, as to what affects behaviour in the long run - it's a nuanced interplay between the two variables which determines how we ultimately behave. To focus on either side too much is to forget objectivity. As such, Part II will examine what the various mechanisms for historical change are.

1 - People Person: Culture vs. Man

"Some are born great, some achieve greatness, and some have greatness thrust upon them."

- William Shakespeare

Whenever we think of history, we naturally think of rulers, religious figures, knaves, philosophers and inventors - extraordinary men and women who, through their unique strength of character, changed how society developed. The Great Man Theory, first popularised by the Scottish writer Thomas Carlyle in 1840, states that had these men not existed, then history itself would be profoundly different [1]. The examples readily pop into our minds: Had Genghis Khan not existed, there wouldn't have been a Mongol Empire; had Martin Luther not put his Ninety-five Theses on a church door, then Protestantism with all the wars and social movements that occurred because of it, would not have been impossible; had Albert Einstein not developed his theories at that particular point in time, the atomic bomb would not have been developed fast enough to be used during WWII; had Rosa Parks not had the courage to stand up against bigotry and racism and remain at the front of the bus, the American civil rights movement wouldn't have happened; etc.

These are all fine stories, but to a great extent they're just that - stories. I'm not denying that any of these events happened, but they weren't as unique or clear cut as they might initially appear to be in their retelling. The Rosa Parks incident, for example, had already happened, several times, in fact. The original person that resisted going to the back of the bus was a woman by the name of Claudette Colvin. Her story was originally silenced and ignored, as she was seen as an uncouth youth who just so happened to get pregnant at the time by a married man. Montgomery's black leaders hushed the story instead, and waited for a more promising face that could conceivably show the civil rights movement in a more positive light, which ended up being the studious Rosa Parks [2].

We could conceivably continue in this vein with some other examples. Albert Einstein was a genius, but hardly unique in the realm of scientific existence. His ideas on general relativity, whilst revolutionary, were already being worked on by other men. To such an extent that there was an ongoing dispute as to whether other people like David Hilbert ought to get a significant portion of the credit, instead of Einstein [3]. As such, whilst very influential in his field, Einstein's body of work might be somewhat overstated in terms of absolute importance.

Much to the chagrin of Ayn Rand fanatics, the completely self-made man, who single-handedly pulled himself up by his own bootstraps, is more or less a myth. Entrepreneurs, and annoying people at dinner parties, love to mention that they alone conquered the odds and succeeded. Forgetting in the process the countless people who contributed to the process, and made it possible.

"No man is an island," as the famous John Donne poem says. Even kings require the help of thousands of people to achieve great fortune and feats. Few powerful men acknowledge this, as they're too busy building their own mythologies. Only the honest ones fully admit that they'd be nothing without having been born in the right time, place and meeting the right people who would help hoist them to fortune. A great story to show this is that of Babur, the first emperor of the Moghuls, who after having conquered the great city of Agra in the mid-sixteenth century held a victory feast. For this momentous occasion he invited everyone that had helped him on his path to becomeimg emperor, and the guests were vast in number (so much so that he called it the grandest feast of his life) [4]. From the lowly merchant that helped him across a river, to generals guiding his troops, every great man needs thousands of people for him to achieve greatness and Babur fully acknowledged it, despite becoming one of the most celebrated leaders in both South and Central Asian history.

This is not saying at all that all of history's great names are incompetent people who just so happened to be lucky and become famous. Whilst that has certainly happened throughout the ages, it's often difficult to see whether one particular person is responsible for actual historical change. For instance, you might be an incompetent leader who just so happens to preside over a Golden Age by complete accident. Your reign would thus be viewed with rose-tinted glasses by future generations wishing to learn from your supposed superior wisdom; whereas if you happened to be a fairly competent leader in horrid times you might seem mediocre, or average at best, by comparison.

It's said that only a poor workman will blame his tools, but one can hardly be expected to build a mountain with a gardening trowel, regardless of how competent one happens to be. Idolizing great historical figures and seeking to emulate them, might hence be a fruitless endeavour if one doesn't take into account the circumstance of the time and place where they lived in. They might have succeeded in spite of their actual capabilities, rather than because of them.

A social movement, unless artificially forced into existence by a cabal of powerful and oblivious elites, is neither late nor early - it arrives precisely when it needs to. Furthermore, being great and capable does not necessarily mean that one's life accomplishments are full of extraordinary feats. Quite the contrary, on paper at least, one's life might be downright boring but still have been a great boon for humanity. Take the *Five Good Roman Emperors,* so called because their aggregate reign of 84 years was a period of prosperity and relative stability. So much so that historians have said that it was the best period in human history. Yet two of the five lead fairly boring lives.

Nerva, the man who instituted the dynasty, was more or less chosen as a stopgap to allow the senate to have more time for horse trading and bribery, to see who achieved power. The prime reason that he had been chosen was because of his blandness, as he hadn't offended anyone in his long career and was fairly innocuous. Miraculously though, he ignored the senate's wishes and chose Trajan, a beloved and capable provincial general, as his successor [5]. He died promptly after, with his only real noteworthy achievement being naming who would succeed him. Two generations later, there was Antoninus Pius, whose rule is called "the uneventful reign" because other than bettering infrastructure and consolidating the holdings of the empire, there's little noteworthy in his career. Despite being at the helm of one of the more militaristic societies in history, he likely never even set eyes on a Roman legion [6]! Yet, he's still considered one of the five greats precisely because so much could've gone wrong, but didn't, as it did with previous and successive sovereigns.

As humans, we have a bias for stories. Little is said about the unsung heroes whose job is merely to fend off life's evils with a steady hand and a consciously-conservative attitude, because they make for boring stories. It's boring to say that because of infrastructure investments thirty years prior, Rome had enough water for its citizens not to go thirsty. Instead, it would make for a much better story for an emperor to jump in the nick of time to save the day, just as civil unrest was beginning to boil to uncontrollable levels. Contented and happy lives make for terrible novels.

Stories, whether they be fictional or real, grab our attention. We like villains, heroes and narratives that explain the world. In our mind, nothing can simply be due to luck and circumstances. We have fine-tuned pattern recognition abilities and we shall use them. As a roulette player "feels" that he's going to win because of this or that reason, we think we can boil down why it is that things happen, rather than just accepting that the environment and circumstances out of our control determine the main direction something develops in, more often than not. It might be because of this bias for action that famous British economist, and the bane of undergraduates, John Maynard Keynes well said: "The game of professional investment is intolerably boring and over-exacting to anyone who is entirely exempt from the gambling instinct; whilst he who has it must pay to this propensity the appropriate toll."[7]

There are indeed people who can change the course of history because they were in extraordinary circumstances, but these are few and far between.

A particularly telling story that shows this is that of Stanislav Yevgrafovich Petrov, who was manning the nuclear early-warning system of the Soviet Union on 26 September 1983. According to protocol, he was to immediately notify his superiors on receiving a nuclear missile alarm, at which point the Soviets would immediately retaliate with all of their own atomic weapons. As luck would have it, a single missile was spotted on that night. If Stanislav followed protocol, he would all but ensure a nuclear war, yet something felt off. The United States wouldn't just send a single missile if it were to attack, it would send hundreds, or thousands, to serve as a decapitating blow. This seemed likelier to be a system glitch, rather than an attack. He thus took a gamble and ignored it, knowing full well that there might be consequences for his actions. Through this inaction, the Soviet war machine wasn't activated and WWIII was averted. Hence this lieutenant colonel might have actually saved the entire world, yet people hardly remember him despite him having only died recently[19].

These people are the Great Men of history, and had you put different individuals at the helm the world might look very different. But even then, their influence is often reduced to single decisions, to a single throw of the dice. It's usually not the case that people can maintain the mythical characteristics necessary to change history over the course of a lifetime. More often than not, chaos happens and we more or less try to pick up the pieces by constructing a story around it, by cherry-picking the events that highlight our narrative. Life just seems so nonsensical that perhaps we should begin to think that it tends to be controlled by the unthinkable and the unknowable - and hence we enter the realm of the Black Swan.

19 He died on 19 May 2017.

2 - An Unsure Thing: Black Swan Driven

"It's hard to believe in coincidence, but it's even harder to believe in anything else."

- John Green, Will Grayson

Perhaps at this point you have now grown despondent. If skill or vision are not necessarily the thing that determines the future, then what does? Is it all truly just random chance which we happen to weave into a narrative? If this is so, then it means that the whims of fortune can often prove to be our downfall, even if we happened to have done everything right.

Indeed, for the human mind obsessed over minutely controlling and optimising all factors, it's a terrifying idea. The ancient Greeks noticed this fear, and it may possibly be the reason for the existence of the tragic drama genre [8]. To vastly oversimplify a whole artform, tragedies can be summed up as: A noble hero, who unwittingly causes his own downfall, and more often than not, nothing could've been done to prevent this as it was simply the wills of the gods that this be so. The survivors of the tragedy are often left to pick up the pieces of their lives and continue living with little fanfare.

At its core, as a social institution, the role of tragic plays was to instil sympathy for people who failed. As the Greek tragic character of Oedipus said, "no man should be considered fortunate until he is dead" - a message that was surely not lost upon the original audience, and one which the modern public ought to remember. The random throw of the dice will often determine our futures in ways we barely understand, but ultimately circumstances are out of our control.

Guns, Germs and Steel, a book by Jared Diamond which I heartily recommend, despite the tedious writing style, makes the case that much of how history ended up developing was somewhat inevitable[20]. Even if we completely disregard race differences between the different peoples of the world, which in the words of James Watson, one of the co-discoverers of DNA, is pretty much wishful thinking - "there is no firm reason to anticipate that the intellectual capacities of peoples geographically separated in their evolution should prove to have evolved identically. Our wanting to reserve equal powers of reason as some universal heritage of humanity will not be enough to make it so" [9], we still have substantial disadvantages in some regions over others, in terms of human development capabilities due to environmental factors.

For example, the geographical layout of a continent enormously affects the potential development of a people. If you happened to be born in a continent with a larger north-south axis (The Americas or Africa) than a west-east axis (Eurasia), then you have the misfortune of various climates instead of a stable one across the land [10]. This makes it very difficult to transport crops and animals as they may well simply not be suited for such wildly different environments. Empires, and even commerce, become much more difficult affairs and as such are reduced in scope, which obviously constricts the developmental potential in that geographic area. Add to it the incidence of dangerous as well as untameable fauna, and you're likely in for a bad time. Furthermore, you might be born in an area of the world that has natural resources but little reason to exploit them to their full extent. Niall Ferguson once made the claim that one of the main strengths that "the West" had over

20 Arguably, when it comes to history, we only truly have a sample size of one, and even though there have been case studies or "natural experiments" over the years, these are limited and may not be representative of anything. So, whilst somewhat on the speculative end of the spectrum, Jared Diamond's claims are among the more robust "theories of history" out there, to such an extent that there have been entire communities debating the book's findings for years.

"the Rest" was that they were driven by competition, or faced extinction [11].

Asia's large planes and flatland, allowed monolithic and longstanding cultures to rise, as the ease of communication between the various areas of the empires made areas interlinked and unlikely to develop full autonomy. Europe, on the other hand, because of its difficult to transverse natural barriers (e.g. the Rhein, the Alps, the Danube) had very real natural limits. Even at the height of the Roman Empire, the Emperor Augustus set firm boundaries as to how extended he thought the Empire ought to be for it to still be a cohesive unit [12]. Despite this edict being more or less followed, it was still far too unwieldy and prone to civil unrest, eventually having to split under the Emperor Diocletian with the Tetrarchy [13].[21]

In either case, despite Europe's inability to remain a single political entity, when compared to its Asian counterparts, this disjointedness proved to be a boon. As with organisms within natural selection, the smaller political units within Europe could use their comparative advantages and fill environmental niches. This set off an arms race, both in its literal and metaphorical sense; as all political entities were vying for supremacy, they more or less had to advance parallel to their competitors or be wiped out. Thus, the bloodbath that was most of European history explains precisely why they had a need for innovative ideas, strategies and technologies, and were more likely to adopt them than other societies.

Imagine an aboriginal man in Australia with Isaac Newton's capabilities. His general environment would pretty much doom him to obscurity if he had been born at any point except the last hundred years. Even if he happened to invent/discover something extraordinary, if there's no immediate advantage for adopting it, or if the change is too costly within the society to adopt, or if it somehow goes against insurmountable social taboos, then any and all of the genius advances would be worthless from a societal point of view. It's no

21 Over the centuries, there had been multiple coups and attempts at separation, which often worked for a couple dozen years. Nevertheless, the first official separation which didn't occur as a direct result of civil war was in 286 CE which more or less marked the death of the Roman Empire, as we commonly think of it.

accident that the greatest centres of culture and learning have historically come about in places of commerce and centres of military power - places wherein people have to develop memes to combat other people's ideas, or face oblivion themselves.

Humans are creatures of habit, much like we will go to the same barber for years on end (despite the fact that he might start charging a bit more over time, and there's little objective difference between other barbers). We will only adopt a new technology when we have no other choice, or if we want to receive specific benefits, and thus we're involuntarily nudged through random circumstance in that direction.

These random and thoroughly unforeseen circumstances, commonly known as Black Swans[22], are the drivers of change on a fundamental level. We do not change unless we have to. Similar to how organisms go into stasis, wherein no real change occurs, whilst the environment remains the same, so do human societies as well. *Why fix what isn't broken?* Yet, when a key change occurs within the ecosystem, all bets are off, and there's punctuated equilibrium - dramatic evolutionary change.

In other words, one could argue that memes, which allow a culture to thrive by possessing them, remain in stasis unless there is a substantial change within the environment. By itself, no innovation is truly circumstantial unless it changes the inherent way society functions, or if it manages to defend against a greater force. For example, there's no need to invent, much less build, aqueducts when one lives besides a safe and sufficient water source. Yet, if there's a drought, or if the society has become bigger than the water source will support, then it's much likelier to adopt a measure that solves the issue - necessity is the mother of invention, after all.

We have a bias for the status quo, and will often fight tooth and nail to defend it. *The more things change, the more they stay the same.* We're always

---

22 Term first coined by the author Nassim Taleb to refer to highly improbable and unpredictable but very consequential events, which fundamentally alter the status quo. For example, the meteor that killed the dinosaurs altered the very fabric of the ecosystem and created new environmental niches which allowed mammals to thrive.

trying to satisfy our biological imperatives with even greater supernormal stimuli. If something would allow us to achieve the same goal in a lazier way, given present circumstances, we will at least attempt to do so.

As such, it may be the case that looking for heroes or grand ideological movements to understand the future of any element in a society, may not be the best way to go about it. It may even be dangerous, as you pay attention to the noise rather than the trend, only to be hit from your blind spot at a random interval in the future. Understanding an object's susceptibility to Black Swan events, is a much more productive use of one's time, as it will allow you to understand how much it will change when it eventually happens.

Nassim Taleb, in his book *Antifragile*, highlights three patterns to which things can react to Black Swan events[23]:

- **Fragile** - Under these conditions, any deviation from the mean is considered likely to cause irreversible damage to the object in question. Your grandmother's precious china does not benefit from randomness, and would much prefer things to remain as they are. Most human institutions fall into this category, given that they're rarely able to cope with a Black Swan event, as they lack adaptability. Reason being that we over-optimise systems to work within a certain set of parameters, once this status quo happens to no longer exist, the system collapses. Typically, the bigger an institution, the more streamlined and centralised it is, the more fragile it is. This is why it's easier to defeat a comparable traditional army over terrorists in guerrilla warfare.
- **Robust** - If one were to ask the typical person on the street whether robust is the opposite of fragile, one is likely to receive an affirmative. Yet, let's think about the matter in detail. Robust objects/institutions/ideas/

23 We must remember that these are signposts on a spectrum rather than Platonic ideals. An element with any of these properties can shift between these states if underlying circumstances change - much like water can become a liquid, gas or solid yet still be the same molecule. For example, an object might be robust to some stressors, but that does not necessarily mean it's immune to all stress available.

mechanisms are indifferent and neutral to whether there's randomness within the system. They do not care whether there are deviations from the mean, as they more or less function the same. For example, an animal's biological imperatives do not disappear irrespective of circumstances. Regardless of whether times are lean, or it's times of plenty, we still need food and water to survive. As such, purveyors of supernatural stimuli (drugs, prostitution, etc.) or just basic biological needs, are robust to change and can only usually be completely wiped out by superior competition, which satisfies the need in a more effective way than how it's being currently handled.

- **Antifragile** - The true opposite of the fragile. These are elements that actually benefit from random change, given that they use volatility to adopt new characteristics which were previously unattainable. No object in the universe is truly antifragile, as there is always some sort of stressor that defeats it. Nevertheless, there are items in the cosmos that not only benefit from mild to strong stressors, but they thrive. For instance, biological systems tend to be more antifragile than fragile because of their ability to adapt. Over a very short time, organisms can change to circumstances quickly and gain from disorder by gaining new characteristics. In other words, antifragile systems utilise randomness to experiment with novel strategies - adopting and discarding according to the benefit given by each strategy. For them, chaos isn't a pit - it's a ladder that brings them to untold heights. A smaller size, redundant capacity to counteract mild stressors, and decentralisation are all hallmarks of the antifragile.

Fragile things break under stress, robust things are oblivious to stress and antifragile things benefit from stress. As such, we may not be able to play the role of prophet and divine exactly how it is that things will happen, but we can assess a system's vulnerability to randomness. It's not a matter of whether a Black Swan event will happen, but when. The more complex a system gets, the likelier that highly improbable events will happen. The more data points interacting with each other, the less time between different iterative states and hence the more generations the interplaying mechanisms have to change the system. Because of this incalculable number of interactions, the unlikely but highly consequential is all but guaranteed to occur at some point in time.

Military strategists, from time immemorial, have been aware that it is impossible to predict the development of a battle, as no battle plan survives contact with the enemy. Instead, they have military simulations to determine a "what if?" scenario and an according countermeasure. The top brass might not effectively understand what will happen, or its origins, but they know whether the system could cope with an emergency, and how they could potentially counteract it. Investors, or anyone wishing to understand future developments, might thus benefit from playing military advisor, instead of prophet, by assessing risk scenarios and whether institutions could potentially survive them with their current capabilities. Attempting to predict with exactitude what will happen is insanity.

Take the beginnings of WWI - who would've genuinely predicted that the murder of an archduke in the Austro-Hungarian empire by a ramshackle terrorist group could genuinely change the future development of humanity? Even after it happened, the markets were fairly nonplussed about the whole affair. It took several weeks for them to register any broad macroeconomic and geopolitical threat [14]. The magnitude of this Pandora's box was barely understood, even when soldiers were amassing.

Yet, as it stands, Gavrilo Princeps - the man who killed Archduke Franz Ferdinand- ended up being arguably the most damaging terrorist in world history, indirectly causing not one, but two, world wars. One could justifiably argue that the powder keg was already there, that the old-world order of globalisation, open borders and massive military alliances was unsustainable, but for any violent explosion to occur we first need a spark. If the spark had never been there, the explosion need never to have happened.

The chance of something occurring does not necessarily mean that it will happen. You could well play Russian Roulette every single day of your life, and never get any more harm than a sore trigger finger. We don't make a habit of playing Russian Roulette, even when offered large amounts of money, because the risks are far too great of it going awry.

As a rule of thumb, we can summarise life, history and human affairs as such: Fragile things will break sooner or later, betting on their permanence is suicidal in the long run. Robust things will remain essentially in the same order of importance, no matter how much time passes. Antifragile systems are nigh impossible to predict, but will tend to do well in the long run, given that their implementation cost (and thus maximum loss) is minor when compared to their potentially infinite upside - low risk, high uncertainty.

He who understands how to harness the nature of these three elements within a system can beat even seemingly unbeatable foes. A perfect case study of this phenomenon was in 2002, when a single military mastermind was able to bring the largest military in world history, with nothing more than outdated technology and some ingenuity, to its knees.

A year prior to the invasion of Iraq, the United States understandably wanted to see how its recent technological and structural advances would fare against a generic Middle Eastern enemy. As such, the military organised the Millennium Challenge 2002 war game exercises. These were an extremely serious affair, costing an estimate of $250 million. The event would work through computer simulations and live exercises, with two participants - the US (Blue) and the generic Middle Eastern country (Red) - fighting against each other with thousands of men under their control [15].

At the helm of the Reds was Lt. General Paul Van Riper, and he did his super-villain sounding name justice, via asymmetric warfare and unpredictable tactics. From the get-go he capitalised on the US military's overreliance on fancy technology and centralised structure. He used couriers on motorcycles to transmit orders to troops, messages hidden in prayers and World-War-II-style light signals to launch airplanes without radio communications, hence completely negating the US' superior surveillance technology.

Then, upon receiving a demand to surrender in the next 24-hours, he correctly assessed that the navy would soon be launched to make good on the threat. As such, using small speed boats he located and pre-emptively attacked the fleet with devastating localised force by way of cruise missiles, low-flying planes, conventional weapons and suicide attacks. Altogether, the opening battle of the war resulted in the US losing dozens of ships and an aircraft carrier with an estimated 20,000 deaths within a handful of minutes. This is a loss only equivalent to some of the bloodiest days of WWI. Just to put the damage into perspective, a carrier alone can cost upwards of $13 billion, and almost twenty years of fighting in Vietnam "only" killed 58,318 people.

Yet despite this overwhelming display of the strengths of antifragile and robust elements, and the exploitation of fragile elements within the military's modus operandi, the entrenched bureaucracy ignored this salient warning of its deep flaws. Instead, it opted for resetting the game and rigging it so that Blue couldn't lose the second time around. Van Riper resigned, left in disgust and wrote a 21-page critique on the ordeal, which was subsequently classified for reasons of national security.

Alas, whilst military strategists are aware of the dangers of inflexible thinking, bureaucracy, jingoism and politicking often takes precedence over common sense. In a later interview, he said that the key to success in war and business was to be "in command but out of control," meaning that if one designed an overreliance on centralised decision-making within an organisation one lost the ability of agents within the system to make adaptive changes to the plan [16]. If everyone is on the page of what the goal is, then the micro-level agents within the system can adapt to best suit their needs, and complete their task more effectively. Short while later, he added the following:

> *"When people asked me about the Joint Forces Command Millenium Challenge 2002 exercise, and the controversy surrounding it, I tell them that as the Red team commander I had an advantage. Number 1 those I work with understood that the universe is made up of two types of systems:*
>
> *There are structurally complex systems - power grids, transportation systems, aircraft and automobiles. Very little freedom in the action of the parts of that system, in fact, if there's*

great freedom of action there's a malfunction. These systems have cause and effect and we understand those cause and effect in a linear fashion. Consequently, we can use the tools and systems analysis for those structurally complex problems and you need to do so, when you are faced with one of those.

There's a larger class of problems that are interactively complex which means that the elements within the system have great freedom of action and often you don't have cause-effect but you have a cascading effect, which mathematically is not computable, after sending so many terms. These systems do not lend themselves to systems analysis they require wisdom and judgement, often they're referred to as "wicked problems" because until you formulate them, understand them, there's no ability to approach them."

Hence what Van Riper did was to understand that the underpinnings of the US strategy relied on fragile systems and predictable cause-effect protocols, and he exploited them by using simple, yet robust, systems (the technologically inferior but innovative communication systems) whilst organising his forces like terrorist cells, where they were allowed to operate semi-autonomously and were thus antifragile.

That is the beauty of understanding network effects. Any successful investor, as with any successful general, will necessarily have to understand whether their potential target has exploitable weaknesses. If so, then organise a strategy that abuses those traits, and if not, then find a way to sidestep those traits entirely.

However, regardless of the position you are in, it is essential to understand the source of any intel. Which is why we will be discussing precisely what mistakes are present in information transmission when existing in a fallible world.

3 - Making Shit Up: Mythologizing and Propaganda

"History is a set of lies agreed upon."

- Napoleon Bonaparte

Given how difficult it is to make sense of society, it's unsurprising that we might cherry-pick and/or fudge the data to allow for a coherent story, even if we have the best intentions at heart. We can easily notice this in ourselves, oftentimes when telling a story of one's experiences, for it to make any narrative sense, we abbreviate, change the chronology of events or outright fabricate sequences so that the story has a beginning, middle and an end.

Theoretically, you could spend an infinite amount of time describing one instant. For example, I am sitting right now typing this on the 17th of September 2016 at 13:30 in a rented apartment in Belgrade. To describe my present situation, I could begin to describe the city, the room I'm currently in, the life events that led me here, etc. Yet, that would quickly become an exercise in tedium for both myself and the reader and I would yet to have even begun to tell a story. Instead, what a good storyteller does is to identify the most important elements to tell a particular tale and only tell those, or as Hemingway put it when giving writing advice "...cut out everything you can. The main thing is to know what to leave out."

All reports in regards to pretty much anything are biased. Humans do not communicate in Platonic ideals, words are open to interpretation and misunderstanding, as well as being malleable. Indeed, it's been suggested that we change memories whenever we access them - as if one were to take a chocolate out of a fridge, manhandle it for a bit and put it back in [17]. Still the same chocolate, still the same memory, but somewhat different in terms of form. One might hence be tempted in thinking that numbers and data are the bulwark of objectivity, instead of fallible human memory. However, even supposedly objective scientific studies have been known to be falsified, both intentionally and inadvertently, to tell a story. You should never take anyone's word as gospel. In pretty much any field of study, the depths of our ignorance are infinitely deeper than the heights of our knowledge. As such, in all likelihood pretty much all opinions on pretty much anything are likely to be wrong to a certain degree.

This is not to say that because all opinions are wrong, there isn't a certain hierarchy of wrongness. The shroud of ignorance might be thick, but it doesn't necessarily make everyone blind. Take Herodotus, as an example, as he wrote the first comprehensive chronology of a people. He was well-read, but much preferred first-hand knowledge so he travelled to far-flung places to learn the truth.

In his travels he was told many myths and legends, some as outlandish as that the population of a country became wolves once a year or that the inhabitants of far off lands hibernated for multiple months a year. He dismissed a good portion of these stories, as he was foremost a sceptic who tried to get reliable sources, but some falsehoods still made their way into his writings, such as the presence of giant Indian ants capable of mining gold. Thus, Herodotus, the so-called "father of history" is also nicknamed as the "father of lies" by modern historians [18].

By wanting to spread the truth, he also happened to inadvertently spread misinformation. But, as with having a faulty lamp in a dark room, it's better to have one than none at all, even if it might not illuminate the whole area and the shadows it cast might make you believe that something else is lurking there. Such it is with Herodotus, he might not have always told the truth, he might have accidentally sent archaeologists and historians on wild goose chases, but his insight has helped us shed light and confirm many findings over the years. So much so that his place in the intellectual tradition of the world is not suspect.

Nevertheless, the fact remains that because of the lies that he spread over the millennia, people's understanding of history, and society in general was skewed in the wrong direction. This might be fairly inoffensive when it happens by accident, and we might momentarily believe in the historical existence of Amazonians and the like. But it is dangerous when history is wilfully co-opted into a propaganda piece, as it creates a precedent and a *raison d'être* to a supposed natural order, that never might have had a reason for existing otherwise.

Almost every culture in human history has a foundational myth that explains their being. These myths might have come about organically through a natural selection of oral histories throughout the centuries. Some of these stories might have even once had their basis in reality, but slowly evolved to a legend of mythic proportions [19].

Take the Aztec's mythic flight from the land of Aztlán as a foundation myth. Legend says their war god Huitzilopochtli, would supposedly grant them glory once they found a land where an eagle was eating a snake on top of a cactus. After over two centuries of roving, they found the cactus in the area of what is now Mexico City and founded the city of Tenochtitlan in 1324 (this myth later became the basis for the Mexican flag) [20]. Whilst the story is likely apocryphal, this purported divine destiny of the Aztecs was used as an excuse to expand their lands and brutally enslave thousands of people. In the words of Voltaire: "Those who can make you believe absurdities, can make you commit atrocities."

Mythologizing, and making everything seem grander in scale, is a powerful political tool. It's why every two-bit king claims that they have a divine right, or why every IPO is sold as the next Google. It legitimises their power by making the supposed glorious future seem as inevitable. In modern times, and in some societies, humans have escaped the stranglehold of religion, but we're so desperate for quick and easy explanations for life - a purpose - that we've created secular mythologies just as well. Think of the communist's epic struggle against the bourgeoisie - by having an enemy they created social order. By having a social order, they created a culture that superseded any other previous tradition. Real events took a secondary importance when pursuing the party goals. Any events that fell outside party doctrine were cleverly concocted lies, no matter their source.

In other words, by enforcing a narrative, it will be difficult to see the world in any other lens. The Western world's foundational myth is, without a doubt, WWII - the Nazis are seen as everything they're not, *ipso facto* anything that can even be placed in their ideological ballpark is instantly evil and no further proof or argument is necessary. Hence the easiest way to discredit any idea is to label it as right-wing or fascist, thereby instantly putting any of the accused on the back foot.

Eventually, the fiction becomes more real than what actually happened, as it necessarily muscles into the truth's territory. Repeat a lie often enough and it becomes the truth. Naturally, the lies will favour the people currently in power. History is written by the victors, after all. But, do not misconstrue this as me implying that there is always a conspiratorial cabal of people wilfully distorting the truth for their nefarious ends. This does happen from time to time though, and there's plenty of evidence showing that historical records are falsified. For example, the Chinese have a long-standing tradition of record alteration, and outright censorship, whenever a new dynastic force comes into play. More recently, it has taken to just deleting records on electronic databases, when they don't fit the current party line [21].

Nevertheless, I mostly suspect this happens as a by-product of the state essentially being their own biographer. Rather than it being a methodical plan to lie to the public. I also believe that private citizens aren't that much more elevated on a moral high ground, when it comes to our personal lives. Take whenever you write your *CV*, you hardly bother putting all your failures and mishaps along the way. Quite the contrary, you polish everything almost beyond recognition of the facts. Surveys have suggested that even as high as a third of applicants exaggerate, if not outright lie, on their qualifications when applying to jobs [22].

It's the argument for why renowned novelist George Orwell famously said that he did not trust an autobiography unless it included unflattering things, as life when viewed from the inside is simply a series of defeats [23]. Even then, in the back of your mind, if you happen to read a miraculously true autobiography, you might wonder that if the author is willing to tell the truth about these unflattering matters, then what truths are intentionally being left out? At which point, your imagination might create something far worse than anything that the author could've written.

Fiction has a much narrower relation with the truth than we might be comfortable with. As a rule of thumb, one should avoid taking anyone's opinion without a mountain of salt, if they stand to gain from convincing you about something. As you're reading this book, for instance, I'm tipping the circumstances in my favour. I'm providing you with a product, a vision of how the world works, but to do that I have to make it compelling. You might have noticed that an abnormal amount of my historical examples are rooted in antiquity, more specifically Rome. I do this deliberately, as I know its history and its rise and fall is a parable for all the civilizations of humanity. Furthermore, in attempting to present a chronological view of the world, I'm glossing over the fact that some events and innovations happened at the same time, or were already in existence millennia before, but were not that important in the past. Instead, I'm presenting the events as the inevitable domino effect of the last outcome.

I do this to make for easier reading, and I don't think it really detracts from one's knowledge of the world. In fact, with a topic so complex, it's a necessity. Otherwise, you end up like the Borges short story, *On the exactitude of Science*, about an empire that wanted a map so accurate that it had no simplifications, yet for that to occur, the map ended up being the size of the entire realm itself. *The map is not the territory*, regardless of what we do it will always be imperfect and an oversimplification. Yet discarding the map outright is particularly foolish as it still gives you an idea of the lay of the land.

The fact remains though, that by focusing on specific data, I am not providing a perfect reflection of the world. At the end of the day, in trying to write an interesting book, I'm selling you an idea. This is why successful professional investors have made it a point not to listen to salesmen, public relation officials or even analysts - they're all being paid to market a product, and hence it's impossible to get an unbiased opinion from them [24].

Historians and chroniclers are no less immune from such influence than any other human. As long as Machiavelli stands to gain from lauding the Medici, he will do so. At absolute best, he might say he's merely bending the truth. This is why *The Prince*, despite being an oft-quoted book, is one that has to be treated as if it were as dangerous as nuclear waste when it comes to using it as a serious historical document. It was literally written as a job application, and thus its integrity is compromised.

The people whose word you ought to trust the most are those that stand to lose nothing if they are not believed, or those who gain nothing if they are.

4 - Hegelian Dialectics: That Thing your Commie Friend Keeps Raving About

"There can be no progress without head-on confrontation."
- Christopher Hitchens

No matter how you slice it, human history is based on conflict. Most people are likely to have ancestors who at one point were slaves, but they are also simultaneously very likely to have the genes of slavers. It's simply a matter of mathematics, for example, if you're vaguely of European descent, then you're related to every European alive in the ninth century who left descendants [25]. Reason being that the number of your ancestors doubles with each successive generation (two parents, four grandparents, eight great-grandparents, etc.) and thus you would rapidly have extraordinarily high numbers of family members, more people than there are today, if they didn't intermarry and "cancel" each other out when tallying your ancestors.

In other words, the blood of both genocidal madmen and saints flows through our veins. This is a testament to just how much variety of ideals can happen with the same genes. At one point, the offspring of the warlords met the offspring of the saints and they had children. We're not simply biological automatons, slaves to our past genes, we're able to take new positions, which would've perhaps shocked our ancestors and may even shock our contemporaries. This is both a strength and a weakness, for unity brings stability but also stagnation, and variety brings adaptability but also chaos.

When polar opposites meet there is volatility and often violent change - when fire meets ice a hard-fought battle ensues where the warm substance is trying to forcefully transfer the kinetic energy of its particles in motion whilst the cold substance is resisting this change via the inertia of its own particles; if fire succeeds in its mission to push the motionless ice particles you end up with water, which is the synthesis of these contrary forces [26]. This is the essence of the Hegelian Dialectic, two opposing forces meet, and in their interaction with each other they create a combination of both opposing forces - a synthesis of both extremes.

Hegel argued that this synergy, wherein the whole is more than the sum of its parts, is the foundation of change, and consequently of history itself. In societies, change occurs by having two opposing memes duke it out. Unless one is evidently superior, what often happens is that in their struggle to the death, they start adopting elements of their competition to keep up.

A good and recent example of such a mechanism is the Cold War, wherein in the latter half of the twentieth century, the American empire and the Soviet Union were pitted against each other. The United States represented capitalism, freedom and a *laissez-faire* means of governance, whilst the Soviet Union extolled the benefits of communism, control over the unruly impulses of human nature and central planners.

Yet, curiously enough, in their fight to defeat each other, they started adopting elements of their sworn enemies. From 1936 to 1981, top income tax rates in the United States barely dipped below 70% with many years going up as far as 92%, meaning that you only really got to keep 8% of your income during those periods [27].

In 1954, at the height of the "Red Scare," with Senator McCarthy accusing everyone and their mother of being commies, Uncle Sam had a right to the lion's share of your income. Hence to fight the evils of big government and central planning, the United States essentially took ownership of most of society's profits. In many respects becoming the monster it was fighting.

Things didn't go all that well for the Soviet Union either, what with having to receive charity from its bourgeois rivals shortly after they were created, just so they could keep their people from starving [28]. Or in 1930, secretly selling their most prized art treasures to American billionaire Andrew Mellon - archetypical Mr. Bigbucks himself - who almost a hundred years later is known as an extraordinary banker, philanthropist, industrialist and politician [29]. They did this as they were in desperate need of foreign currency. Politics is where ideologies go to die. Leaders, when confronted with the burdens of power and keeping the right people happy, will almost always make small, seemingly logical concessions on their ideological stances, and inch-by-inch they lose their soul until nothing but the rhetoric and grandstanding remains.

Overall, the Soviet economy was always a mess, and it was never able to fix itself. Given that they voluntarily eschewed the use of markets, the most extraordinary and complex computing mechanism in human history, their economic plans depended on a lot of guesswork and quotas. Unsurprisingly, this had horrible side-effects where material was misused. As American economist Paul Craig Roberts put it [30]:

> *"The Soviet Union wasted its resources, because the success indicator for Soviet managers allowed them to be successful even though their output was poorly related to the needs of users. Soviet output basically satisfied no one but the statistician measuring it.*
>
> *The Soviet manager's success indicator was a measure of gross output, such as weight, quantity, square feet, or surface area. Gross output indicators played havoc with assortments, sizes, quality, and so on. Nikita Khrushchev complained of chandeliers so heavy "that they pull the ceilings down on our heads.""*

Their main problem was always that they simply didn't know what the consumer wanted, or needed, until it was too late. Nor did they have a way of measuring their economic production to any sensible degree without assigning random amounts of materials to be used, which simply promoted waste. Personally, I think a better argument can be made for a modern communist state capable of instantly logging and predicting the needs of consumers based on statistical models. Similar to how there are online retailers nowadays that leave their inventory purchasing decisions entirely in the hands of algorithms, which allows them to operate more effectively as this allows them to react immediately to consumer demands [31]. Add some blockchain technology[24] to purchases to measure consumption habits immediately, customer reviews to measure consumer satisfaction, automation technology, 3D printing, alongside a shareware licensing agreement on intellectual property, a technocratic and meritocratic democracy, a pseudo universal income and a free economy in luxury goods, and I could see a communist state actually work.

As it stands though, many of those elements are in their infancy and will likely not be fully developed in the near term. Hence, I have my doubts we'll be living in a Star Trek-esque utopia any time soon. Point still stands though, such a utopia would necessarily have to be a hybrid of the lessons that history has taught us; mixing in elements from liberal and socialist models and isn't completely either one of those.

Money, for example, is a necessity in any modern civilized society. Imagine if all the world's problems were solved, we would live in a world of such abundance that not a single person goes hungry and everyone has access to what could now be considered an upper-middle-class lifestyle. Yet, what happens when people want to live at the beachfront? Or what happens when people want to do something eccentric, which costs a lot of material resources?

Curbing such desires isn't the way to go about it. After all, it was the tinkerers and the hobbyists that gave rise to the Industrial Revolution, had these men not had the means to express their eccentricities we might've been robbed of great advances. Furthermore, beachfront properties will exist with or without money. Being that this theoretical utopia works under the principles of liberalism and merit, rulers can't just hand them out to their sycophants and enablers, as the rulers of old might've done. Hence, a far more rational

---

24 A decentralised ledger system which underpins the Bitcoin currency and easily keeps track of all transactions that have ever happened in that particular currency's history.

course of action is to put a price on them, and whoever wishes to spend their resources on them are free to do so.

Ultimately, the Soviet Union attempted to bend their social structure so much that it eventually snapped. The rhetoric and grandstanding simply lost any realistic means of maintaining face and they became more capitalistic whilst still maintaining a lot of the state-owned enterprises. These would then become the bedrock upon which the Russian Oligarchs would build their own kingdom after staking their claim on the ruins of the Soviet Empire [32]. Much like local bigwigs had done with their fiefdoms in the Roman Empire as it fell, they consolidated their holdings to defend them from other usurpers, which would then evolve to become kingdoms. Necessity bred opportunity, and thus society changed.

Progress is a compromise between ideals and reality. No two people will ever completely see eye-to-eye on any one issue, and unless one side is violently obliterated, sacrifices will be made and a new status quo will come into existence, which balances both opposing viewpoints. This new status quo, commonly known as "Overton Window," will dictate the acceptable range of discourse that the public is willing to accept.

For example, in this day and age, you'd be very hard-pressed to find people in the Western world who unironically support slavery. Yet, as we will discuss in future chapters, the abnegation of slavery didn't quite come out of a love for our fellow man, but a cold mathematical fact - that human slave labour was simply not worth the cost incurred by the maintenance of the system, and it made more sense to simply not have slaves.

It is thus how inch-by-inch, compromise after compromise and battle after battle, that the Overton Window changes. For good or ill, societal change happens because of the constant struggle between each other and the environment.

PART III: DEATH OF A CAVEMAN: SOCIETY AND BUREAUCRACY

Society and all it entails, in statistical terms, is an outlier when we consider the overwhelming majority of human existence was during prehistory. Our brains and behaviours were custom-built to cope with those primeval periods, not the relative stagnancy and predictability of living in civilized societies.

Naturally, because of this, we ought to be suspect of the suggestion that is usually peddled to us that sedentary societies were an inevitability, and everyone jumped ship once agriculture was developed as an idea. In fact, some hunter-gatherer tribes, such as the Sentinelese and Pirahã, are still in existence today. As is usually the case, there is far more nuance in real life than the narratives given to us by tired and overworked teachers allow.

Nevertheless, once the majority of humans decided to settle down, and societies grew beyond the number where they self-policed by social pressure, we needed clear hierarchies and laws to make the new system work. To do this, the ruling class needed a method of coercion to control any dissidents. As such, to be successful, any proto-modern state will necessarily usurp, co-opt and monopolise all possible means of convincing or coercing people to reduce their chances of losing power. Hence, civilization partially begins once the state has achieved a monopoly on violence and has created a bureaucracy to control it. Over the next few chapters, we'll see what these systems are and what necessities drove their creation.

1 - Alcohol and the Malthusian Trap

"To Alcohol! The cause of, and solution to, all of life's problems."

Homer Simpson, The Simpsons

In 1798, the Reverend Thomas Robert Malthus wrote *An Essay on the Principle of Population*, wherein he posited the simple maths that might lead to a very bleak future - food growth tends to grow arithmetically, whilst population growth is exponential. This led to a very chilling conclusion: sooner or later there'd be more people than there'd be food for. Needless to say, reaching such an unbalancing point would in all likelihood lead to severe social strife with starvation, death and social unrest until order was somehow established. Fortunately for us all, this nightmarish prediction did not happen in our lifetimes as technology and new farming methods averted it. Of course, Malthus' spectre is always hiding in the shadows, waiting just until we get comfortable to unleash its hell on Earth. The second that population growth outpaces our capacity for food production innovation we're in trouble.

Previously, we've discussed that hunter-gatherers might've originally been the "original affluent society," as with relatively little effort they might've been able to lead lives of plenty. As such, despite there being evidence of agriculture being developed on multiple occasions, it was sometimes ignored as a permanent option and lifestyle. Nomadic tribes may, for example, see it wise to plant self-supporting crops in an area they will visit in the future, but may not consider it worth the effort to tend their bounty for the rest of the year. The life of a full-time farmer is not a pleasant one, after all, it requires very long hours and a lot of drudgery. It would take a lot of external motivation to force people to abandon the relative freedom of the hunter-gatherer in exchange for the bleakness of the average farmer's life; where boredom, back-breaking labour and stress were the norms for most of human history.

In fact, I dare say that up until fairly recently if you'd given the average hunter-gatherer a choice in the matter, they'd run for the hills at the first chance. Such was the case in 1815, during the British colonization of Australia, when the colonial administrator Lachlan Macquarie wanted to settle the aboriginals in the European way of 'civilized' life. Hence, as an experiment, he tried to settle sixteen of the indigenous peoples on a small farm with huts and a boat. Yet, over a surprisingly short timespan, the aborigines lost the boat, ignored the huts and went into the wilderness once more. Having tried the mundanity of modernity, they opted for the variety of the wild [1]. Of course, this was used to point out to their supposed inherent failings. Yet, what if it's something else entirely? What if civilization might not be all it's cracked up to be?

You could even make the argument that the average European was better fed in the pre-Neolithic revolution than when farming became widespread. If you analyse the stature achieved by the average man in a given era you can get a rough estimation of the quality of their nutrition. As such, it's interesting to note that the average male European nowadays is around 177cm-178cm (5'9" in freedom units), whilst the average male 16,000 years ago was 179cm (5'10"), thereafter with the advent of farming, heights plummet drastically over the next few thousand years with the lowest point being in the late Neolithic, from 5000-3000 BCE, with an average of 161cm (5'3") for males. Not even Bronze Age kings (in 1450 BCE), the billionaires of the ancient world, were immune to this decline in height and were only 171cm (5'7") - a far cry from their hunter-gatherer ancestors. It took well into the modern era, with all the technology and proper nutrition that entails, to eliminate that discrepancy [2].

Be that as it may, there's one thing that might tip the balance and make the whole thing worthwhile, to some: Booze. Fully nomadic societies do not have access to alcohol, or at least not in any sizeable quantities, as one needs to ferment vats of fruits or grains for extended periods of time. As such, if you enjoy a nightcap, you're doing yourself a disservice by being a hunter-gatherer - you'd either have to trade with the sedentary cultures at a marked-up price or you'd have to go through the trouble of foraging for the materials and transporting them wherever you go. On first glance, this argument might seem insane. Could the entire future of civilization solely have been determined by our alcoholic grandfathers? It's doubtful, despite it being an argument that's been debated for the last fifty years by some anthropologists, but it definitely might have helped push the momentum in the right direction for civilization [3].

Beer, for example, is not a nutrition source that rots quickly, which means that it can be stored and used as needed. Furthermore, not only is it a dense source of calories but it's also one of the best social lubricants known to man. Unsurprisingly alcohol was used in any and all social settings, be they secular or religious, hence one could see the appeal of sedentarism over the nomadic lifestyle. Not only that, but a hunter-gatherer needs proportionally a larger area to live off the land than a farmer does. Upon adopting agriculture, populations exploded with population density increasing 1500% from the hunter-gatherer levels [4]!

When human beings were all still hunter-gatherers, each needed about a thousand hectares (100 km2) of land to support themselves [5]. As such, there is a natural limit to how big hunter-gatherer societies could potentially get. If there were to be a random shortage in wild game, nomadic tribes would necessarily have to adopt one of four strategies in order to survive:

1. Become full-time farmers, as that way the land you live on can support the density of your population. The main downside is that farming is very hard work, you have to be at the beck and call of your crops or they will die off. In essence, you substitute the variability of the wild for the certainty of the civilized.

2. Move elsewhere where there are better opportunities. An issue with this is that after a certain point there will be few desirable and habitable locations that are uninhabited by other tribes. This means that this strategy might lead to violent conflict.
3. Steal and plunder from full-time agrarian societies. The problem with this is that if you are too violent in your raids, you might wipe them out, and then you're back to where you started. However, the problem if you don't wipe them out though, is that they will arm themselves, build defences, and they are statistically likely going to outnumber you. If you are dangerous enough, they might even start a militia specifically designed to fight you off.
4. Trade with agrarian communities, but given that they outnumber you, tend to have superior weapons to you, and have this obnoxious habit of claiming ownership over land they might not even be using whilst being willing to defend it against trespassers, you're at their mercy.

As the perspicacious reader might have noticed though, there's a bias towards agriculture in the long run. The last three options are temporary, as sooner or later the same problem will lead you to repeat the cycle of assimilation or destruction. That said, once you've committed to agriculture, it might be difficult to go back to your hunter-gatherer lifestyle, past a certain point, even if the wildlife levels normalise again to what they used to be before you were driven to agriculture.

Agricultural societies tend to have more children than hunter-gatherer societies. A number of factors contribute to this. The main one is that female hunter-gatherers have children once every four years, as they have to carry and take care of the baby - their biology even goes as far as inhibiting the pregnancy. Breastfeeding causes prolactin secretion. A feedback loop then occurs which goes straight from the nipples to the hypothalamus. If there is nipple stimulation for any reason (in males as well as females), the hypothalamus signals the pituitary to secrete prolactin. Prolactin in sufficient quantities causes reproduction to cease, thus becoming a powerful contraceptive [6].

The reason why pregnancies happen during this 4-year period in agricultural societies is that breastfeeding does not occur with enough regularity for it to affect the reproductive system, as hunter-gatherers do it constantly - this happens about a minute or two every fifteen minutes, wherein babies are carried on slings and sleep with their mothers. This does not happen in more established societies, as babies can be left in the house or other safe locations. Consequently, females in agricultural societies have no truly effective contraceptive system[25]. Add to this that there's less of a disincentive to not have many children, as an extra pair of hands in the farm can increase your marginal utility by more than it costs (which incidentally is the calculation that lead to the invention of slavery, but we'll get to that), and the population increases exponentially.

The problem occurs when you wish to switch back to being a hunter-gatherer society. If enough time has elapsed, your society has grown far too big to comfortably allow for the existence of a single hunter-gatherer community. At which point, you either have to have a portion of your tribe branch off elsewhere, or you have to accept that there's no turning back. Once you've gotten on the treadmill of agriculture and stayed there for a while, the rat race can't stop.

Agriculture, rather than the pioneering success that it's sold to be, might have simply been a pit which we fell down into and were unable to claw out of. We gave our freedom in exchange for security and, in many ways, we've been miserable ever since. Becoming domesticated gave us ulcers, bosses and drudgery. The hunter-gatherer life might not have been glamorous, or perhaps even pleasant, but it was never boring, or stressful[26].

---

25 I'm painting in broad strokes, Mediterranean cultures, for example, used a plant called "Silphium" to avoid pregnancies. It was purported to work much in the same way as the morning-after pill. Nowadays it may be extinct, we don't precisely know, so its effectiveness, beyond what ancient sources tell us, is in doubt.

26 Of course, there were stressful situations, but stress as a constant source of anguish which destroys your body and kills you was close to nonexistent, same as obesity.

2 - The Specialisation Of Labour And The Root Of All Evil

> "Oh, you hate your job? Why didn't you say so? There's a support group for that. It's called 'EVERYBODY', and they meet at the bar."
>
> – *Drew Carey, Drew Carey Show*

All the pieces are now set, and our society can finally begin to take shape on a more permanent basis. Yet we soon begin to see the limits of unspecialised labour. Whereas before, everyone more or less had to be able to do the same work due to the needs and capabilities of the tribe, there's now a whole catalogue of jobs to be done: the newly domesticated animals need tending, the buildings need to be planned, built and repaired, the various tools of life need to be crafted, the food needs cooking, etc.

All in all, it makes far more sense to have everyone work to each according to his ability, to each according to his needs. Skilled artisans should not plough the fields, as their time is valuable. In other words, they can bring far more benefit to the society by not doing so and focusing on their skillset; given that they have a comparative advantage in their own trade, when compared to the average person. There's a slight issue with that though. When communities were small, you could more or less keep track of social relations. You could rely on social pressure to eliminate any person who would attempt to take advantage of the community and not do their fair share of the work. With a ballooning of community sizes though, it became impossible to keep track of all of the social relations[27], and thus one could not rely on social ties to ensure everyone contributes equitably. Before this period, it made perfect sense to be altruistic, given that with each contribution you increased your standing in the community and you would, in turn, receive help when needed.

Pre-agricultural societies are largely egalitarian, downright communist even, but such societies quickly disintegrate when they're no longer self-policeable and you can take more from the society than you put in. Wealth disparities generally increased with the domestication of plants and animals and with an expansion of the socio-political arena [7]. In economics, this phenomenon is known as "The Tragedy of the Commons" - meaning that whenever there's a common space with ill-defined obligations and rights, people will seek to maximise their personal benefit at the detriment of the society as a whole. As such, people take more than their fair share and the whole suffers.

A good case study is that of the farmers with common pastures, when animals are taken to graze there it makes little sense to not have as many animals as possible for the individual farmer. The best solution in the long run though, is for everyone to have a reasonable number of animals to benefit, but also to maintain the viability of the field by not overgrazing. Nevertheless, if a single person "cheats" by having more animals than the average, he will take out of the community more than he puts in [8]. The Nash Equilibrium strategy[28] that yields the best results for the individual person, given that single person's behaviour, thus becomes for everyone to cheat, as one would otherwise forgo the benefit of essentially stealing from society without repercussions by having more animals and getting them fatter than those who don't. Thus, everyone ends up in a worse overall position in the long run by following their own interests in the common space, as the grasslands don't have enough time to replenish and they're used beyond the point of recovery.

---

27 The cut-off point is somewhere between 150-250 individuals, as we previously mentioned regarding Dunbar's Number.

28 Game theory strategy where the optimal outcome of a game is one where no player has an incentive to change his chosen strategy after considering his opponent's choice.

A system thus had to be devised to counteract people's ability to shirk work and obligations. The farmer produced crops, these were proof of his investment in the community, the artisan had his work as proof of his benefit to the community, the builder had his buildings as proof, etc. To eliminate the mental accounting book that every citizen must have had, to keep track of his obligations and expectations that he had of the community from that point onwards, the proof would be in the pudding. You would own the fruits of your labour, you would have private property, which would inherently signal your standing in the community by providing palpable proof of your investment.

No longer would you be able to receive goods or services on credit, in expectation that you might somehow repay it in future via some act of reciprocal kindness. Now, unless you were directly blood related or friends, you had to exchange something proportional to what you were being given, or receive nothing at all. For instance, if you wanted a pot by the master artisan, you would have to give him something proportional to the effort and materials that he was expending, say a chicken.

The problem with that becomes fairly obvious. The master artisan might not like chicken, but that's the only thing we might have, as a potential client, to pay with. As such, we would have to search for someone exchanging a good or service for chicken, which in turn might interest the master artisan enough to trade me the pot. This systemic problem, known as "the double coincidence of wants" quickly becomes very cumbersome and it incurs a lot of transaction costs. A lot of potential trades simply do not occur, given that it's difficult to have all parties agree on an exchange.

The seemingly obvious innovation to solve this problem is the invention of money - a universally accepted, non-perishable means to store value. We are correct in assuming that it's the solution to the problem, but we are wrong in assuming that it's an obvious innovation. A surprising number of civilized societies did not have money, developed it well after they were established, or merely used it as a means to trade with other societies and didn't use it within their own borders. Civilizations on this list include the likes of the Egyptians, the Spartans, and the Incas.

Money, in whichever form it may take, be it precious metals, gems, bottles of alcohol, cowry shells, paper or cigarettes, at its core is a means of tallying how to divide resources. In game theory terms, money is a hard to fake signal of one's commitment and loyalty to the community, as it indirectly shows how many goods and services your involvement in the community has helped accumulate. At its core, money is supposed to be a means by which we quantify reciprocal altruism - or the costs incurred by an organism in the expectation of future benefits from the receiver of said service. Because of this, wealth by itself is almost seen as a virtue, and thus many wealthy people are admired because of their material possessions. Power has often historically stemmed from the riches one commands.

However, despite this seeming like a logical argument, agricultural societies have an inherent flaw with such a tallying mechanism of social favour. At its core, this system makes the false assumption that one is being paid for one's work, and not for that of others. After all, one could always coerce people into one's service and reap handsome rewards for their troubles. Thus, with the advent of civilization, slavery became an all too common occurrence.

The agricultural revolution created an imbalance in labour inputs and production outputs. For the first time ever, you could receive more out of the food production system than you put in. It used to be that, on average, if you put in a day's work you, then you got about a day's worth of food. Under such conditions, it makes little sense to go through the trouble of enslaving people. At absolute best, by forcing people into slavery, you'd barely get enough resources back, to warrant keeping them alive [9]. Not only that, but you had to go through the trouble of policing them and ensuring that they wouldn't rebel. From a purely economic standpoint, slavery hardly makes sense under such conditions[29].

The surplus of food created by agriculture opened the floodgates for untold

29 I'm glossing over sexual slavery, as that is much more easily achieved and doesn't necessarily require an agricultural state backing the institution. This is why even chimpanzees go on raids to capture females.

misery. Not only could you now easily feed your workers with the work of a handful of slaves, but you could have them focus on other non-essential or dangerous occupations, such as mining. A few people might die in the process, but in the overall arithmetic, you would still be ahead. Unsurprising that slavery was the rule, rather than the exception to most civilizations. The only societal development which truly put a dent into the institution was the industrial revolution, but that is many thousand years of history, and many chapters of this book, into the future.

At its core, to create a stable system of slavery, two essential things are needed: governments and a military, both of which we shall discuss over the next few chapters.

3 - Bloody Murder: A Brief History of Violence

"What is best in Life? To crush your enemies, see them driven before you, and to hear the lamentations of their women!"

– *Conan, Conan the Barbarian*

I remember once as a teenager browsing the philosophy section in a bookshop, coming upon a book by the 14th Dalai Lama, Tenzin Gyatso, and flicking through it. Needless to say, that if one is in need of practical advice, looking for it in the form of a quasi-god figure that has never lived a normal life, is likely to result in very out of touch material.

To paraphrase the quote that stuck in my craw, he said something along the lines that if human beings had a natural compunction to hit each other, we would have no fingers and simply have fingerless stumps to pummel each other with. In the process of making a nice sounding point about morality, the Dalai Lama threw logic out the window. The ability to punch is no less human than the ability to hug your loved ones (which you can still do even if you only had stumps for arms). Violence is as much a part of human nature as kindness and caring are. It should not be promoted, but neither should it be ignored as a natural desire and important social mechanism.

We are far from the only animals who do this: chimps, for example, organise border patrols to safeguard their territories from other encroaching males. If their territory is trespassed, the punishment is death [10]. Not only that, but when social tension rises past a certain point, they've been known to have multi-year long civil wars, such as the Gombe Chimpanzee War which lasted from 1974 to 1978 [11].

Truth is that violence, assuming that one has the capacity to win and dominate the confrontation and ensuing fallout, is a powerful means of controlling people and making your desires be met. By eliminating your potential competition, not only do you immediately eliminate them from causing you further trouble down the line, but you also signal to potential dissenters what may happen if they try to rebel. The survival instinct is as powerful in humans as it is in any other creature. As such, we tend to shy away from outright suicidal tactics, unless a meme has managed to supersede our natural impulses by creating an exceedingly effective supernormal stimulus (the religious indoctrination and fanaticism of suicide bombers, for example). Thus, if a ruler regularly, but selectively, shows his capacity for violence without abusing it, people are much less likely to outright revolt. Having overwhelming force, when compared to your rivals, allows you more direct control over the direction in which society develops.

It's not without reason that despots cling to the rule of the sword, over the affection of the masses. The mob's love is fickle, in their eyes you are only as good as their most recent impressions of your rule. For better or for worse, you will always be blamed, even if you have nothing to do with the current situation. The military, on the other hand, knows well that their fortunes are tied to the continued existence of the current regime, and hence they are likely to remain loyal to whosoever holds the purse strings - as the ruthless emperor Septimius Severus suggested on his deathbed to his psychopathic children: "Be harmonious, enrich the soldiers, scorn everybody else" [12].

Such a strategy is untenable in the long run though. The Severan dynasty followed this suggestion to the letter, which proved to be their downfall. As a consequence, the Roman Emperors grew increasingly out of touch with reality, going as far as acquiring god complexes, murdering an entire delegation of representatives and looting a city because someone dared write a comedic play about them [13]. In the meantime, the army drew ever increasing bonuses until it essentially bankrupted the government.

This is why honour, tradition, duty, nationalism and religion are ideas that are often much favoured by successful governments. These not only legitimise the monopoly of violence that the state strives for, but will make any attempt to contradict "the mandate of heaven" an act of treason. People will go out of their way to self-police these doctrines and will willingly indoctrinate their children in them. As such, people will be more loyal to the state without the ruler having to resort to bankruptcy through bribery.

In fact, it may even work exceedingly well, to the point where people willingly pay for their armament. For most of human history, private individuals bought their own weapons and armour, often with the implicit understanding that their social standing would bear a direct correlation with them. This is why, since the time of Stonehenge, you're likely to find sumptuous burials with decorative weapons, even when the person is ineligible for combat (incidentally this is often the reason you sometimes find graves of supposed female warriors - whilst they did exist, they were the exception far more than they were the norm[30]). In Ancient Athens, for example, men had to buy their own equipment, and this was seen as an honourable duty [15].

Economists are often baffled by non-monetary incentives, forgetting in the process of disregarding reality that people's priority is not for wealth, but what emanates from wealth - status and power. Once more, wealth is a surrogate - a parallel metric - for measuring our position in the social hierarchy. Surprisingly enough, professional armies, as we know them, are fairly new concepts. There were several failed experiments in an attempt to have a standing army. Nevertheless, they mostly depended on conscripts or untrained volunteers until Philip II of Macedon, the father of Alexander the Great, laid the groundwork for his son's empire [16].The concept more or less

30 This is not me being sexist for the sake of being sexist. Even in modern times, where the army doesn't usually involve hacking at people with cumbersome pieces of metal, women - **on average** -are unable to meet the physical requirements. To the point where the armed forces of some countries, in an attempt to seem more inclusive, have reduced the prerequisites to join. [14]

petered out for a couple of centuries, but was officially retaken by the Romans in the Marian reforms, which completely changed the functioning of the army [17]. Arguably, the increasing superiority of the Roman fighting style allowed some of the more notorious expansions in the history of the world.

Thus, the monopoly on violence is the cornerstone of society. The ability to inflict violence on others, and the loyalty emanating from this capacity, is what keeps other pretenders to the throne in check and allows for continuity, expansion and normalcy. Nevertheless, other societies will quickly adopt the warpath as well. By militarizing one's society, one gains but a momentary advantage, which one needs to capitalise on. Once two societies start to compete for the strongest military advantage, we enter Red Queen territory.

When the first societies are attacked, the survivors will build defences. As such, we have the first hillforts, settlements that are more or less impregnable through a combination of natural defences and incredible engineering feats. Now, raids are much more difficult, attacking a settlement becomes very complicated, given that few men can mount a hefty resistance to a seemingly overwhelming force. As such, the best technique becomes to simply wait them out, let disease and famine do what their men would've done. There are good grounds for why the word siege derives from *sedere*, Latin for "to sit"; reason being that they're very slow, and may well take years, so deciding to siege a town becomes a very high-cost affair and not something to be taken lightly.

This stalemate between offence and defence remained for several hundred, possibly a thousand, years until the invention of the first siege engines - machines whose sole purpose was to overcome defences. This shifted the game and made it possible to have massive expansion for the aggressors, given that enemies could be decisively beaten much quicker.

As such, from fractious and independent city-states, warlords emerged which made vassals of their culturally-similar but ill-prepared neighbours. Over time, this domination became symbiotic and there came a time where the conquerors and the conquered were indistinguishable, as happened with the Romans and Etruscans. Yet, greed soon turned their eyes to other societies altogether different from their own, and hence from their conquest they created empires.

Eventually, their reach exceeds their grasp, as empires can only be so large without industrial or slightly pre-industrial levels of technology. Thus, hubris and overextension often proved to be the end of them. The empires collapsed and the torch was passed to a new civilization to try to build an even more glorious one. Yet despite every warlord having that twinkle in their eye when they heard about the empires of old, extremely few were able to surpass the raw extension of the original Asian and European powers, until technology caught up with ambition.

Mechanisation allowed for the spectre of empire to extend like never before. It also had the secondary, yet not unwelcome, effect of creating emotional distance between a person and the brutality they could inflict. There's clearly a difference in kind between killing a single person in cold blood and dropping an atomic bomb on a city. In the first scenario, there's a twisted sense of intimacy in the act of murder where you're witness to every convulsion and desperate attempt at drawing another breath, whilst you're close enough to feel their warmth and you can even smell them. In the second scenario, you flick a switch and somewhere far away there's a ball of hellfire which obliterates entire communities and makes the first murder look like the work of an amateur. Or as Harry S. Truman put it: "The atom bomb was no 'great decision.' It was merely another powerful weapon in the arsenal of righteousness" [18].

The distance between the target of violence and the perpetrator is visible in the incidence rate of PTSD among modern militaries. In the United States we have the following rates of incidence per 1,000 people in the different branches of the military: Army (land/infantry) 1.43%, Marines (naval infantry) 0.97%, Navy (sea) 0.37% and Air Force (air) 0.34% [19]. It doesn't take a mathematical genius to see that the difference is very pronounced. People in direct contact with the enemy will necessarily cover more of the psychological cost.

As such, the more technology a society amasses, the more chaos they can inflict without being witness to it, or even being aware of the toll it takes on a society. For those of us that live in highly-developed industrialized (or "first world") nations, widespread death, disease, poverty and violence are quite distant from our everyday experiences. In the modern world, even the hint of unexpectedness is enough to unsettle some folks - tell a German his train is five minutes late and see how he reacts. Hence, when modern soldiers are confronted with the savagery of war, it's unsurprising that a portion of them cracks.

In the US, it's been estimated that when soldiers engage in a firefight, the survivors have a 154.8% higher probability of suicidal ideation, a 55.6% higher probability of depression and a 140.9% higher probability of developing post-traumatic stress disorder (PTSD). Worst still, getting wounded or injured in combat is associated with a 124.1% increase in the probability of depressive symptomatology and a 225.2% increase in the probability of PTSD. In addition, seeing a coalition/ally member or civilian killed, dead, or wounded has adverse psychological consequences for those serving in combat zones.

However, observing the killing, death, or wounding of the enemy has no independent adverse psychological consequences. Even more interesting, killing or believing to have killed someone is not significantly associated with any mental health problems after accounting for intensity of firefight and deployment length [20].

This shouldn't really be a surprise. Studies, like the Milgram experiment, have shown that most sane individuals are capable of murder when directly ordered to do so by an authority figure [21]. It's not the vanquishing of the enemy that leaves people awake at night, it's having to pick up the pieces of the consequences, as well as the gruesome break from their normal lives, which is truly damaging. It's really hard to care about paying your taxes on time after you've seen what brutality the average human is capable of when given the right setting and motivation.

At the risk of indulging in some speculation, I suspect this has to do with the agency of control. In ancient times, you more or less knew when a battle had begun or had ended. Recent psychological studies show that what causes semi-permanent damage on a person, is not stress per se, but chronic stress [22]. If your system is always on alert, your anatomy works overtime pumping adrenaline. This is very taxing on the system, and you become susceptible to all manner of diseases - both physical and psychological. In modern times, you have to be always on your guard as a drone or a sniper hiding in the bushes can kill you whilst you're smoking a cigarette.

On the other hand, in ancient warfare, up until the invention of gunpowder, there was more of a direct sense of control. When in formation, you defended the person beside you, and they defended you. As such, this agency of control, which has been mentioned as being imperative for our correct mental wellbeing, was not compromised [23]. Thus, I imagine that we weren't nearly as susceptible to such mental maladies as nowadays - we're still the same creature with the same susceptibilities and desires, but we operate under very different environments. In our day-to -day lives, we were much more likely to see death, and even our religious institutions, which brought solace to us, often involved bloody ritual sacrifice. We were fully aware of our own mortality and the preciousness and rarity of a peaceful society. Nowadays, we have more stopgap measures to prolong peace and lifespan, and are more likely to take them for granted. So, whilst not entirely immune to it, we were far better able to cope with death and tragedy in ancient times than people from the modern age.

Having said this, I believe we cope with tragedy in much the same as people of old, given we're still fundamentally human. Or as Philip Gibbs put it when talking about his own experience with coping with the mental stress of WWI:

> *"It was astonishing how loudly one laughed at tales of gruesome things, of war's brutality - I with the rest of them. I think at the bottom of it was a sense of the ironical contrast between the normal ways of civilian life and this hark-back to the caveman code. [...] It was, I think, the laughter of mortals at the trick which had been played on them by an ironical fate. They had been taught to believe that the whole object of life was to reach out to beauty and love, and that mankind, in its progress to perfection, had killed the beast instinct, cruelty, blood-lust, the primitive, savage law of survival by tooth and claw and club and ax. [...]The war-time humor of the soul roared with mirth at the sight of all that dignity and elegance despoiled."[24]*

For better or for worse, war was always a force that drove us to test our limits. That's the tragedy of war, it's one of the few things in a society that can utterly put aside our differences and focus us all on achieving a single goal. It isn't until one is in palpable fear of death that one's mettle is tested, that is where the brave and the cowards are separated. The forces that created the conflict might be artificial in nature, but the strife and the cultural advances that come as a result of it are very real.

True kindness is only possible as a result of sacrifice; true insight and creativity are only possible when putting aside social conventions that disappear in the turmoil of conflict (be it internal or external, which is true enough for the individual as well). Truth is, as a society, we may need violence, war and strife to avoid cultural stagnation. To advance as a civilization, we need an external foe, otherwise our tribalism takes over and we squabble over minutia between each other until we eventually enter into cultural stasis and stagnation.

Indeed, it's been argued that the only thing really capable of promoting social mobility are catastrophes. Epidemics, pandemics, the collapse of the status quo through Black Swan events and violence have been argued to be the few things actually capable of changing people's lot in life [25]. Otherwise, politics becomes a compromise between the rich and powerful, wherein the disenfranchised and poor are used as pawns and horse trading. Best they can hope for is for their interests to marginally align with a populist who will wield their collective menace as a cudgel to gain power, and then stab them in the back when they become too loud and the populist becomes part of the establishment.

The point should not be misconstrued as promoting every war or conflict, quite the contrary. Conflict is an undesirable state, but it is a necessary one to create unity and stability in the long run. Initially, this might sound counterproductive, but allow me to elaborate. Imagine a forest, wherein naturally driftwood and similar flammable materials are produced as a by-product of the correct functioning of the ecosystem. If forest fires are actively combated at every turn, this deadwood will accumulate over the years.

Eventually though, some element will slip through the defences and light the whole thing ablaze. The ensuing chaos will cause far more damage than simply having allowed the local forest fires to occur and allowing themselves to burn out.

Wilfully losing a battle to avoid losing the war is a sensible strategy, yet it is an unpopular one. In the US, 98% of all fires are extinguished and aren't allowed to burn themselves out. Yet, despite a near perfect record in fire suppression, the six worst fire seasons in the last 50 years have all occurred since 2000 [26]. Fact of the matter is that nobody wants to be told that their property has to be burnt down for everyone else's benefit, and thus flammable material accrues until no force can adequately contain it.

Nations too, in their day-to-day operations, produce volatile and dangerous material in the form of memes. These might have been created at the internal level due to the different interactions between the demographics living in the nation, or as a result of the interaction with other entities at the international level. The most effective sovereign will understand that immediately stamping out dissent and conflict may not be the best course of action, as it simply drives it underground and may reappear when you are in dire circumstances. Sometimes, allowing things to escalate and consequently gaining the necessary permissions to attack it in full force, may be the best and most effective way to go about it. Not only that, but by not attempting to stop every single conflict, they don't become a rallying cry for all of one's enemies when they do succeed in escalating. Instead, they become small and isolated, limiting their potential damage to manageable portions.

To be able to do this though, you must have the infrastructure in place to support and defend the necessary monopoly on violence. The next section will cover the development of bureaucracies and their unintended by-products.

4 - State Of The Art: Culture, Tradition, Philosophy And Religion

---

"Art is the lie that enables us to realize the truth."

- Pablo Picasso

In the strictly ascetic sense, tradition, culture, philosophy and religion are thoroughly useless affairs in one's life. One needs sustenance to live, but could easily live a lifetime without ever having heard Beethoven's 5th Symphony. The story of the Greek philosopher Diogenes is a perfect example of this ethos.

Far from being the heroic figures one sees on marble busts, philosophers in Ancient Greece were often loathsome figures. They sometimes accosted random people in the marketplace, whilst likely smelling foully, and asked them on the nature of love, beauty and justice. If they so happened to fail at this surprise exam (not least because the poor victims likely wanted to be as far away from them as possible) their answers and name would be mocked for all eternity in the inevitable philosopher's treatise, where their conversation would be replayed and edited, so as to show them in the worst light possible.

One of the worst of these philosophers was Diogenes. He was a thoroughly detestable figure who preached virtue by haranguing everyone's lack of morals and decency, despite having been kicked out of his native city for debasing the currency. Afterwards, he settled in Athens and took to living in a barrel in the marketplace, with his one possession beyond a barrel, being a bowl so that he could drink water. There, he had all the freedom to annoy people at his heart's content, even going as far as urinating on those whose answers he didn't like, defecating in theatres and masturbating in public.

One day, it was pointed out to him that he could very easily drink from a stream without the bowl, as he could simply cup his hands together. Upon hearing this, he immediately threw the bowl away. Say what you will about him but at least he was consistent, and genuinely seemed content. So much so that legends say that Alexander the Great, upon meeting him, said that had he not been born the conqueror of the world, he would've well liked to be Diogenes, as he lived a very contented existence [27]. Diogenes, in turn, answered that had he not been born Diogenes, he would've likely also wanted to be Diogenes.

Tradition and culture, like any meme or gene in competitive environment, have their own preservation and propagation as the prime focus. Naturally, some rules are not designed with our satisfaction or wellbeing in place. It makes rational sense to ignore such regulations when we can get away with it, but do it too much and you lose the one trait that separates one from man and beast - civilization.

Take feral children as an experiment. From time to time, nature conspires to give us an image of what we would be like without the civilizing forces that hold our baser natures in check. For one reason or another, young children sometimes end up in the wilderness or outside the confines of human society. On rare occasions, these children don't die from exposure or wildlife but they're adopted by animals. They may even adapt to their circumstances extremely well, to the point of walking on all fours and imitating animal sounds. When they're inevitably found and brought back to civilization, they often have severe communication difficulties [28]. You could arguably have a more intelligible conversation with Koko the gorilla, than an unlucky feral child, even after attempting to educate them.

Human development tends to happen within a certain window, if the factors aren't developed in their rightly time, then we may fail to develop it at all [29]. Culture is a mishmash of useful and pointless adaptations. Nevertheless, it provides for a net positive influence overall, as it provides the fruits that make life worth living. I would posit that all animals: cats, dogs and possibly feral children, can lead happy lives, wantonly following their hedonistic desires. But I would also argue that there is something lacking from such a superficial existence - they lack significance and meaning.

There is nothing that a creative mind abhors more than a vacuum, and thus we fill existence with useless tradition and pageantry to find meaning. In the words of British author Stephen Fry: "It is the useless things that make life worth living and that make life dangerous too: wine, love, art, beauty. Without them life is safe, but not worth bothering with."

Whilst avowedly an atheist, and a sceptic of fantastic claims, I now see that I might've been a tad too hasty in promoting the elimination of religion as a teenager. It is absolutely true that supposed divine words have been used to defend some of the most horrific acts in human history, but it is also true that man's superstitious nature likely gave us art and civilization. Open any art history textbook, and you will quickly see a pattern: Most memorable art ever created was to exalt magic and the supernatural - to exalt something otherworldly and far greater than us.

How do you convince people to bond together when family ties are not strong enough? An easy solution is to create an even bigger family, which includes all people who believe in the same creed. I'm genuinely jealous of the sense of belonging and purpose that religious people seem to feel. That seems to me the cornerstone of civilization, that sense of supra familial bonds, where kindness extends beyond superficial boundaries. As the Greeks used to say, "society grows great when old men plant trees whose shade they know they shall never sit in." Homo economicus has no desire to plant trees it cannot use himself, but we Homo sapiens depend on the irrationally altruistic to move forward.

We may nowadays take that sense of community and belonging for granted, as we intrinsically believe in nations, political parties and communities. But when untold horrors could have been lurking just a hillside away and violence was rampant, taking comfort in the community who shared your memes was a powerful experience. Someone once pointed out to me that a church organ might well have been one of the loudest and most unique sounds people experienced in their whole lives, outside of naturally occurring phenomena like thunder. Is it any wonder that all this pageantry was developed to separate the mundane from the exalted? It's also been suggested that religious affiliation, as it changes the very fabric and functioning of a community, has a deep effect on economic development. Max Weber, for example, suggested that the West had the Protestant work ethic to thank for its affluence [30].

By its very nature religion, tradition and culture provide a bulwark for rampant and dangerous innovation. It only changes when it has a need for change, not simply for the sake of it. Change for change's sake is an irresponsible philosophy. There are far more ways to screw something up than to make it better. This is why bloody revolutions and Dark Ages are so plentiful in the pages of history, whilst Golden Ages are so rare. When allowed to make random, unprecedented changes, chances are that they will be bad ones, as the ideas have not been properly tested and polished to make them successful. When confronted with a risky situation that requires no immediate action, inaction is a valid solution, until there's better information.

As history will attest, medicine was useless for most of it, worse than useless - dangerous even. Not only were most treatments ineffectual, but could likely harm a patient permanently, perhaps even kill them. This is why true physicians, and not charlatans, develop a deep respect and fear of the potential damage that a treatment could bring and thus become reticent of interfering with nature unless absolutely necessary - the Hippocratic oath is to do no harm, after all. In Greek this is known as "Iatrogenics" and much like doctors accept that they don't understand the whole system and their meddling might only make matters worse [31], so should one accept the glacial pace at which society sometimes develops unless absolutely necessary. Respecting nature, and its ebb and flow, leads to much more stable structures than by trying to violently overthrow it.

Often meddling with a system that one does not understand leads to the exact opposite outcome one wanted to incentivise. This phenomenon is commonly referred to as "the cobra effect"; so named because in the 19th century the British Raj began a policy in Delhi of paying a bounty for every cobra captured and killed, which yielded horrible results. The reason being that enterprising people began breeding cobras for profit. Yet upon realising what was happening, the government immediately shut down the programme. The cobra farmers, upon hearing this, found it easier to free the venomous snakes, rather than kill them. As such, a policy specifically designed to eliminate cobras actually ended up increasing their population [32]. This story is useful in showing how overly ambitious an ill planned social policy can often do more harm than good.

Do not misunderstand me though, government regulation is necessary and it can nudge people to do the right thing. But rather than taking action for the sake of taking action, one should attempt to be as scientific about drastic changes within a complex system, as one can manage. For example, the colonial rulers could've run small scale studies to see the unintended consequences of the policies, or study the incentive mechanisms in place. Instead, some bureaucrat somewhere had an idea and made a mess of things. Conservatism isn't simply a political stance, but it is just as much a survival strategy. As one only changes what is necessary, and little more, one attempts to ensure that what works doesn't get meddled with.

Sometimes though, a Black Swan, an event of such stratospheric magnitude that the rules are impossible to maintain, will happen - consequently punctuated equilibrium will occur, and taboos will be broken with astonishing rapidity. At the risk of adding Egyptologists to the list of people this book has offended, I shall ask you to compare the astonishing changes that have happened in the last hundred and fifty years, and the stagnancy of Egyptian culture for most of its history. It may surprise you to learn that Cleopatra was born (69 BCE) closer to the moon landing (1969 CE) than to when the pyramids were built (the Great Pyramid of Giza having been built c. 2560–2540 BCE).

In the meantime, Egyptian culture and art more or less stopped developing for long stretches of time. Hundreds, if not thousands of years could pass, and life more or less looked identical. There wasn't any particular need to do otherwise, the culture had found its niche and settled in. Imagine as if society's belief were a pendulum, each shock affecting the speed of the swing and direction. Eventually, if the pendulum becomes too robust, too heavy to be moved by smaller influences, it will remain in a point of balance, until it's yanked off its resting position by a much stronger force.

A great civilization is not conquered from without until it has destroyed itself within. More often than not conquerors would take the fruit of their spoils and grow soft, possibly even adopt the culture of the conquered, only to repeat the cycle once more when an even bigger force knocked on their door. The only thing constant in life is change, that is the essence of civilization. Finding the right balance between volatility and stagnation is very difficult, requiring both good statesmanship and a steady hand.

Yet, there are some trends and cultural advances that are rarely forgotten no matter how much time passes, and only keep increasing as the inherent nature of civilization demands it. For example, the trend has historically been for nations to become larger. At its zenith, the vast Roman Empire had a measly c.50 million people, nowadays a country of similar population size is Kenya. It's depressing to think how much societies used to accomplish with so few means. American actor Orson Welles might have been onto something when he said: "The enemy of art is the absence of limitations." Hence, with numerically the same number of people, the Roman Empire managed to be one of the bedrocks of civilization with advances in art, philosophy, politics and technology while Kenya remains a backwater of the world.

Whilst obviously it was comparatively easier to create new technological advances back in the day, it also stands to reason that the basis of a good society often rests on the quality of its institutions and overall operational philosophy, as such we will be addressing the reason why some societal structures are more efficient than others in the next chapter.

5 - Bureaucratic Oversights: Trade, Laws and Taxes

"We cannot expect people to have respect for law and order until we teach respect to those we have entrusted to enforce those laws."

- Hunter S. Thompson

Once groups created the philosophy necessary to allow the unification of disparate groups, many societies achieved wealth and power beyond their imagining. Their militaries grew with the plunder, and the population ballooned because of the surplus of food, and kidnapping people from other tribes. By that point, the community has long since ceased to be something that is regulated by the common decency of humanity, if there ever was such a thing. To add insult to injury, the more complex a society becomes, the more likely a Black Swan is to occur.

As such, there have to be contingencies in place for when trouble comes. One such contingency is the development of central granaries, which store food in times of plenty and dole out rations in times of need. In the Fertile Crescent, the area spanning from Nile River valley in Egypt to Mesopotamia, where much of the early advances in civilization occurred as a lucky happenstance of history, we saw such a system emerge. To keep track of the system, these cultures invented a primitive form of bookkeeping. This was nowhere near as advanced as the double-entry ledger system that was developed during the Renaissance period in Europe, which is still in use today. Furthermore, most ancient numeral systems are utterly incapable, or at the very least ill-suited, for complex mathematics.

Here's a fun plan for the afternoon, if you have nothing better to do: try making any calculation in Roman numerals, other than basic arithmetic. This would give you an approximation of the inherent difficulties with using ill-suited mathematical tools for performing calculations.

We owe a debt of gratitude to those people that brought us the Hindu-Arabic numeral system, whose simplifications made maths more streamlined, without which modernity might be impossible. Before this had happened though, mathematical truths had to be proven through raw insight. It's not without reason that the Pythagorean theorem was the best kept secret of a fanatical quasi-religious cult. Rather than just simple mathematical formula, the Pythagorean theorem was devised through very careful and complex meditation. Its raw complexity, and its seeming magical properties in explaining the natural world, almost undoubtedly proved its divine origin. In the words of American astrophysicist Carl Sagan: "They believed that in their mathematics they had glimpsed a perfect reality, a realm of the gods, of which our familiar world is but an imperfect reflection" [33].

It's hilarious to think that modernity has managed to strip away its awe-inspiring difficulty through simplification and more efficient visualisation techniques, that the biggest group of people who occupy themselves with it are high school students who mainly only begrudgingly learn it to pass their exams - completely unaware that they're learning secrets that might've even gotten them killed in another time.

As it stands, the original proto-bookkeeping accounts were little more than pictograms where they tallied out how many units they had of one particular resource. Something curious eventually happened though, either out of laziness or as a time-saving mechanism, the pictograms used to identify the units started to become more abstract. After a while, the pictograms were more phonetic than iconographic, thus you could use the phonetic sound of concrete words to write something intangible down [34]. For example, if you were to use this system in English, whilst very limited, you could still use everyday objects to express ephemeral concepts:

Eye + bee + leaf = I believe

From that point of abstraction, it's a somewhat easier jump to write an alphabet that is completely devoid of any association to any other words, but the ones being spelt out with it. This whole development of the written word is hardly set in stone though. In fact, it only developed five times in human history, and the progenitor cultures were the Egyptians, Chinese, Easter Islanders, Sumerians and early Mesoamericans [35]. The rest of societies either had to design an offshoot or make do without it. Take the Aztec Empire, which possessed no written language despite governing over five million people in the sixteenth century, as an example. Despite such a necessarily complex bureaucratic system, theirs was mainly an ideographic proto-writing, which required insider knowledge for its interpretation [36].

At the end of the day, when one depends on prior cultural understanding for the decipherment of a message, one is already on the back foot. It's much like when you hang out with friends, and one blurts an inside joke to which the others aren't privy to. Despite their best efforts to convey the meaning, at the end of the day "you just had to be there." Which is why to this day, many of the writings remain a mystery, as nobody out there can explain the social context necessary for the understanding of the message.

It certainly helps to write things down to convey your meaning in a precise way without assumptions of much prior knowledge other than language and literacy. Knowledge hence becomes transportable, wherein your exact meaning can be conveyed without the need to parse and interpret. It's because of this evolution to a more rational method that the writing systems eventually evolved past mere accounting and started conveying more complex things such as contracts, laws and taxes. Initially, the written word was hardly ever used to express anything artistic. Oral tradition was the mainstay for storytellers, either of a mythical or secular nature.

On the other hand, laws were literally written in stone, and among the first ever longform examples of writing in human history. The Hammurabi Code is among one of the oldest and most well-known examples of legal systems in the world. It stands as a testament of our attempts to tame man; given that man-made laws are attempts to deal with recurring problems without knowing how to solve them permanently. Surprisingly though, despite not being an economic document, a good portion of the code concentrates on financial matters, like inheritance rules, wages and trade. It's odd, when one considers the often-barbaric content of the rest of the material (like cutting a child's arm for hitting his father), that the Babylonians would be interested in matters of high finance [37].

Nevertheless, with some historical perspective, it makes perfect sense. The most conclusive sign that you control an area unchallenged, is the ability to effectively charge taxes and control economic development. People will not usually wish to hand over their wealth unless they're receiving the carrot or the stick in return. To tax regularly and successfully, one needs to have a firm grasp of the area, otherwise your wishes will all but be ignored. The mountainous terrain of Greece, for example, historically made it a very difficult country to rule. Geopolitically, it's a country that has been very difficult to invade. On an infrastructural level it's a nightmare, as the hilly terrain impedes everything from post services to tax collection. It's not without reason that, even nowadays, tax evasion is considered a national sport [38]. From personal experience, I can attest that to this day even moving between the islands in the off-season is a nightmare. Often you have to wait half a week, or thereabouts, for a ferry which then gets cancelled, or postponed, due to the bad weather.

To return to the point that I made earlier, it's not an absolute necessity to be understood by everyone in one's society. Literacy and numeracy rates varied widely throughout history. Sometimes, as in the glory days of Roman society, it was so widespread that it wasn't uncommon for even slaves to be literate [39]. At other times, it was a rare and privileged skill reserved for the elite.

One group of people consistently retained the literacy and numeracy advances though, and that is merchants. Regardless of the time and place that you pick, there they were with a thirst for knowledge. Not because they were necessarily interested in highbrow culture, but because knowing basic maths, and being reasonably well-educated about the world gives you an edge over dimmer merchants. If, as a by-product, you're enjoying the finer things in life more, so much the better, but that is not the priority.

Incidentally, this line of reasoning is one of the prime motivators for the wide scope of this book. Why else would I go through the trouble of talking about topics as diverse as biology, psychology, history and investing? Sometimes, the topics are directly related to the whole picture, sometimes they just make it clearer, but they're all important in understanding what makes a person and, by extension, a society, tick - the economy is the aggregation of an innumerable amount of unconscious mechanisms working in lockstep with each other, much like the gears in a clock.

A mathematical model, a rule of thumb or a forecast is worth nothing, or is even dangerous, if you do not understand the environment it was crafted in, as otherwise you do not know the potential flaws within the system. There's a reason why in the entryway to the ancient Delphic Temple, where the legendary oracles would tell you a cryptic prophecy about your affairs, the message "Know Thyself" was carved[31] [40]. It initially seems like a platitude, "of course, who doesn't know themselves?" most will scoff.

Yet beyond seeming theatrical and mysterious for the sake of it, the oracles knew why understanding the circumstances and oneself is very important. A story was told that the ruler of Lydia (the western half of modern-day Turkey), King Croesus, decided to consult the oracles of Delphi before going to battle with the Persians. They responded with their typical obfuscations and unclear statements, and said that if he were to attack the Persians a great empire would fall on that day. Croesus took this to mean that the Persian empire was doomed to fall, and thus he grew overconfident in his tactics. Cyrus, the Persian king, was not so cocky and took advantage of every opportunity offered to him - in

31 Incidentally, most of the Delphic Maxims are worth looking at and thinking through, just in case you're looking for material to meditate on.

the end, he proved to be the victor. The overconfident King Croesus, thinking that he need only show up, lost - not knowing himself, his army and his enemy proved to be his downfall as well as that of the whole empire [41].

When I discussed wise tradesmen who used knowledge of their world for their benefit, I was not talking about your average market stall vendor, they will rarely ever achieve much beyond their local sphere, as they lack the motivation, imagination and/or capital to do so. I was instead talking about a merchant who's well versed in the ways of the world - someone who's seen it all and done it all. I was talking about people like Thales of Miletus who not only understood the cosmos but profited from it.

Thales of Miletus was a philosopher by trade, but many in his social circle pestered him that this was hardly a real occupation. As such, he sought to prove them wrong, he hatched a plan to show that he did it by choice, and had just as much talent to successfully do other things. He bought the right to use every olive press in the vicinity of Miletus and Chios, well in advance of harvest season, thus he got it at a relatively low price. Some time later, the harvest proved to be very fruitful, and there was a large need for olive presses, at which point Thales offered owners to buy back the rights for the use of their own assets. They did so gladly, despite their naturally being a hike in prices to the benefit of Thales.

Nevertheless, through his education and observations, he knew that such a gamble would prove to be profitable. Aristotle posits that Thales, with his knowledge of astronomy, had seen in Winter that the weather would be unusually warm in the Summer. More modern thinkers, like Nassim Taleb, have posited that he was ignorant of any such development, but he positioned himself in such a way where his potential losses would be marginal at best, with a huge likely upside, as he was buying the right to use the olive presses, not the obligation [42]. Personally, I think this is an irrelevant point in the tale, the fact remains that regardless of what mechanism he used to fuel his investing prowess, it was his higher understanding of some field of knowledge (be it mathematics or astronomy) which lead him to profit immensely from the deal.

This is the type of person that ultimately triumphs over the markets and the economy. This is the type of person, whose extracurricular interests lead them to make connections that no other person would've, or could've seen otherwise. The real world is not divided up in neat little boxes, where one topic doesn't bleed into the other one. I still remember in my days as an undergraduate when I quoted historical examples in the subject exams where I had to explain how economies work in a given situation. In return, I would get a bad mark from the lecturer and with a straight face get told that "history has no relation to economics."

We ignore the lessons of history at our own peril. The merchants, the men of wisdom who profited from people's ignorance, understood that this is folly. Knowledge is power, and thus the centres of trade often became the centres for learning - Carthage, Athens, Alexandria, Baghdad, Aachen, Constantinople, the city-states of Italy, the Dutch Republic, and so on, were all enterprising in their own right and were merchants before scholars, despite greatly aiding civilization. These centres of commerce beckoned to all men of ambition, by promising wealth and freedom. This allowed for people and ideas to cross paths with circumstances they would have never imagined, and often created golden ages of unparalleled growth and development by finding unique solutions to problems.

The simplest, and most effective, way to stagnation and intellectual atrophy is to become jingoistic and shut oneself off from outside forces, hence allowing the scheming elites to exercise undue influence over the behaviours of their fellow citizens. On the opposite end of the spectrum, there is trade, freedom of speech, freedom of thought and a movement for the intelligentsia, which has historically been one of the best means of prosperity for a society. Needless to say, this wealth is likely to make the leaders of a society very rich men. I wonder, what is the usual outcome when a small elite gain great power and influence?

6 - The Holy, Rich and Morally Dubious Kings

"Three great men sit in a room, a king, a priest and a rich man between them stands a common sellsword. Each great man bids the sellsword kill the other two. Who lives? Who dies?"

- *Varys, Game of Thrones*

Power is an illusion, ultimately its existence rests upon the eyes of the beholder. It is a confidence trick. Paradoxically, people's trust in the worth and the authority of your word is what determines how much of it you possess. Given that authority stems from such ephemeral forces, typically men seek out well-established "kingmakers" and ally themselves with them, absconding the other sources in the pursuit of mastery of one. Sometimes, the sources of power come bundled with each other, as the leaders seek to monopolise all sources of power - not only are they the ultimate military commander, but the representative of God on Earth and the embodiment of his nation's culture. If they are successful at that task then the only way to rise in the ranks is to play by the elite's rules. Throughout history, as the introductory quote implies, there have been three main well-established sources of power in human societies:

- **Wealth** - This is the quickest means of achieving power, yet it is also the most unstable one. The people who choose to master this element do so by appealing to people's greed. The motivation of the followers of those who offer their riches is to one day become wealthy themselves. Nevertheless, given that people's loyalties literally have a price, they will have few qualms about jumping ship once a richer Maecenas comes along, the well runs dry, or people convince them that there are more important things in life than gold.

  The Medici family in the late fifteenth century, for example, achieved great influence in the Florentine Republic through their endless wealth. But, at one point, their patriarch, the aptly-named Piero the Unfortunate, proved too arrogant and ill-equipped to handle the difficulties of leading the Republic, and the whole clan was ignobly ousted.
- **Politics** - This is the realm of the charismatic, feared and beloved. One's success will mainly depend on opportunism and convincing the mob, or people already in power. The people who choose to master this element do so by winning the minds and hearts of the people by crafting a narrative. The motivation of the followers of such rulers is the avoidance of pain and the promise of a better future by following the leader's ideals. Their methods vary, and can be anything as barbaric as coercion or as exalted as diplomacy.

  In the late fifteenth century, Cesare Borgia managed to control half of Italy through diplomacy, bribery, charisma and war. It's not without reason that Machiavelli modelled the ideal Prince after him. However, he made too many enemies along the way, as well as breaching far too many social taboos, and hence lost the support of his allies. Eventually, he was defeated and imprisoned for depending too much on this one source of power.
- **Tradition** - This is by far the slowest and most difficult means of achieving power. Often the upper echelons have been set in stone by castes, divine rights, inheritance or precedent. They're also very likely to rely heavily on nepotism. Furthermore, given that the main source of their appeal

is permanence, continuity, stability and simple inertia, it is challenging to do anything radically different. These leaders will rarely be able to simultaneously be a great reformer and a bulwark of the establishment.

Girolamo Savonarola, for example, was the simple Dominican priest who managed to oust the Medici. He did so by claiming to be a prophet and using religious fervour to gain power. Having said this, he proved to be far too out of touch with reality, and far too inflammatory, so the Pope had him executed.

All examples I gave achieved power roughly in the same place and time, and all three suffered through ignominy because they were unable to wield the maelstrom of competing interests. *When you play a game of thrones you win or you die.* Regardless of whichever path one wishes to follow to achieve power, there is a very simple question that one has to answer beforehand though: *Why would anyone go through the trouble?*

In the earlier sections of this book, we've established that men have a biological need for competition because of testosterone; this hormone increases risk-taking behaviour, aggression and similar traits that are associated with those of authority. Women are more commonly in the minority in positions of power, as they lack the inherent drive for dominance, whilst possessing other biological predispositions, such as reproductive pressures.

Natural selection has honed the desire for power and authority in men because those males who had it were better off evolutionarily. The reason evolution has benefited those who succeed at becoming powerful is because it all but guarantees access to the rarer and more sought-after resources, and because you can more easily break social conventions to your benefit. The difference between being crazy and eccentric is a matter of money and power at one's disposition. For example, if you date a woman forty years your junior, you might be seen as a creep and vilified, if you're just a random guy; but if you add a magazine empire to the mix, then you're Hugh Hefner and that's just what you're supposed to do.

In the civilized world, these advantages of power go from being marginally beneficial, in the largely egalitarian prehistoric age, to completely outclassing their less fortunate peers by orders of magnitude once agriculture is established. We have, for example, argued in PI-Ch9 that there has historically been a gender gap in reproduction, which became more pronounced with the advent of private property and systemic forms of power. Women easily managed to reproduce, whilst men often failed - the worst being during portions of the Neolithic Revolution when for every 17 women that reproduced, only one man did. It's been argued that this stark contrast happened with agricultural societies, as no matter how charismatic or well-endowed Chad McCaveman is, he's still ruled by Dunbar's number and the lack of an army backing his flagrant abuses on egalitarianism. In other words, location and timing are extremely important - there's no point in being more charismatic and appealing than all others when your audience consists of at most 150 or so people, where only a handful of those would be sexually active and available females.

Hence agriculture, private property and civilization gave rise to stark hierarchical differences, like nowhere else in history, as benefits marginally add to the elites by each additional person in a group - the bigger the pool of peasants, the larger the potential tax revenues, assuming all other things are equal. Just to put this into context, there's been circumstances throughout history where kings have such lavish lifestyles that when they visit an area that is unused to their living standards, they cause long-standing economic disruptions by their very presence - like a super dense economic black hole ruining the natural clockwork of the cosmos.

The life story of Musa Keita I, sultan of the rich Mali Empire in northwest Africa at the start of the fourteenth century, showcases such devastating inequality. According to Islamic tradition, every devout adherent of the faith who can afford it must go to Mecca at least once in their lifetime. This is such an important pilgrimage for Muslims that one earns the title of "Hajji" on completion of this journey. As such, in 1324, Musa went on a hajj (pilgrimage) to Mecca. Accompanying him, he brought a vast caravan of 60,000 men and 12,000 slaves, along with countless riches. He shared his wealth freely, following another pillar of Islam - which is to be charitable to the unfortunate. Nevertheless, he gave so freely that gold suddenly plummeted in value, as everyone along his route was quite swamped with it. On coming back, and seeing the misery he had caused, he tried to rectify it by borrowing money at exorbitant interest rates, thus functioning as a quasi-central banker by eliminating liquidity and making gold scarce - this is the one and only time in human history where a single man truly determined the price of gold in the Mediterranean [43].

It could well be argued that all governments are kleptocracies, stealing from the taxes that they took from others and doing with it what they wish. This is not to say that they were, or even are, all evil. Assigning morality to such things is difficult, all the more so because you will rarely find people who genuinely view themselves as a scourge on society [44].

To modern audiences, it seems bizarre that the rulers of a society should even consider not living in a palace, a mansion, or a similarly ostentatious building as we inherently accept that authority carries with it privileges of luxury. Steven D. Levitt and Sudhir Alladi Venkatesh, of Freakonomics fame, once had the opportunity of shadowing a crack cocaine drug-dealing gang in the 1990's [45]. What they found, contrary to expectations, is that the vast majority of participants in the drug trade made below minimum wage. The real profits, regardless of whether times were good or bad, were reserved for the elite. As one of them elegantly put it: "You got all these niggers below you who want your job, you dig? If you start taking losses, they see you [as] weak and shit" [46]. Or put differently, if a leader were to downgrade their lifestyle and live like the common folk, they might be seen as a pushover or unsuccessful, thereby losing authority.

It may be that once the Pandora's Box is opened by an overly greedy leader, it becomes all but impossible to go back to egalitarianism, as power would necessarily and inherently draw a distinction between the haves and have nots. As a consequence, I'm inclined to agree with Jared Diamond, wherein he suggests that a government is only a kleptocracy if it is not doing things that the populace wants and finds fair. If a populace is happy with a ruling class, even if they happen to live in unparalleled luxury, then that is their privilege for their service to the community [47].

Yet, perhaps we have unwittingly unearthed a less talked about extension of power. If one manages to climb to the top of the hierarchy, one becomes the exception that provides the justification - the *raison d'être* - for the society. They are the one who writes the rules, and could easily simply write themselves out of the obligation of having to follow them. Typically, this will be done in the name of the common good, and thus they will live in the "state of exception," where laws only vaguely apply to the leader [48]. In fact, the extent of power will be directly correlated with how brazenly the ruler(s) can flaunt the rules.

Think of it this way, if you had to attend an important formal business meeting and showed up hungover whilst slovenly dressed with a five-o'clock shadow and actually got away with it, then that is proof that you're a powerful individual. The other businessmen would only tolerate such a flagrant sign of disrespect to the pre-established rules if your value to the organisation far exceeds theirs.

This is why political figures, celebrities and wealthy people rarely end up in serious legal problems, that is unless their transgressions are truly heinous to the society, or another more powerful person conspires against them. Power is a maelstrom, it's an unconscious mechanism that is constantly fluctuating. Trying to grab onto power is akin to trying to grab a stream of water, as it's a zero-sum game[32], where all players are desperately trying to increase their share.

In this game of chess, you will naturally have pawns, which will inadvertently be used in an attempt to expand your influence. These pawns will often be put in situations that are contrary to their wellbeing and will be your first line of defence. Often, you won't even have to cajole them into doing so, as they'll decide on their own to come to your aid. Whether you call them "self-appointed

32 A zero-sum game is a situation wherein each player's gain (or loss) of well being is precisely balanced by the losses (or gains) of the other player. If the total gains of the participants were to be summed up and the total losses were deducted, they will equal zero. It's akin to a cake, the bigger someone's slice, the less there is for others.

guardians of the grand narrative" or "useful fools," as the communists called liberals for doing their bidding without noticing [49]; some people are so tied to an ideology that they will help simply because you have power and influence, and will do so without even an expectation of a reward beyond being a driving force for those ideals. In an economic setting, useful fools are the die-hard fanatics who are bullish on an asset, even despite evidence to the contrary. Thus, even when the price has bottomed out, they will continue buying it, hence the "dead cat bounce" where an asset price momentarily bounces after having reached rock bottom.

Those are merely the ones who unwittingly do your bidding, as for people under your direct control, you can make them do anything if they truly believe in your authority. In the earlier chapter on war (PIII-Ch3), we briefly discussed the findings of the Milgram experiment, wherein people voluntarily murdered other participants at the behest of a person in a lab coat. This is one of the main keys in understanding the pageantry associated with power.

I always used to wonder why it is that people in power have always seemed to be in a secret contest to look as ridiculous as humanly possible. Power seems not to be a means, but to be an end to wear silly hats with impunity. Having said this, theatricality and deception are powerful agents. Wearing ridiculous clothing achieves exactly what the Milgram experiment showed: the outrageous clothing creates a disassociation from the normal. The people trusted the scientist in the experiment because he was wearing a lab coat, and we've been brought up to believe that scientists and doctors, who often wear lab coats, know what's best for us. As such, rather than relying on our own judgement, we tend to defer to the person who seems to be in charge and also seems to know what they're doing, letting them have to carry the burden of our decisions.

In the words of Mark Twain: "Clothes make the man. Naked people have little or no influence on society."[33] Furthermore, how we dress not only

---

33 I'd somewhat disagree with him though, the hope of having naked people in my bedroom tends to be very influential in my day to day life.

influences how we're perceived, but how we think. Wearing a lab coat, which has been associated with the uniform of a learned man, increases your ability to carry out tasks relying on attention [50]. Is it such a stretch to think that wearing a crown or holding a sceptre will make you act in a more regal manner?

"Enclothed cognition" and the roles that our environment hoists upon us may well explain how we behave in a society. We intrinsically understand the roles provided by us, and we play them to the terrifying hilt. A perfect case study of this is the Stanford prison experiment, wherein participants were put into a pseudo jail, and were arbitrarily separated as prisoners and jailers. They were told to act the part as well. Short few days later, the experiment had to be called off because riots were being staged and violence had erupted due to the ill treatment of prisoners. The jailers then fought back against the rebellion with torture and cruelty, despite knowing that none of the prisoners had actually done anything to deserve it. (Seems that when Stanford psychologists aren't handing children marshmallows to children, they're promoting inhuman treatment of undergraduates.) This undeserved punishment due to arbitrary roles is a key in this though. All participants knew that they had been randomly put in these roles, yet the circumstances were so convincing that everyone played their role with frightening accuracy [51]. No man's an island, as we behave based on contextual data, by seeing how much social leeway we are allowed - if we're given the whole rope, we'll hang ourselves with it.

In the hierarchical totem pole, we more or less know where we stand - we know who are our social betters and who are our social lessers. If you disbelieve me, let us do a simple thought experiment. Take a group of ten people, assign them with a number on a card, and paste it on their foreheads without them knowing where they stand in the scale. Now, tell the group to each find a partner with the highest numerical value possible. Naturally, the person with the highest value will be swarmed by everyone.

The person with a 10 will immediately realise that they have a very high number, if not the highest one, so they will only settle with a similarly high numerical value. Now, assuming that they don't immediately settle for the first viable option available to them, they would more or less find a partner very close to themselves in the sequence. Each person that followed successively would follow suit, with the lower end of the numerical hierarchy, growing increasingly desperate and eventually settling for the lower tier [52].

Reality is not as clear cut as this model would imply, people can convince others that they possess a higher value than they really have, as there is an asymmetry of information between the agents within the system. Or as comedian Louis CK put it in one of his stand-up shows:

> *"There are millions of people out there who we've all unanimously decided they are lightspeed ugly and nobody kisses them on the lips even! Nobody touches their genitals in their entire lives, they just wash them and then they die. That's what happens. [...] That's the way everyone's mean - nobody fucks down. People fuck up or across [...] some women fuck down because a guy talked them into thinking it was up though"*

Nevertheless, the vast majority of people will eventually signal their real respective values over time, whilst screening for comparable partners. *Assortative mating*, as this phenomenon is called, is a very real and well-established feature of human behaviour - we like hanging out with people who can actually understand our trials and tribulations.

Here's where it gets interesting though, imagine that you had done the experiment with a million people, instead of ten. After pairing off, the experiment would continue and they'd produce children with a random value, as children are not identical to their parents. That said, if the people in the higher rungs of our quasi-society had any power, they would decidedly seek to protect the rights of their children to remain in the elite subgroup - they would more or less accidentally institute nepotistic practices, but would have to disguise them, so as to not anger the rest. At its core, this is the basis of aristocracies and similarly hereditary privileges, whose sexual and social mechanisms we will be discussing in the next two chapters.

7 - The Keys to Power: Why Politics is a Corrupting Influence

"Any man who must say, 'I am the *king*' is no true king."
- *Tywin Lannister, Game of Thrones*

The first and foremost priority of a new ruler is to survive and solidify their own hold on power. Anything else is of secondary concern when there's the Sword of Damocles dangling overhead. Far from this line of thinking being paranoid, all good rulers must be acutely aware that almost every single one of their courtiers would gladly stab them in the back, if their own self interests did not align with their monarch's.

Look no further than Roman Emperor Commodus' murder, where he'd been terrorising the populace with impunity for years until his mistress found a list of people he wanted murdered and, much to her horror, discovered her own name was on it. Thus, alongside with some of the other people on the list, she hatched a plan to assassinate him. The first attempt failed, but eventually a wrestler called Narcissus strangled Commodus whilst he was taking a bath [53]. The fun bit of the tale is that he had been roleplaying as a gladiator for years by fixing matches, wounding combatants before the fight even began and so on, so being wrestled to death whilst butt naked and vulnerable brings its own little ironic twist.

In either case, the moral of the story is that, as a dictator, it is imperative to keep your court in good standing, and the easiest way to do so is by bribing them with large portions of the nation's treasury. The populace be damned if you have the support of elites, access to superior armies, and their standing in society depends on your continued well-being. After all, it's quite rare for a revolution or coup to succeed without the support of the elites. Even a supposed proletariat uprising, as happened with the creation of the Soviet Union, required extensive German meddling and resources to succeed [54].

Power is a fickle mistress that comes in many forms, but rarely does it come in the form of absolute obedience. Hence, the main threat to one's power are other elites, who possess the necessary connections and funds to present a threat. This is a problem when one realises that the elites are necessary to keep the system running. Any society that goes beyond Dunbar's number requires a fixed hierarchy, with a clear delegation of duties, as it's simply unmanageable otherwise. Or they're extremely prone to Black Swans when they're overly centralized and dependent on the whims of a single individual.

Think of how Spanish Conquistador Hernán Cortés was essentially able to take over the Aztec empire overnight by taking the emperor Moctezuma II as his sole hostage [55][34]. In a similar situation, when the Roman Emperor Valerian was abducted by the Sassanids (the last kingdom of the Persian Empire), the Romans vowed revenge but hardly caved in to their enemy's demands, despite their emperor supposedly being ridiculed and used as a footstool; all in all, business went on as usual with only some minor hiccups [56].

A robust society needs tax ministers, governors, generals, spiritual leaders, capital managers, etc., and they all require a certain degree of autonomy to be able to work effectively. In other words, an effective leader gives the people in his court power and the discretion to use it. Of course, this is a double-edged sword as, with more freedom and power, men often have delusions of grandeur. The crisis of the third century, also known as Military Anarchy or the Roman

34 It has to be said though that the Spaniards overplayed their cards, committed flagrant abuses and were eventually ousted with such force that they were almost obliterated. Yet, a few years later the Aztec Empire was utterly destroyed by the Spanish counterattack, which depended on extensive native help.

Imperial Crisis (CE 235–284), is a perfect case study of this issue[35]. Whenever the emperor was far away, dealing with some other insurrection or dilemma, and a general won a fight, both the populace and the army often hailed him as the new Caesar, which quickly led to civil war with the original emperor. By giving enough power to his subjects for them to deal effectively with foreign threats, they often became threats themselves. It's a miracle that the Roman Empire survived at all, and it was only really thanks to the superhuman efforts of some emperors that it did, as there was a period where it was cut in thirds [57]. The reason behind it was that by that point the empire was far too large and hence nobody ever seemed to be on the emperor's list of priorities, unless he happened to be there in person.

It thus stands to reason that the best way to keep the peace is to align both your own and your elite's motivations. Only an insane person would murder their meal ticket. This is why elites are willing to accept silly things as hereditary power transfers. For instance, the son of a great conqueror and warlord is unlikely to be as extraordinary as his father, yet those in the ruler's court accept that his son is a worthy heir because they've benefited from the status quo.

Rocking the boat by agitating that another worthier successor follows the conqueror is likely to lead to violent volatility - possibly even civil war, as happened when Alexander the Great died heirless and left his empire "to the strongest." [58] When your own position is comfortable and likely to remain so in the foreseeable future, it makes little sense to risk the potential slight increase in status when your head can end on the chopping block if you don't succeed.

Accepting the snotty brat, whose only real merit may just have been being the lucky sperm, then makes perfect sense. This holds true even if the last deserving and competent heir was several generations of lucky sperms ago. As

35 If you haven't already heard it, and you're even remotely interested in the Romans, I highly recommend Mike Duncan's podcast "The History of Rome" for a thorough study of all the human drama.

such, because elites benefit from the existing status quo (by simple virtue that they're already elites and most other people are not) they have a vested interest in metastasizing and stopping cultural changes that don't directly benefit them.

Whosoever dares defy these entrenched interests risks death or fall from grace. A sizeable percentage of a nation's income is spent on keeping these elites happy. When a leader decides to alter this balance and divert resources to the common people to help build infrastructure, or help them by easing their financial burdens, he is kicking a hornet's nest.

A regime change becomes palatable to a member of the elite once it's clear that their position in the social totem pole is not fixed and they stand to lose power and influence through their inaction. At that point, their best interests are in direct opposition with the person in power, and they become dangerous. Gather enough of these people together, and a coup is all but guaranteed.

Aspiring leaders will often promise the world, in essence writing blank cheques to whosoever will pledge their support to them. But when the new regime happens to make it to the top, and people want to cash their promised rewards in, he realises that his social capital is nowhere near enough to make good on his promises without stepping on powerful people's toes. Political honesty is like oxygen, the higher you climb, the rarer it is.

Politicians thus lie as a matter of course, even if at one point they actually meant what they said. The farther away that the populace is from the means of wealth creation, the worse off they will be. If, for example, a country depends on natural resources and not the labour of their populace for their wealth, then the wellbeing of the people at large is irrelevant. Any resources diverted to the commoners is a coin not in the purse strings of the army of the pre-established elites; do that often enough and they'll start sharpening their knives to safeguard their position, regardless of whether you have good intentions.

This is the nature of the "resource curse," where the richer a country is in natural wealth, like oil, diamonds and precious metals, the less likely the elites will ever think the wellbeing of the common person is worth considering. After all, their lives are already laced in gold, their armies are well-equipped and if the plebeians dare complain then their lives are forfeit. They thus have no incentive to build infrastructure such as hospitals and schools that would help the masses. Consequently, an abundance of resources that aren't directly tied to the production capacity and wellbeing of a people promote autocratic and totalitarian states.

When the main source of your wealth is, say, oil, (or even more controversially foreign aid from well meaning but naive donors) why bother educating the masses or giving them political freedom? Whereas if your society is dependent on creativity and innovation, then helping your people improve their lot in life is the wiser choice. Because of this, tyrants are far more likely to surface in areas with an economy dependent on natural resources, where poor management can be offset with the inherent qualities of the region.

The disadvantage of such an undiversified operation is that if the world suddenly decides that your resources aren't worth as much, because a better substitute has been found, your whole regime might collapse like a house of cards. When was the last time your life depended on salt, spices, guano or whale blubber, for example? Yet, in their heyday, wars were fought over them, as they were such a lucrative staple that it was worth sacrificing people's lives to obtain or to keep them.

Whereas, if the wealth of the country depends on industry and human capital, the situation is reversed. The elites actively benefit from keeping their populace content with social programs. Japan was a pioneer when it came to inventing welfare programmes in the 1930s - like providing widely-accessible healthcare - not because of the goodness of their hearts, but because they needed healthy and able-bodied young soldiers and workers [59]. In other words, despite being a military society hell-bent on violent expansion they had to take care of their populace. After all, Japan is not an island known for its natural resources and hence its success or failure primarily depends on its people and organization. Which is why several decades before, the Emperor of Japan decided to embrace rapid industrialization in what is now known as the "Meiji restoration," as isolationism and atavism had miserably failed in the centuries beforehand [60].

As a general rule of thumb, governments (as institutions and unconscious mechanisms) will do the least they can get away with, whilst still maintaining the reins of power. This is even assuming that some people in power have your best interests at heart, which is in sincere doubt more often than not. Hence, depending on the goodwill of the government is often dangerous, if not suicidal.

The Dutch Republic prevailed over the Habsburg Empire because having the world's first modern stock market was financially preferable to having the world's biggest silver mine [61]. With freedom, people could focus on their strengths, instead of being forced to mine for silver, and thus they were better off on average. This benefited everyone, elites included, and allowed for a fairer and more dynamic society by aligning the interests of both the wealth creators and the elite.

At the risk of quoting a jingoistic warmonger and incompetent politician, I'm inclined to agree with Former British Prime Minister Winston Churchill when he said: "Democracy is the worst form of government, except for all the others." Democracy, for all its faults, somewhat aligns the wishes of the common man with those of the elite - otherwise they get voted out.

Lucky sperm dependent government styles have the distinct disadvantage that the quality of their leaders massively varies from generation to generation. Marcus Aurelius, one of the so called "five good emperors" and of the most important moral philosophers of all time, gave birth to Commodus who transformed Rome "from a kingdom of gold to one of iron and rust" with his vices and excesses [62].

If monarchies or dictatorships were to somehow be able to consistently guarantee men of the calibre of Augustus or Napoleon, without civil war, I'd be squarely for them. As it stands though, stable mediocrity with political and financial freedoms seems preferable to playing Russian Roulette with society every twenty-odd years.

8 - Diamonds are a Girl's Best Friend: Marriage, Love, Monogamy and Prostitution

"I didn't find out what happiness means until I got married- and then it was too late."

- Anonymous

Despite starting to feel like the jerk who tells children that Santa Claus doesn't exist, you can be at peace, for I shall not be saying today that love doesn't exist. Quite the contrary, in fact, love is a very strong emotion and I imagine that it may well be one of the principal motivational sources for people. The history of humanity would surely be much poorer without the love-struck fool, who will write heart-warming literature, play wonderful music, paint awe-inspiring pictures and produce monumental feats of creativity and character all in the hopes of wooing a woman.

Yet "love" is a fascinatingly convoluted word. The ancient Greeks had no less than four words to describe the feelings smooshed together in this one Anglo-concept[36]. Firstly, there was "*Storge*," which was related to the natural sense of empathy and caring one feels for the family and close friends. Secondly, there

36 Seven in fact if you want to split hairs, though I prefer not to be as pedantic. As my editor put it: "There is also ludus, pragma and philautia." But usually it's kept at four, such as by CS Lewis, and I'll keep it as such. Take this as an example on how an author can outright omit certain bits of information if it doesn't suit their narrative.

was "*Philia,*" which was meant as the feeling of affectionate regard between equals, fraternal love which was beyond everything else, dispassionate, communal and friendly. Thirdly, there was "*Eros*," which was the intimate love that makes you appreciate beauty and seek truth and a sense of being in it, though it was primarily erotic. Fourthly, there was "*Agápe*," which was the spiritual and communal version of love, such as the love originating from God for his creation - this is seen as the highest form of love as it is primarily selfless and generous [63].

If you were to tell an ancient Greek that you were marrying for love, they'd fire back with a question: "Which one?" Our modern western interpretation would immediately jump to Eros, the intimate love, but then people have often stayed in horrible marriages "for the children," thus lust seems often not to be the prime motivator, despite initial evidence. Currently, modern society seems deeply confused as to the purpose of marriage. Nowadays, a wedding is a deeply improbable promise made between two people in front of a crowd to try to make it stick, at least a bit longer than it otherwise would have. In fact, there's evidence to support that the more ostentatious the wedding, the more fraught the relationship is likely to be [64].

We like to make grand claims about having a love that lasts forever, and we even give expensive diamonds as signs of such undying affection. If we were to put this into game theory terms, these are difficult to fake signals of one's commitment - if a man were to follow the commonly-accepted standard of three-months' salary to estimate the price of a ring, this is indeed a serious sign of commitment. Incidentally, these types of difficult to fake signs of commitment can also be found in the indoctrination of terrorists, when they are called upon to prove one's commitment to the cause [65]. This partly works because of the heuristic judgements we discussed earlier (PI-Ch6), or more succinctly because of the sunk cost fallacy. If we invest heavily in something, we will value it far more and will be unwilling to put it aside even if it has severe downsides, this is regardless of whether the investment is economical as with a stock, or emotional, as with a marriage or a terrorist suicide pledge.

This indoctrination, coupled with our natural compunction to demonstrate the honesty of our desires and wanting to remain consistent in regards to people's perceptions of ourselves, is why we took to buying expensive diamonds to show our commitment. This is despite the fact that the tradition was largely manufactured less than a hundred years ago by the De Beers diamond company's marketing department so as to artificially inflate the price of diamonds [66]. In PII-Ch3 we discussed how myths are made to promote certain behaviours, and this is simply a modern example thereof, about how a story can make us behave in strange ways. This is especially concerning when we consider the fact that diamonds are not rare, they're common enough for them to be stockpiled in fear of them being capable of collapsing their perceived value by flooding the market. Furthermore, the resale value of a diamond, unless you have the crown jewels or other legendary items, is negligible compared to their purchase price.

Yet, in our eagerness in promising commitment, we forgot to ask whether we should even bother nowadays. Marriage has historically been little more than an economic contract, much like the loan contracts of ancient Mesopotamia. Wedlock is simply an easy way to merge two powerful familial units, and to align their incentives with each other. Love, in the intimate and sexual sense, was hardly ever part of the picture.

In fact, it was seen as downright odd. There are even records of a Roman senator falling into ignominy for embracing his wife in front of his daughter in broad daylight. Even a minor show of affection was suspect and possibly even damnable, as your spouse was primarily there for political purposes [67]. If you wanted love, you went with courtesans, slaves or mistresses, and people tend to have the good sense of keeping those indiscretions to themselves. It's not without reason that female slaves in ancient Rome were suspiciously freed whilst young, fertile (and likely pregnant) at much higher rates than male slaves achieved their liberty. It also bears saying that while virtually none of the female slaves had jobs around the house, female slaves commanded high prices if sold in youth [68].

As I hinted at before, when I first started talking about sex, humans are not biologically predisposed to monogamy, but neither are they prone to wanton sex either. Biology has a promiscuity spectrum ranging from the dull and safe pair bonding of the penguin, to the rapacious tournament competitions of gorillas. Human beings are somewhere in between the pair bonding and tournament species spectrum. Collectively preferring variety, whilst not abandoning the comfort of the familiar.

We're all suckers for a good love story, but rarely ask what happens after the "happy ending." Truth be told, if biology is any determinant, the brain will return to its pre-infatuation levels within a year or two [69]. This does not mean that affection ceases to exist, just that it commonly isn't a passionate feeling anymore.

In the meantime, the male brain is primed for novelty and will seek new partners which excite his libido. This is a phenomenon known as "the Coolidge Effect," wherein a male mammal's sexual desire is reinvigorated solely when presented with a new partner, this happens to a good proportion of mammals, including rats and even humans [70]. Women, on the other hand, are typically far more stable in their romantic affairs, theirs is often a problem of quality, not of quantity. Although it must be said that men and women have similar rates of cheating in relationships, women have far more opportunity to do so, yet do not [71].

If we were to try to test for the inherent behaviour of each sex, we should look no further than the natural experiments provided to us by homosexual communities, given that they exercise their sexuality without direct influence from the opposite sex. The results of looking at the data are startling.

In gay communities[37], wherein for obvious reasons there is no female counterbalance to men's sexual appetites, it's not uncommon to have upwards of a hundred partners over a lifetime [72]. Gay communities have a chronic lack of faithfulness. Not so in lesbian communities, wherein so little sex happens that psychologists have legitimately coined a term for it - "lesbian bed death" [73]. The average lesbian struggles to get ten female sexual partners over the course of a lifetime [74]. On the other hand, we have the statistical average lifetime sexual

---

37 This is assuming an environment where they are not persecuted, and they have relative ease in finding others with their sexual inclinations.

partners for heterosexual couples, which bounces around depending on study but is usually above ten, but below twenty. To further add complications, men tend to overestimate the amount, whilst women tend to underestimate [75].

The data does seem to paint a very clear picture in this case, women are far more selective than men regarding whom they sleep with. This does not happen due to the common assertions that some people like to throw around, like the fact that women are "frigid" or don't enjoy sex. In fact, I'll even side with Greek mythology on this one, and agree with what Tiresias said when asked by Zeus what gender enjoys sex more, as he had experienced being both at different points in life: "A man enjoys only a tenth of what a woman feels" [76].

Nevertheless, the fact remains that the data suggests that men have to seduce women into the idea of having sex. From a biological point of view, this makes perfect sense, a man's potential investment in having offspring can literally end within a few seconds. A woman's, on the other hand, is a commitment of several years. Hence, there is an imbalance between the dangers and potential benefits of sex.

The risk of a potential pregnancy must be balanced out by the benefits one receives as a consequence of copulating. Because of this, it shouldn't really be a surprise when people jokingly say that prostitution is one of the oldest professions in the book. In Mexico, we have an expression "entre broma y broma, la verdad se asoma" - "between joke and joke, truth shows its face." Evidence does suggest that prostitution has existed for longer than humans have been around.

Chimpanzees are known to passively exchange food for sex within a community. This is not done directly, but is partially based on accrued social capital - *if you've put into the community, you get to put it in* [77]. Other primates are far crasser in their dealings. There was a rather amusing study once wherein the innate economic behaviour of capuchin monkeys was researched. To do this, they were given silver discs which could be exchanged for various treats. However, upon understanding what the coins meant, one enterprising capuchin monkey exchanged the silver discs for sex with a female in the enclosure. Upon noticing the behaviour, the killjoy researcher, took steps to avoid the possibility of prostitution within the confines of the study [78].

In human beings, the lines are particularly blurry. Is paying for drinks, for example, not a mild variant of prostitution and a weak signal to show that you can provide for a woman if she were to end up with you? Or is this just my cynicism? Historically speaking, the most powerful people in a society tend to be old men and young women.

Young, beautiful women have historically tended to have very high chances of social mobility, as there's always the chance that they will catch the eye of an elite. Young, charismatic men, far less so [79]. Partially, this is why gender ratios are skewed according to one's social class: Couples in higher social positions tend to produce more males, whilst couples in lower strata produce more females. If you're rich and powerful you have a slightly higher, though statistically significant, chance of having a male (billionaires have a 65% chance of siring a son when having kids, for example). The opposite holds true if you're poor [80]. It's even been hypothesised that parents are able to unconsciously affect the likelihood of the gender of their children [81]. The idea being that if you're at the top of the social totem pole, your children are likely to have status as well, ergo they'll likely also have the means of impressing women. But if they were male and born into a low social position, the deck would be severely stacked against them and consequently they wouldn't really be good marriage prospects.

For most of human history, marriage was about resources. This is why the institution of marriage as we know it, only really began at about the same time as private property. It also took a very particular and specific form, much like we know it nowadays [82]. True, there was polygamy in some societies, but by and large it was many females, and a male - in the few cases where it wasn't so, the husbands would mostly be related [83]. Also, regardless of where you go, laws have usually been incredibly male biased, they used to hand a slap on the wrist to an unfaithful man, but used to penalise severely an unfaithful woman, sometimes even with death.

This would imply that one of the primary points regarding the role of marriage is ensuring legitimacy of the produced offspring. A woman can know with absolute certainty that they're the biological parent, a man less so. It's why in polygamous societies, a king's harems were guarded by eunuchs and hidden away from prying eyes. Nevertheless, there was usually one primary matriarch, whose offspring were considered more legitimate than the rest.

The reason for the extreme oversight regarding legitimate offspring is simple: if you did not expressly give instructions about the assumed hierarchy of your offspring, you risk civil war every interregnum. Sometimes, even this wasn't enough, which is why it wasn't uncommon for Ottoman sultans to murder all their sons but one, when they were about to die. If the father failed to do this, it wasn't unusual for the legitimate son to finish this job and imprison his brothers [84].

Polygynous societies, where a ruler could potentially have hundreds of offspring, seem inherently unbalanced [85]. Furthermore, if the practice of polygyny isn't solely for the person at the top of the social pyramid, it's also likely to create social problems. Can you imagine how frustrated a peasant is likely to get when the local aristocrat is on his seventh marriage, and they haven't even found a single person to marry? The more unequal we perceive a situation to be, the more likely we are to use force to rectify matters [86]. This happens in circumstances even as inconsequential as flying first class vs. cattle class; where if the VIP area is visible from the back, there's a higher likelihood of violence erupting on the plane [87]. Airlines avoid this by keeping the plebs at bay with a curtain so hopefully they forget about the nice treatment the patricians at the front have.

Now, with that in mind, picture the frustration of someone who sees the asymmetry in access to women and will never be able to even dream about changing their circumstances, as social mobility is practically non-existent in such cultures. These groups of men, who through no fault of their own, have no access to women but the ones discarded by the elite (if they happen to be the lucky ones), will grow envious and frustrated. This frustration will not be stoically taken in stride, but is a societal timebomb. As we discussed in PI-Ch9, men die disproportionately between puberty and their mid-twenties, these deaths often happen due to sexual competition, given that men engage in risk taking to improve their social standing. The most terrifying part is that this frustration is wieldable for political gain!

During WWI, for instance, retired Vice Admiral Charles Penrose-Fitzgerald came up with a brilliant marketing strategy to make young men willingly jump into the meat grinder as "there is a danger awaiting them far more terrible than anything they can meet in battle." The plan was quite devilish as it used sexual competition to shame men into enlisting. Groups of attractive women were tasked with walking around and pinning white feathers on men who looked fit to fight, yet weren't wearing a uniform, whilst making as big of a ruckus as they could manage. Through this drama everyone would know that this young man had been branded as a coward of the highest order, and by a beautiful female no less! Incredible to think but that stupid stunt and white feather was likely responsible for killing thousands of men [88].

It doesn't take a genius to put two and two together: if someone were to harness this pent-up aggression by creating a meme that functioned as a supernormal stimulus, they could quickly become a danger to the fabric of society itself.

A recent example of a successful harnessing of these violent forces is the creation of ISIS, all it takes is the promise of forty virgins in the afterlife, and some rousing oratory, to convince young men to do your terrifying will [89]. To hell if the region tears itself asunder, what matters to the person leading them and promising them that they're doing Allah's work, is that one day they get to be king of the ashes. As such, most of modern civilization might have defaulted to a monogamous structure of marriage because of polygamy's inherent instability. The societies that did not adopt said monogamous structure, tore themselves down over time. Instead of a figurative ball and chain, monogamy may well be one of the most important behaviours in human beings to create long lasting stability[38].

38 Of course, people cheat, both men and women. Nevertheless, transferring to a monogamous system from a polygamous system puts the blame of being single to the individual, rather than the social level. Hence the frustration is directed inwards, rather than outwards.

PART IV: THE HIDDEN CLOCKWORK: AN ANALYSIS OF UNCONSCIOUS MECHANISMS

Throughout the course of this book, thousands, if not millions, of years pass, whilst we have only read a sentence or a paragraph regarding historical eras and events. Because of this singular luxury, we have been able to see the unique interplay within the factors that affect us; how one event far off in the future is foreshadowed at the beginning of the play. It's akin to a domino effect wherein no object is acted upon without just cause.

Yet, in retelling the tale I have often invoked the phrase "unconscious mechanisms" as an explanation of the events, much like a priest would've proclaimed "God wills it!" when asked to explain a natural phenomenon. This sort of answer may temporarily placate people, but will not satiate the truth-seeker in the long run. Saying that an "unconscious mechanism" did something is no more helpful than saying that Zeus, Thor, Allah or Yahweh did it.

Unconscious mechanisms are systems that create order and efficiency, despite the fact that there is no design committee deciding on the patterns it ought to take. Ultimately, they are amoral, uncaring, ruthless in pursuing their purpose and exist only because the universe has immutable laws that must be followed. If there is a God up in the cosmos, it's not a loving and caring one who is particularly interested about the wellbeing of individuals; instead, it is one who very much seems to care about order and the efficiency of systems. Even within the confines of religion, "free will" has limitations. We cannot, for example, bend the laws of time and space or shrink to the size of ants. Quite the contrary, much like when Henry Ford said "You can have any colour of car you want, as long as it's black," our cosmic dictator might've well said, "You can do anything you want, as long as it follows the rules of nature." Within those rigid bounds, we're free to do as we please, yet for every action there's an equal and opposite reaction. If we try to build the tower of Babel, which shall reach the heavens, we should not be surprised that what goes up, must eventually come down.

The rules of nature govern everything in our lives, even that which seems arbitrary. For example, from the rules of physics we get planets, which formed when matter started attracting itself through gravity. Given that a mass particle's gravitational attraction is equal in all directions, as shown in Newton's formulas, the most logical result is that they will eventually coalesce into a sphere. The reason is that a sphere is the geometric shape with the minimum surface area to volume ratio, and is thus the most efficient possible shape to densely pack things together, given the natural limitations of our universe. This is why planets are round, and not square or any other shape. If you were to build a planet with a different shape, and it was large enough, the unconscious mechanism within its gravitational force would collapse it back into a spheroid object.

An unconscious mechanism is the process by which a system goes to its point of equilibrium, where all the forces acting upon it are in balance. Furthermore, every unconscious mechanism will work in tandem or attempt to fight back with every other mechanism that is affecting the point of equilibrium. Think of the gears in a clock, where one gear has to be set in motion via the natural rules of the universe for all other gears to work. Or, if you're more interested in the macroscopic end of the spectrum, think of the immutable rules of nature that drove particles to coalesce into the astronomical bodies, and the chemical reactions that arose in those astronomical bodies that could perpetuate themselves. These chemical reactions could only take so many forms given their limitations, and thus they developed behavioural patterns best suited for their environment and purpose, these behavioural patterns eventually gave rise to memes that were subject to similar selective pressures, and so on.

This is why I do not consider it folly to discuss evolution, religion, war, love and sex in an investing book - in fact, I consider them essential. These are all unconscious mechanisms that affect each other. One of the cardinal sins of modernity is neatly packaging subjects into different boxes; when out in the wild, outside of the classroom, they are deeply connected. Understanding the relation of these patterns is what makes you truly capable of comprehending reality and by extension become a better investor. This is why in this chapter I shall be explaining the characteristics of the unconscious mechanism. Perhaps, at the very least, being aware of them might make one pause before coming up with fanciful-sounding theories based solely on utility maximisation, interest rates and supply and demand curves.

1 - The Weatherman's Lament

"It's tough to make predictions, especially about the future"
- *Yogi Berra*

In 1720, after having invested in the rise of the *South Sea Company*, Sir Isaac Newton made a hefty profit when he exited the market. Yet the syren's call of profits proved irresistible and he decided to reinvest his net worth in this rising star. Then, the unthinkable happened - the stock collapsed, and wiped out a good portion of Newton's wealth along with it. Despondent, and as a tragic epitaph to the whole affair, he said: "I can calculate the motion of the heavenly bodies, but not the madness of people" [1].

Newton, on paper at least, was a far cry from your irrational investor. He was a mathematical genius, a savant who invented calculus before turning twenty-five. If there was anyone in the history of humankind who should've been able to make sense of the Gordian Knot of economic modelling, it would've been him, especially with such a vast economic incentive, yet he failed miserably. Avarice was his downfall.

Be that as it may, it is disingenuous to single out Newton in this matter. He was far from the only person to fail to do so. Economic historian Peter Temin makes the case that bubbles can happen even if the market were to be populated by rational people, and he went on to say that the South Seas Bubble was no exception [2]. As long as profits are made, people will find explanations and rationalisations for their good fortune.

Furthermore, it may even be the case that failures in our decision-making processes happen because we overestimate just how rational and intelligent we are, alongside with just how much access to information we actually have. "Know thyself" is oddly difficult advice to follow. Possibly, it is because of people like Newton, and their astonishing success in the non-financial world that blinds us as to the depths of our ignorance. After all, with a few simple maxims and general equations he managed to marry something seemingly so disparate as an apple falling on someone's head and the movement of entire galaxies.

It seems reasonable to think that if something so complex as the movement of the cosmos is explainable through the beauty of simple mathematics that markets and similar unconscious mechanisms would be a piece of cake in comparison. Reductionist theories, wherein you simplify your models by isolating all variables from each other and grow obsessive about getting ever more precise measurement systems, work well up to a certain point and in some circumstances.

Yet, much like when you listen to a populist politician, the broad strokes of what they have to say usually have a valid point. Nevertheless, their stirring rhetoric will usually abscond nuance in favour of mass appeal; and in painting reality in such a broad brush it eventually loses all texture and all relation to reality. For example, economists love to mention that people want to maximise their utility, thus it stands to reason that gaining more access to resources has no detriment whatsoever[39]. This assumption is sensible, up to a certain point, but it breaks down past it. If I started giving you an item, say chocolate bars, you'll be very grateful...initially. If I continued giving you chocolate bars, stacking them in small towers in front of your front door, you would actively start hating me for it and dreading the sight of any more chocolate bars. In fact, your well-being would actually decrease with each

39 They do make the concession that your potential marginal utility decreases with each unit, but they never make the logical leap of assuming that too much of something is just as bad as having too little. As such, according to classical economics, your marginal utility when receiving resources is on an asymptotic downwards spiral with 0, but never quite reaching it.

marginal chocolate bar that I would give you.

Regular economic theory would argue that you would simply trade the excess resources for other ones you're in dire need for. But think about it, just storing said chocolate would be expensive, in and of itself, and who in their right mind would buy heaps of chocolates from a random stranger? Either establishing a store or attempting to find a potential bulk buyer might take so long and make you incur a greater opportunity cost than whatever you would stand to gain. Mick Jagger was wrong it seems, not everything worth doing is worth overdoing, as it may well have the opposite intended effect.

Complex systems with interdependent variables defy simple linear mathematical relations - an input will not necessarily always yield the same output. Or put in layman's terms: the phrase "the hair that broke the camel's back" is wrong, well before the camel's back breaks, he is in an unsustainable position. In this overburdened situation, it will injure itself in the long run if its burden is not considerably lessened, regardless of whether a hair is added or not. Even then, it might be able to complete its task with the heavy load without an issue. But then collapse a day or two later, seemingly without just cause. There isn't a situation where a camel's back necessarily has to reach breaking point for failure to occur, it vastly depends on its past and present circumstances to determine what might happen in future.

Despite the failures of linear models to adequately explain the world, many princes in ivory towers have been somewhat reticent of abandoning, or at the very least limiting the use of such simplistic models, due to their ability to be easily solved. In other words, you can easily use said models to make predictions about future states. Like most prophets in history though, they tend to get things wrong.

Over the last half century, there's been a growing rebellion. Most surprisingly of all, it was a meteorologist, rather than someone who stood to make a fortune from revealing system mistakes, who first came up with this new investigative front. Still very much in the fringes of science, but gaining popularity due to its applications in all complex models under the Sun, Chaos Theory is very much a new way of understanding the world. Its assertions are deceptively simple, but its consequences are terrifyingly complex.

In the early 1960s, Edward Lorenz sought to understand how air moved in the atmosphere, so as to understand what drove climate. As such, he simplified the behaviours of the weather down to a very crude set of three equations. He would run said model in a clunky analogue computer, which brute forced the calculations and took time to come to its conclusions. One day, in the winter of 1961, rather than run the whole simulation back to the point in time he wanted to examine, Lorenz took a shortcut. He simply input the initial conditions, as the exact point he wanted to simulate, by copying the numbers from a printout he'd made earlier.

A short while later, he came back and examined the results with puzzlement. The program had been the same, and there had been no error in inputting in the data. Nevertheless, the second round of results differed vastly from the first run. So confusing were these results that he even thought that the computer might have malfunctioned. Yet, he soon realised the truth. In the computer's memory, up to six decimal places were stored as data points. On the printout, for the sake of brevity, only three were included. Lorenz had entered the rounded-off numbers, thinking that the minute difference was irrelevant [3].

In other words, a measurement difference which would often not even be noticeable in the real world (even with the best available equipment), had compounded and created a completely different scenario. This has troubling consequences in the real world. Even if God himself had given you the very equations that explained the universe, if you didn't have access to all data points at one point in time with infinite precision, you would still make wrong predictions. Furthermore, as more time passed, the more incorrect your predictions would become, as the errors would keep compounding on each other.

Approximate data in a chaotic system, does not lead to approximately accurate results - it leads to wildly different results when enough time is given for errors to compound. As such, much like the weather, economic forecasts will likely be wrong in the long term. That said, they can also be wrong in the very short term. Reason being that there's "noise" within the elements of the system and no scale change or improvement in methodology will likely make the data any clearer, because the errors are built into the variables themselves [4]. There's no true Platonic ideal of what certain values ought to be, as naturally, they fluctuate within a certain range. For instance, healthy human body temperature is said to be between 36.5 and 37.5 °C, there are just too many factors at work for there to be a true stable equilibrium value that applies to all humans; and hence, there is a range of stability instead of a "perfect" number. In most elements that you could possibly measure within a system, there will be a variance. Because of this, it's natural to ask what values we are meant to use in our models, and if we include an error range does this not guarantee that we will have the wrong conclusions?

I am truly sceptical of people's ability to comprehend, or even accurately predict results in complex systems, except in the short- to medium-term, before the errors have time to compound on each other[40]. There's only a small window of accurate and useful prediction, longer scales are guaranteed to be wrong because a small unaccounted variance aggregates and changes the whole result.

To make matters worse, this conclusion is generous enough in assuming that we have the right models and semi-accurate data points in the first place. Forecasting in chaotic systems works well until it doesn't - you may be right today by sheer luck, but there's no guarantee you'll be lucky tomorrow. Now, imagine if you built a dependence on accurate predictions for your continued well-being, say if you were a derivatives speculator in Wall Street. In such circumstances, even getting a single decimal point out of place can cost you a king's ransom.

At the risk of one day becoming akin to the people who said that the airplane and the horseless carriage were impossible, I'll put forth that no matter how much computational power and data one has, it is impossible to predict the future unless one is essentially omniscient already. Furthermore,

40 Even then, these results would be approximate and not accurate.

if you were to make your predictions known, the markets will adapt to them and thus would throw a wrench into your pre-established models.

The world just seems far too complex to defy simplicity, and it cannot truly be reduced to separate components. A perfect case study of such a complex system is the fertilisation of the Amazon. One would be forgiven to think that the desolate Sahara Desert and the lush Amazon Rainforest, on the other side of the globe, have no relation with each other. However, recent studies have come to the conclusion that the Sahara's dried out lake beds have essential nutrients that are transferred to the Amazon in dust through air currents, which end up fertilising it. In other words, if the Sahara didn't exist, there might not even be such an exuberant rainforest, and with it an important producer of the world's oxygen and biodiversity would also be non-existent. To fully understand one aspect of the planet one pretty much has to understand the planet as a system [5].

I don't think it's a reasonable assumption that we would ever know about all these unconscious mechanisms with enough precision to build a perfect framework correct enough to predict with exactitude. The sanest course of action might be a simple admission of ignorance; to admit that "one only knows that one knows nothing," as Plato would put it. In future chapters, where I discuss investing, I will discuss how one can build robustness to our own ignorance of the pertinent facts. For now, suffice it to say that one has to pay attention in what sort of system one is playing:

- **Linear systems** have a direct proportional output based on their initial input, and they are easy to model. Most systems that you find in textbooks are linear, and are only truly applicable in circumstances where you can isolate the variables from each other. For the most part, these ought to be reserved for educational purposes to make ideas clearer as a thought experiment, *one should rarely actually take them seriously as a means of representing reality*. Even then, whatever conclusions they produce, should be taken with a crate of salt.

- **Non-linear systems** have negative and positive feedback loops. In other words, the relation of the separate variables can cause interferences and synergies, which produce effects disproportionate to their inputs. These systems are difficult to model, and to quantify, due to their complex nature. Most systems you find in nature possess non-linear traits. One should be sceptical of all short- and long-term model conclusions that they produce, as they are guaranteed to be wrong to some degree. For one to be truly able to solve the next state of the system, one would have to know all other states that the unconscious mechanism has been in with exact precision.

There are good reasons why in school and successive academic pursuits we end up ignoring feedback loops and non-linear systems - they're excruciatingly difficult to solve. Yet we ignore them at our peril. We would be wise to remember that the world is more complicated than our simplifications. Sometimes the same input yields dramatically different results, and it is all because of a difference of timing.

2 - All in Good Time

"A wizard is never late, nor is he early, he arrives precisely when he means to."

- *Gandalf, Lord of the Rings*

Whether you're writing a comedy sketch or attempting to find a sensible investing strategy, timing seems to be everything. Over the course of one's investing lifetime one receives a deluge of trite advice such as "buy low, sell high" - implying that people have been genuinely stupid enough to attempt to do the opposite. Truth is nobody genuinely wants to mistime their behaviours, but it happens nonetheless because we don't really understand the natural variance of unconscious mechanisms.

We're like boxers in a ring, flinching to punches that never come, but then getting walloped by an unexpected left hook. Statistically speaking, you're unlikely to ever accurately buy when the market has bottomed out, or sell when the market has peaked. Reason being that a disproportionately small amount of days will account for a large proportion of your returns over an investing career. The international bank JP Morgan made the argument that had an investor purchased an index fund of the S&P-500 on January 3, 1995, ten years later they would've made an annual return of 9.85%. Nevertheless, had this investor missed the ten best days within this period, they would've only made a 6.10% return; worse still, six of the ten best days were within two weeks of the worst days [6]. This means that one would've surely ended up missing the ten best days, had one tried to time the market, and it would've cost them almost 40% of their potential profits.

It stands to reason that you should never completely exit the market. If one's an enterprising investor, and one has yet to decide exactly which stocks are worthwhile investments, it might be worth momentarily putting one's money in diversified index funds, which are as safe as investments can be given that you're investing in the economy as a whole instead of a single company. In either case, if the initially-invested lump sum is not enough to reach one's wealth goals within an acceptable timeframe, then one needs to continue adding a set percentage of one's income to one's investment, regardless of whether the market is up or down. This sub-strategy is termed "dollar cost averaging" and it seeks to minimize the effect of volatility on purchases of financial products by reducing exposure to certain forms of financial risk. In other words, this strategy acknowledges one's fallibility and the inherent random behaviour in the unconscious mechanism that is the invisible hand. This strategy simply takes away a person's ability to make stupid mistakes and gives one the best returns in the long run, by averaging out the good with the bad.

As bizarre as it might seem, comedians use a similar hedging strategy to safeguard themselves from flopping. When they have a comedy routine, they go on stage with all their new material. By their own admission, and even in their professional judgements, they often don't know which jokes are the ones that will make the audience laugh the most. As they go on their comedy tour, they will sometimes alter the timing of a joke, or the way that it's told, even outright eliminating a joke based on the audience's reaction, and they might also improvise something on the fly, only to perfect it in subsequent shows [7]. So, by the time that they tape the comedy special and have it air on HBO or Comedy Central, they've let unconscious mechanisms perfect the comedy shows for them. Simply put, world experts (in any field) do not know how certain elements in a system will behave when out in the wild, thus they structure their work in such a way as to benefit, or shield themselves, from randomness. Their projects are designed in such a way that over time they will only keep the positive random changes - they do not know when they will happen, they only know that they will.

Whether we want them to or not, fortune and probability rule our lives in ways we barely comprehend. Yet, even the processes of chance follow rules. In this case, there are two insights that Benoit Mandelbrot, one of the greatest mathematicians of the twentieth century, developed that apply to trends and data streams dependent on prior conditions [8]:

- **Noah Effect** - Its name is derived from a reference to the biblical flood that killed everyone on the planet off, save for a select number of people. In other words, it refers to the fact that a trend can be broken abruptly because the underlying situation changes. For example, if a stock starts at the price of $100 and then falls to the price of $8 due to bad news, it doesn't mean that it was ever sold for a price in between $100 and $8. A new "normal" can be established erratically and without earlier signs of it happening because a Black Swan occurred.
- **Joseph Effect** - Its name is derived from the biblical story of Joseph predicting to the Pharaoh seven years of plenty, followed by seven years of famine. This refers to the fact that data in a time series, where present and future states are dependent on prior conditions, contain a "memory" or a persistence of earlier events. "The signals fade in time. But it can take months, years, or decades for a signal to become unremarkable. Such is long-term dependence [...] Every event, no matter how remote or long ago, echoes across all other events." [9] For instance, if a drought has lasted a long time, it's likely to continue lasting a long time because it creates a self-perpetuating system. Hence, in many systems, the longer something lasts the likelier it is that it will remain so, by the circular logic that it has already been able to do so.

These effects might initially seem contradictory. The Noah Effect saying that there will at some point be a random change that affects the status quo, whilst the Joseph Effect advocates that nature tends to favour inertia. Nevertheless, there is a subtle interplay at work here. Elements within a system will tend to remain the same, until they suddenly don't - this is one of the many reasons why it's so difficult to predict things. Forecasts are reasonably accurate whilst things remain stable, when even a blind man could see what's ahead without resorting to complex mathematics. But when there are uncertain times ahead, and an accurate prediction would be very useful, even the most knowledgeable of people will tend to get it wrong.

Remember our discussion in earlier chapters where we talked about how evolution occurs by leaps and bounds, by punctuated equilibrium, but most of the time species remain in stasis without any noteworthy changes. This is how the unconscious mechanism operates, a cycle of stagnancy followed by a punctuated and violent overturning of the status quo. Or in the words of science historian James Gleick [10]:

> *"The "Noah" and "Joseph" Effects push in different directions, but they add up to this:* ***trends in nature are real, but they can vanish as quickly as they come."***

3 - A Matter of Perspective

"You can never see with your eyes on Earth. Look through Heaven's eyes!"

- Jethro, The Prince of Egypt

There's an ancient Indian fable, where a group of blind men is trying to make sense of an elephant they'd come across. One touched the side of the beast and proclaimed it was a wall. Another grabbed a tusk and thought it must be a mighty spear. The third grabbed the trunk and thought it to be very snake-like. And so on and so on, with each man making silly assertions about what an elephant was truly like. It bears saying that all men had a valid case for making their argument but they failed to understand the creature as a whole. This ancient Indian fable explains the failure in our individual understanding of the world. Every so often, we might see flickers of divine truth, but for the most part, we're barred from peering into the realm of verity.

A single-word solution to this dilemma might quickly pop into one's head - "numbers!" Surely, these objective measures cannot ever be wrong, when wielded correctly. The history of the modern western world is a testament to number's power. I do not deny this, but much in the same way that I support the rule of law, it doesn't mean that I support fascism. Fancy-looking equations will dissuade all but the most battle-hardened critics, or dumbest of your opponents. Thus, many faulty arguments are draped with the veneer of mathematical legitimacy whilst their underlying assumptions are wrong even before they leave the starting line. Mathematics by itself is not foolproof and requires a smooth operator to work properly. Maths is a tool, not the solution.

Take something as objective-sounding as measuring the length of the coast of Britain. Surely, there isn't much to be disputed about something like that, right? In fact, it has been argued that essentially any measure of a coastline, if it gives a finite number, is infinitely wrong, or rather depends on your measurement system [11]. Reason is simple, if you were a surveyor trouncing around Britain's perimeter with a meter-long divider, you'd come with a certain finite number. But if you were to do the same with a half-a-meter divider, you'd arrive at a much larger result. In fact, the smaller increments you use to measure the coastline, the larger the result becomes. Theoretically, with a precise enough measuring system, the coastline is infinitely long! How does this make any sense?

"An observer trying to estimate the length of England's coastline from a satellite will make a smaller guess than an observer trying to walk its coves and beaches, who will make a smaller guess in turn than a snail negotiating every pebble" [12]. By caring about minutia, your assertions have the potential to become infinitely complex. In other words, even something as seemingly objective as analysing the length of a coastline is partisan and depends on the point of view of the observer.

In creating a predictive model and assigning a coefficient to a certain variable, you are inherently being partisan. Whether or not you're assigning appropriate values is up for debate. The point of the matter is that even with things that appear clear cut we have difficulty assigning precise numeric values that are not up for debate. Then, to add insult to injury, you expect others to believe that you can correctly model the behaviour of a whole complex system with enough precision that your predictive abilities are not little more than guesswork? Please!

The key to surviving through the natural rebalancing of an unconscious mechanism is to position yourself in such a way that the potential losses of your position pale in comparison to your potential gains. In other words, you might not win every battle, but in the long run you will win the war. It's why it's said that "the house always wins." The statement isn't true in the literal sense - it's impossible to win every single time, yet in the long run, they do. Casinos structure their games in such a way that the statistical probability is in their favour. The house will **always** win when given enough time, there's no other outcome given the restrictions of the system.

It is essential to side with the forces that are irreplaceable. Ideologies and different methods of analysis might be developed, but there are some patterns that remain true regardless of what happens. I can guarantee you that even in a hundred years, no matter how much society changes, people will still need food, technology, entertainment and status symbols; which means that they will need the resources to produce and maintain those elements in their lives.

The trick is not to get side-tracked by following any one particular company supplying these trends all too much. These are fads that will be quickly snuffed out of existence and betting on the survival of most of them is little more lucrative than gambling. In the words of Oscar Wilde: "Fashion is a form of ugliness so intolerable that we have to alter it every six months." Instead of listening to the partisan data and the fluctuating will of the public, focus on the factors that need to exist to supply said needs. The clothes themselves might change every six months, but the materials they're made from can remain stable for centuries. As such, the material suppliers of fads end up benefiting more than the people who are promoting the fads themselves.

For example, in 1848, during the California Gold Rush, hundreds of thousands of people flocked to find the supposed mountains of gold flowing from the streams. In almost a decade, despite the massive uproar, few people made a fortune, or even any money, from prospecting. On average, only half the miners made a modest profit, after taking all expenses into account [13].

Having said this, many fortunes were made in that time and place because they capitalised on the phenomena. The ones who ended up becoming rich were usually the ones providing services and goods to the gold-addicted populace [14]. Once more, it was the merchants supplying the materials, who reaped the profits from the variable behaviour of the crowds, rather than participants of the mania. A general store owner could sell mining equipment, clothes, dry goods or household goods based on the needs of its customers, regardless of whether or not one particular well ran dry. Or railroads could shift from transporting mining material to whatever else became in vogue. Point being that learning the underlying material needs of a trend, not merely the trend itself, leads to far greater stability and performance in the long run.

We must always remember that consistent gains are far better than volatile returns. You shouldn't look for one lucky throw of the dice, but you want to make profits today, tomorrow and all the days thereafter. It's fool's folly to try to invent schemes to sidestep the necessity of time and proper business acumen required. It's difficult to not get partisan data, as I've explained over the course of this section of the book. Thus, I suggest a simple heuristic to overcome this needless complexity when making financial decisions: Occam's Razor.

This logic tool can be defined as follows: "when deciding between multiple explanations, that which requires the least assumptions is likelier to be correct" [15]. In other words, trying to predict specificity of trends and trying to time them is likely to be a fool's errand; even after the dust is settled it often becomes very difficult without a heap of guesswork. How many warehouses full of fidget spinners and selfie sticks do you think exist nowadays? Surely there were hundreds, perhaps thousands, of entrepreneurs who thought that one particular upwards swing in that particular niche was their path to riches. Yet I really can't explain why either of those plastic gimmicks gained as much attention as they did, or why they died so suddenly. I'm on Newton's on this one, the madness of crowds is beyond my comprehension. To this day, for instance, I could not tell you why it is that Myspace lost against Facebook when it had more functionality, wider market distribution and more capital. Everyone has their pet theory, but trying to parse through the wreckage after the hurricane came through might be missing the point.

Instead, one should focus on universal needs. In technology, at least for the foreseeable future, there are certain raw materials that are essential like plastic, silicon and copper, no matter what company it is. These are not bad investments, assuming you pick a random well-managed and competitive supplier, you're likely not going to do badly in years to come. Same goes with computing power - the need for it is only growing exponentially, so well-managed suppliers of it are not going to quickly collapse.

These are the ways one avoids falling for the public's whims. The mob is fickle and unpredictable in their wants and desires. But regardless of what shape the new developments happen to take, they tend to depend on factors which remain stable and profitable for many years. The inherent forces within the system guide it to a point of equilibria - through the path of least resistance.

4 - The Path of Least Resistance

"The heights charm us, but the steps do not; with the mountain in our view we love to walk the plains."

- Johann Wolfgang von Goethe

One of the hallmarks of a bad writer is making their protagonist superhuman. This "Superman Effect"[41] not only limits the story choices you can make, as there's no character development left to be done, but it ostracizes the audience. We like to root for the underdog, because we see from our day-to-day life that it's difficult to succeed when the deck is stacked against you. Hence, it's very cathartic to see a character overcome the odds, despite their flaws, and the inherent difficulty thereof.

We find it cathartic precisely because a long shot in real life usually doesn't pan out. The underdog usually does not win. In reality, smart and capable villains die happily in their beds of old age, or are eventually supplanted by even worse monsters. Much like a ball will always roll down a hill, circumstances tend to follow the path of least resistance, unless compelled by an even greater force. And even then, only so long as the strength remains to fight against the inherent decay and devolution of the system.

This is why it's easier to make $10 million once you're rich, than it is to make

41 This type of characters are commonly called "Mary Sues" because of a fan fiction character that was written precisely to lampoon this type of failure in writing.

$1 million whilst starting from nothing. Assuming that there's even social mobility, you still have to overcome the fact that there are limits to how much money you can save. The poorer you are, a proportionally higher amount of your income is just spent on surviving [16]. Add to it the fact that you likely have the "Ghetto tax" to contend with, where you pay more for comparatively the same products than wealthier people, and you have a recipe for disaster [17]. Ironically, it's expensive to be poor.

It's not that "evil" corporations are putting them down, by giving them higher interest rates on loans, for example. It's just that people with their profile statistically have a higher chance of failure to repay loans than other demographics. Thus, the unconscious mechanisms that have profit maximisation as an end goal have to make up for this higher rate of failure. It might outwardly look the same as racism, sexism, classism or any other such "-ism," but ideology never entered into it. A logical computer, incapable of understanding the concepts of race, sex and class that had no information other than the expected value of offering a certain financial product to a certain demographic, would come up with the same result.

Whereas, if you're wealthy, you likely have a higher income that stems from a stable job; therefore, if you were to fail to make payments, you likely have assets that can be repossessed. So, companies are much more permissive, and tolerant, which results in much lower costs. In other words, nothing breeds success like success.

Yet not because something seems probable or likely, does it mean that it will occur - you could feasibly play Russian Roulette your whole life, whilst dying from food poisoning in your old age. A large probability of something occurring does not equal certainty. The theoretical logical computer, for example, might not give out loans to a poor man with a brilliant idea, who might've used that idea to create a multi-billion-dollar business; whilst it might also give a loan to a rich drug addict with a gambling addiction. It does so on logical grounds, because on average that behavioural pattern is profitable - poor people are likely to default on their debts, and rich people are unlikely to do so. But individuals and specific circumstances rarely translate into a nice and clean equation with an expected outcome.

One of the great failures of a lot of models is that they quantify inputs as always having the same output. Reality is much more brutal and unfair, as the underlying mechanisms and situations the inputs find themselves in are prone to change. The same input can lead to vastly different outputs at a different point in time. Think of someone like Vincent van Gogh, who toiled all his life while barely being able to sell a single painting [18]. His brother, Theo van Gogh, was a renowned art dealer who subsidized his manic-depressive way of life until he shot himself. The big irony being that after van Gogh committed suicide, his paintings catapulted in fame through his memorial exhibit and they are now among the world's most expensive paintings.

As depressing as it is to say, you can be both extremely talented and a hard worker, but have nothing to show for it by the end of your life. One's talent will not necessarily ever be acknowledged. This is particularly irksome, as we inherently like to believe in the idea of a meritocracy because of the social mechanisms that we talked about in *Part I* relating to reciprocal altruism. Our very biology primes us into believing that we ought to be rewarded in direct proportion to the quality of our work. Yet, the problem is that a perfect meritocracy implies perfect knowledge of the capabilities of someone. But our world has become far too complex to be able to devote the time to singlehandedly pick the most qualified person for a job. Instead, we depend on the wisdom of the crowds, hearsay and our institutions to tell us whom to spend our time on.

Allow me to put it into context with something near and dear to my heart: writing. It's been estimated that about 90% of Americans believe that they have a book in them and want to write it [19]. If we take only the adult population of the United States, that means that there are 220.77 million potential new books. Funnily enough, this 90% number is higher than the 76% of people who say they've read for fun over the past year, meaning that there are at least several million people in the US who want to become an author, but don't actually like reading [20]. If only one in a thousand of these people manage to have a rough draft, and publishes it during their lifetime, that's still an enormous number of new books. What percentage of those would you think are actually any good?

It used to be that there were gatekeepers in place to supposedly protect us from the onslaught of garbage. For centuries, the usual path to success as an author was usually to get an agent, have that agent get you a publishing deal with a publishing house and then hope for the best after they made major changes to every aspect of your book. Most people did not make it through the process.

It wasn't necessarily due to a lack of talent or marketability either. JK Rowling, author of the 25-billion-dollar franchise *Harry Potter*, got rejected by twelve different publishers [21]. Then, to add insult to injury, after she had already created this billion-dollar wizarding-empire, she tried to write under the pseudonym of *Robert Galbraith* and got several rude rejection letters, some even offering her sources on basic writing tips [22]. Say what you will about her as an author and person, but she clearly had the capacity to become part of the big leagues, but without stubbornness and a good amount of luck, the *Harry Potter* franchise would've ended in some drawer somewhere. How many such franchises were locked away, I wonder? Whether you liked it or not, this is simply how publishing was done. If you didn't please the gatekeepers, you had no chance of ever becoming widely known.

That is until about ten years ago, in May 2009, when Amazon - the world's largest bookseller - opened the floodgates for any person to sell their books on their platform. From then on, literally anyone can put whatever garbage they want online, so the gems are lost amidst a sea of faecal matter. There was even a recent example of someone who gamed the Amazon algorithm and got a literal photo of his foot into becoming an *Amazon Bestseller*.

Every time one looks to buy a book online one inadvertently bogs through this fetid mire. So naturally, rather than try to pick books at random, we look for something that already has signs of approval. This becomes a bit of a Catch-22 for any aspiring author - for someone to decide to read your book, the reviews have to be good, but for there to be any reviews at all someone has to have read it. Hence good reviews are incredibly important for any aspiring author today, and thus I cherish each and every one that I get[42].

In either case, that is why if you happen to have any notoriety whatsoever, you're likelier to get attention and sell books, when compared to a nobody without a platform to raise himself. All other things being equal, familiarity is an incredibly powerful advantage. Over time, this can become a bit of a self-perpetuating cycle - "the rich get richer, and the poor poorer."

Imagine that for your own amusement you terraformed a planet and raised lab-grown humans with our current level of knowledge. In this world nobody would be born famous, or have a bigger platform to start with, or anything of the sort. Beyond their genetics, they would be identical in terms of a starting position. Yet, over time, things would begin to change. Through sheer random chance the work of some of the artistically-minded people would be viewed more - for example, their name could start with a double A and thus would be likelier to show up in alphabetically organised systems.

Through this random quirk, they would gain more exposure and occupy more mental real estate. By doing so, there's more attention on their work, and soon enough, their level of influence is in a different league of those that didn't gain from the random boost. Advantages compound on each other, as one book sold is proof that at least one other person is willing to spend their time and money on it, two books sold doubly so. Hence to not have reviews, or an audience, is worse than being invisible, as people will wonder what is wrong with you and why you don't have a following. As such, small changes in initial circumstances can yield vastly different outcomes. Not only that, but they can compound over generations, as we discussed in PIII-Ch6 when we discussed how the concept of hereditary aristocracies came into existence. The son of a successful artist has a much better chance of launching a career dependent on wealth or status, by simple virtue that his parents have already done the heavy lifting for him. Even by marginal association to their fame he has a radically different starting point.

This phenomenon, where some benefit is given to someone (or some

42 Wink, wink, nudge, nudge ;)

object/idea) according to how much they already have, so that the winners in the system keep "winning" more and the losers do not get anything, is called the "preferential attachment hypothesis" and it is a well-established phenomenon in nature. Even language has such an organisational style where the twenty most commonly used words account for a lion's share of what we say [23]. It doesn't solely happen in English, but every natural language that has been studied - even ones that haven't been deciphered by archaeologists and linguists.

The modern age, in its desire to fix all maladies, has tried to rectify biases of sampling and truly create a meritocracy where you get what you give. In its stead, it created a different problem altogether - a tyranny of numbers. The motivation was sound - substitute flawed human decision making for a cold, efficient and unthinking algorithm. The problem is that, as a product of the human mind, it becomes difficult to extricate the biases of the model's creator from the model itself.

For example, recently Amazon tried to train an algorithm to sort out potential job candidates by analysing their CVs. The programme learned the ideal candidate by analysing former hires and got to work, assigning 1-5 stars on prospective hires (much like customers do when reviewing products on Amazon) [24].The funny thing is that by doing so, it started flagging words like "female" and rejecting resumes for the inclusion of that phrase. Reason being that most successful hires in the tech industry are male. Being the gender dimorphic species that we are, due to all the factors we discussed in part I, *on average* men tend to focus on things and women on people. It's even been shown that how men and women write erotic fiction highlights this mental bias; as men tend to focus on the mechanics (who is putting what where), whilst women tend to focus on the emotions and sensations of the counter [25]. Ergo, it makes perfect sense that either gender would be overrepresented in some industries.

However, this was obviously extremely unfair for actually qualified candidates who were being rejected because they attended a "Women's basketball team" or something of the sort. Simply because the word "woman" was flagged. The system didn't care for the morality of its actions, it was asked to find hires similar to the ones already in the company and it did. So we should be careful of trusting algorithms fully as they can make us unable to see through our preconceptions, as we might then just be judging all books by their cover. Not only that, but equations and faulty models can legitimize the wrong conclusions as they obfuscate matters by adding an extra layer of complexity, consequently they become cargo cult sciences.

A "cargo cult science" is a reference to physicist Richard Feynman's discussion about science and its flaws [26]. Cargo cults are religions from the South Sea Pacific islands that sprang up in WWII when American bombers landed with a bounty of supplies and excited the natives with their superior technology and abundance of material goods. After the American *GIs* left, the natives immediately went to work clearing the jungle, and building the infrastructure that would accommodate planes coming back with an even bigger bounty - they built runways out of wood, headphones out of bark and twigs, etc. All would seem to be in order, the execution looked to be perfect, with the caveat being that planes did not land no matter how much the cultists tried.

Learned people often behave much in the same *modus operandi* as these cults. Reason being that they can fail to ask themselves whether their underlying assumption about the world are correct. Economists are particularly notorious in exhibiting this behaviour. As such, American economics professor Paul Krugman once said that one of the biggest failings of economics is that it often mistakes beauty for truth [27]. He continued in saying that economists tend to fall within the margin of error whilst things remain static and it's unimportant to get it precisely right, given the stability of the system. But, when it's essential for them to get matters accurately though, there's nary a prediction that does so.

The behavioural economist is likely to identify this failing as an aggregate of the heuristic judgements mentioned in PI-Ch6. Firstly, their perceptions are **anchored** to the most recent instances about the world, as such they don't find any **available** evidence that contradicts their assertions. Secondly, they

substitute the question about whether their current models work at all with whether they're elegant and coherent in and of themselves. Their initial success in predicting the future within a very reduced sample size fuels their **optimism,** and they become more reckless with their gambling. Yet, when there start to be instances of the models not working properly and the economic system crashes, they'll **frame** the matter in a different light. "It wasn't the models that were at fault," they will claim that there are interferences with the model because of a momentary Black Swan event, and it'll soon come to pass. Finally, when it's clear that the models don't adequately reflect reality, they will seek to tweak the models, rather than abandon them wholesale, as the **sunk-cost** of the time money and effort, appears too great to let it go to waste. As such, the economist simply amends the perceived fault of the algorithm, and stabler times come, independent of the economist's models. The new status quo is blamed on the amended model, and the cycle is repeated *ad nauseam.*

On their own, none of the heuristic judgements would've been fatal in the creation of the model. Economics, whilst not a fully-fledged "hard science," does contain enough of the scientific method's underlying epistemology to quelch individual failings, given enough time. In aggregate though, the heuristics prove too much of a compelling narrative and hence they override any academic rigour which we would've otherwise wanted to reach, as it often becomes little more than confirmation bias.

However, economic forecasting as a whole should not be written off. There are various fields in economics that overcome their inherent limitations and manage to be true to reality. Game theory, for example, might have been partly responsible for averting nuclear Armageddon by providing both sides with a clear framework of mutually assured destruction - once the numbers were crunched, and the missiles were armed, neither side had an incentive to actually use nuclear weapons, thus creating a Nash Equilibria [28]. Game theory works by creating a theory that is adaptable to the circumstances, its predictions are often accurate due to their Delphic quality. Nevertheless, they're not precise, as they don't go into specifics about the cascade effect of the likely consequences of Cold War.

Whereas on physics and similar sciences, you have the luxury of identifying and separating the forces you want to test. In economics, you cannot separate elements and forces quite as readily, as all factors are inextricably linked and thus the whole is greater than the sum of its parts. Take Max Weber's interpretation that the Protestant work ethic was one of the reasons capitalism was so successful, which we discussed in PIII-Ch4. How exactly should an economist quantify such a nebulous term as "the Protestant work ethic"? Ignoring it altogether seems negligent, as culture clearly does change behaviour, and logically consumption and production of goods and services, yet accepting it within the purview of classical economics brings its own set of problems. There have been attempts to quantify it, but none that are compelling. What happens if the actors in the model have a different underlying philosophy to go along with it, or a different interpretation of the philosophy than that which the model was created in? Can you truly export economic models across international boundaries and expect them to work? Would a Protestant Chinese get the same boost to production as a Protestant American?

The human factor is among the biggest question marks in the variables embedded in the models. Therein lies the main problem with economics, and the *raison d'être* of the behavioural economist. As former Secretary of Defence Donald Rumsfeld put it, there are: Known Knowns, information that we know we know, but we rarely consider; Known Unknowns, information that we know that we do not know; and Unknown Unknowns, or information which we do not know that we do not know [29].

Absence of evidence does not imply evidence of absence, which we often seem to believe when designing models that seek to forecast events. Our models and predictions should leave room for the unknowable and the unthinkable. Black Swans happen eventually, whether we want them to or not. In making decisions under conditions of uncertainty, the consequences must dominate the probabilities. We never know the future [30].

PART V: PROTO MODERNITY: ARE WE THERE YET?

The world has changed much since humans first decided to mostly abandon their nomadic ways. The bands of roving marauders would still be a problem for centuries to come. But, by and large, humanity decided to focus on building civilization instead of building cultures solely dedicated to theft and pillaging.

Rulers often flirted with bringing order to large swathes of land through violence, and some even accomplished it. Over the millennia, these empires allowed cultures to share commonalities with each other and it created a sense of a people, an ethnicity with common beliefs, goals and preferences. More often than not though, these imperial policies proved to be overly ambitious and Black Swan shocks chiselled away at the governing infrastructure until they collapsed or remained in stagnancy.

This is where the story for this chapter begins, with the Roman Empire at its deathbed. Comatose and moribund some remnants of it would keep alive well up to 1453. The starting symptoms of the illness are difficult to pinpoint; however, by the third century AD, the writing seemed to be on the wall. Almost the whole century was spent on a civil war, where every two-bit general and governor tried to earn the throne. The established volatility, anarchy, violence and autonomous functioning of small regions, which with time became kingdoms, proved to be the rule rather than the exception over the coming century. After millennia of petty squabbling, Western civilization would rise up from its ashes to conquer the world through some unprecedented advances.

1 - Crawling out of the Abyss of the Not-so-Dark Ages

> *"Strange women lying in ponds, distributing swords, is no basis for a system of government!"*
>
> *- Monty Python and the Holy Grail*

After the decline and fall of the Roman Empire, the world was plunged into an age of seeming stagnancy. Colloquially, this is seen as being the fault of religious dogma, snuffing away the last embers of curiosity in the West. That said, I don't think this provides a satisfactory answer.

Whilst I'm up for some Catholicism-bashing as much as the next guy, the evidence simply does not support a purely religious interpretation for the almost millennium long stagnation. Now, it is true that religious fanatics destroyed knowledge, as happened with the destruction of the Serapeum of Alexandria in 391 CE, which housed the remnants of the majestic Library of Alexandria [1][43]. But this sort of barbarism has happened without fail throughout history, even

43 The original library was a spectacular achievement of a government promoting scholarly knowledge. Whenever a book was found on a person when entering the port of Alexandria, it was temporarily confiscated so a copy of it could be made and housed in the library. As such, it housed knowledge from most of the known world. Furthermore, it contained scientific advances that under the right situation could've changed the world, as it happened when the insights were rediscovered millennia later. For example, Heron of Alexandria's works included elements of clockwork automata and the beginnings of a steam engine but went largely ignored. Had this not happened we could've had the technological foundations of an Industrial Revolution over 2,000 years ago [2].

in the seemingly most enlightened of ages. Surprisingly, this still held true in the Renaissance, when admiration for the ancients was at an all-time high. Pope Urban the VIII, of the Barberini clan, went as far as destroying Roman works for their raw materials; prompting a popular saying to be created: *Quod non fecerunt barbari, fecerunt Barberini;* or in English: "What the barbarians didn't accomplish, the Barberini did." [3]

Widespread admiration for the past, with its culture and teachings, is a relatively new phenomenon. Even in the modern age, it's nowhere near as sacrosanct as one would like. A trip to Greece should be enough to dispel this notion, as you'll find shopping centres built on top of Greek and Roman ruins. Or on the other side of the world, in Mexico, you'll find a gigantic supermarket owned by Walmart besides Teotihuacan, one of the most important pre-Hispanic Mesoamerican cities. This is despite the tremendous economic incentive to keep ruins intact because of tourism money. So, when the remnants of the ancient cultures are just lying there and the present inhabitants see them as worthless, or even an affront to their beliefs, is it any wonder that they destroy them and use their materials for something else? The *modus operandi* of groups like ISIS, whilst nowadays the exception that wantonly destroys culture in the modern age, was far more common than we care to admit throughout history. I dare say it's a miracle that we have any records at all from ancient cultures.

Having said this, cultural genocide tended to be random, instead of wilful. The Parthenon is a good example, which survived up to the seventeenth century in relatively good standing. Yet, it was used as a gunpowder magazine, and a Venetian mortar shot set the whole thing ablaze. This wasn't an attempt by the Venetians, Turks or even the Greeks to erase history. It was instead an accident of circumstances, and not a conspiracy. Or think about the *Archimedes Palimpsest,* which is a copy of an otherwise unknown work of Archimedes of Syracuse, which was overwritten with a Christian religious text by 13th Century monks [4]. How, or why, the monks got their hands on the text is difficult to say. It does point to the fact that this type of document simply wasn't seen as worthwhile to preserve. As such, they drifted from hand to hand, getting forgotten in musty basements, libraries, attics, and being found again, only to repeat the cycle every couple hundred years. Eventually, someone who failed to recognize the document's importance used them for their base materials, and destroyed them.

So, whilst there certainly was persecution of "heretical ideas," simple apathy might explain the loss of countless works of immeasurable historical value far more than a millennia-long witch hunt. If anything, the few educated men that remained were associated with religion in some shape or form. The persecution of scientific ideas was nowhere near as bad as is commonly perceived in popular mediums. It obviously did exist, but it's mostly exaggerated. Take the Spanish Inquisition's record to show the breadth of the exaggeration. It is usually said to have been the most barbaric of any such organization in human history, but its actual effect was laughable when compared to the hype.

Much like when you see the kill count of historical serial killers one is shocked to see a mere handful. Jack the Ripper, for example, only killed five people - you could easily beat that record in an afternoon if you put your mind to it [5]. As for the Spanish inquisition, in its 356-year history, depending on whom you ask, they killed between 1% and 3.3% of the 125,000 people they tried, which hardly seems like the numbers of a supposedly bloodthirsty institution [6][7]. Furthermore, whilst it did use torture to elicit confessions, it did so far less than contemporary institutions and it did so with several restrictions [8]. Nobody expects the *(surprisingly reasonable)* Spanish Inquisition!

In terms of religious persecution for the Western World, one of the worst time periods was arguably the Protestant Reformation, which was well into the heart of the Renaissance, and surprisingly not the Middle Ages, which are commonly marred by the stereotype of religious intolerance. Contrary to the everyman's understanding of the topic, heresy during the Middle Ages was a complex topic. Sometimes kings became so powerful that they defied the Pope, or established their own competing Pope (Wikipedia even has a long list of antipopes!). Some areas steadfastly maintained pagan beliefs, or mixed them in with Christian dogma. Hence to say that any dissenting opinion was promptly eliminated through violence anywhere and at any time, is misrepresenting the truth.

So, whilst religious fervour certainly had an effect on the world, we're all but forgetting what was lost when the Roman Empire fell. To paraphrase the ideas of American mathematician and philosopher Ted Kaczynski there are two types of technology: small-scale technology and organization-dependent technology. Small-scale technologies are tools that are able to be produced, maintained and used by a single person. A simple bow and arrow, for example, requires craftsmanship but a single craftsman could build one. Technological regression in that sort of technology is almost unheard of. Compare that to a refrigerator, which is organization-dependent technology, not only would you have to get the resources to build one (which are often found in different parts of the world), you would also have to have the technical knowledge to construct one as well as infrastructure to power it [9].

In other words, modern advances are simply not feasible, or practical, without an advanced technological and economic system backing its production and use. As such, if society were to collapse, the technical knowhow for building a refrigerator would quickly disappear in a generation or two. If a technical design book were to survive, it would be mostly worthless, except as a curiosity. Most people would simply not see it worth preserving, as its survival has no further effect on their life. This is what was lost when the Roman Empire fell, all the infrastructure on which technological advances were built simply ceased to exist. Their aqueducts fell into disrepair and were never rebuilt. The technical knowhow to produce cement and roads were lost through disuse. The Roman system of urban sanitation was forgotten, hence until recent times, the sanitation of European cities was inferior to that of Ancient Rome [10]. Even nowadays we're benefiting from technology rediscovered from 2,000 years ago - Roman concrete is not only cheaper than the traditional Portland cement, but it's more environmentally friendly and has a longer longevity [11]. Seems the ancients still have lessons for us.

As such, even if there wasn't an active persecution of thoughtcrime - or even when knowledge was actively promoted as in the Carolingian Renaissance - you would still have to restructure your whole society to make up for this fall from grace for there to be any grand technological advances. The ensuing reshuffling and building of your own infrastructure, that isn't dependant on a central authority in a far-off region, could take centuries. Hence, any and all technological and philosophical advances you could reasonably make would be of a much smaller scale. Add to this the fact that every two-bit aristocrat would be vying for power and you could start excusing the whole period for its perceived stagnancy.

Even warfare became much smaller in scale, the authority figures commanded a reduced pool of available recruits, and thus had to reduce the scope of military operations. By way of example, one of the largest battles in the Middle Ages, the Battle of Grunwald in 1410, had the Kingdom of Poland and the Grand Duchy of Lithuania paired up against the State of the Teutonic Order [12]. Altogether, they might've had as many as 66,000 men (if we use the largest force estimates). Whereas sixteen centuries before, in the Second Punic War, Carthage fought against Rome in the battle of Cannae. In total, both sides combined had around 136,000 men [13]. This means that a single side in a conflict, which happened millennia before, had almost as much, if not more, manpower at their disposal than some of the powerhouses of the continent in the Middle Ages combined. It's also worth noting that Rome ended up winning that war, despite the wholesale slaughter of almost all their men that battle.

The limited amount of manpower is partially the motivation behind building castles. Without modern siege equipment, and a gigantic army, castles were defendable by a surprisingly small amount of people. The quintessential example of such a case of castle defence was the siege of Corfe Castle in 1643 where Lady Bankes née Hawtry successfully defended the stronghold during a three-year siege with five men, later reinforced with eighty, against a force of around 500 wherein they managed to kill and wound over a hundred of their foes whilst only losing two of their own [14].

Is it any wonder that it took immense advances in financial technology and a resurgence of classical beliefs to counteract the loss of economies of scale[44] that happened when the Roman Empire fell?

---

44 The reduction of a unit cost in a product or service due to a larger production capacity. By using technology to scale up and make production more efficient goods fall in price.

2 - Paper Trading: The Rise of Planet Finance

"Money is a terrible master but an excellent servant."

- *P.T. Barnum*

In 2016, the total economic output of the planet was circa $75.87 trillion [15]. The market capitalization of listed domestic companies was $64.9 trillion [16]. The total debt outstanding was around $217 trillion during that period [17], and the total derivatives[45] outstanding was $544 trillion at the end of 2016, meaning that its value alone is seven times more than all the stock markets put together [18]. In other words, the world of finance is increasingly becoming disconnected with real life, or at least abstract promises and ephemeral concepts are perceived as holding more value than physical items.

Niall Ferguson put it best in his book *The Ascent of Money: A Financial History of the World*, when he wrote that "Planet Finance is beginning to dwarf

45 These are financial contracts deriving value from the performance of an underlying entity. They were initially meant to safeguard suppliers from the fluctuations of the resources that they used in production by guaranteeing the delivery of a product or service at a given time and price. In this way, they could stabilize and, somewhat more accurately, predict their future earnings by essentially setting in stone the production costs. Nevertheless, derivatives have mainly evolved to become a vehicle for rampant speculation, where large institutions essentially bet on outcomes to occur. This can be very profitable, with profit margins well above the average returns, but they're also very dangerous as they're costly when they're misused. As such, value investors, like Warren Buffett have unironically called them "Weapons of Mass Destruction" for their perceived capabilities to produce damage.

Planet Earth. And Planet Finance seems to spin faster too. Every day two trillion dollars change hands on foreign exchange markets. Every month seven trillion dollars change hands on global stock markets. Every minute of every hour of every day of every week, someone, somewhere, is trading. And all the time new financial life forms are evolving."

Hundreds of years ago, if you were to see a decrease of 50% from one day to the next in the monetary value of an economy, you could reasonably expect a war or some sort of armed conflict to have occurred. Infrastructure, manpower and production capabilities would likely have massively decreased, and obviously had an effect on economic output. This shift would be palpable, you'd likely be able to see the signs on the streets of such a cataclysmic event.

Yet, in the last few centuries, you could have such an event happen and, if you were to walk around the communities, you wouldn't notice much of a difference. The factories would all be there, the workers would still all able-bodied and willing to work, and the infrastructure would more than likely be capable of supplying for people's needs. The only real difference is that in one particular room, where people meet and scream at each other, people are suddenly shouting radically different numbers at each other, than they did yesterday, due to some perceived change in circumstances. Nowadays, it's computers whirring and buzzing with different algorithms at each other, but the point still stands - economic capabilities have been somewhat severed from monetary returns.

We have progressively built more castles in the air with ever more complicated stories to keep them aloft. Usury or, in more modern language, charging interest on loans has always been a bit of a social transgression. Think of it this way, when you charge interest on a loan, you are implicitly creating more capital than there exists money. Assuming that there is no new money being created to offset this, it eventually becomes physically impossible to repay the debts that exist within a society - there simply aren't enough resources available to do so. In other words, you're all but ensuring that there will be serfdom as people will have to keep slaving away to service the ever more difficult to pay amounts, which only keep increasing because of the interest rates.

People who don't understand finance in any shape or form, upon hearing this, immediately exclaim that charging interest on loans should be illegal. But such assertions are missing some nuance. If one prohibits others from charging usury, then one has little motivation to lend money, as they incur an "opportunity cost" since they could have otherwise invested or done something productive with the money. A family member, or even a friend, might be able to do this out of kindness or obligation, but a businessman who doesn't know you personally and has no reason to trust you? No chance. Yet, the need for the loan would still be there. Hence, where there aren't efficient capital markets available, loan sharks have a field day, and aren't afraid to break some legs to cash their dues, as they already operate outside the legal framework anyways.

This is why social communities increasing past Dunbar's number, a phenomenon which we talked about extensively in Parts I & III, is such a big deal. The innate rules of fraternal love, community cohesion, etc. will only take you so far before they're taken advantage of by less scrupulous people. Psychopathy, and being uncaring to the plight of others, is thus somewhat of an advantage the further away we get from community and family bonds, which happens the larger the society gets. This is hardly hyperbole either, the modern jobs that have the highest incidence of psychopathy are as follows: CEO, lawyer, media (TV/radio), salesperson, surgeon, journalist, police officer, clergy, chef and civil servant [19]. I don't think it's a coincidence that a good portion of the professions on this list have substantial influence in how we live our lives either. In the words of evolutionary biologist David Buss, talking about Linda Mealey's theory that psychopathic behaviour is an adaptation designed to take advantage of a community's innate goodwill [20][21]:

> *"Psychopaths pursue a deceptive or "cheating" strategy in their social interactions. Psychopathy is more common among men (4%) than women (1%). Psychopaths pursue a social strategy characterized by exploiting the reciprocity mechanisms of others. After feigning cooperation, psychopaths typically defect. This cheating strategy might be pursued by men who are unlikely to outcompete other men*

> *in a more traditional or mainstream status hierarchy. A psychopathic strategy can be maintained by frequency-dependent selection. As the number of cheaters increases, and hence the average cost to the cooperative hosts increases, adaptations evolve to detect cheating and inflict costs on cheaters. As the prevalence of psychopaths increases, therefore, the average payoff of the psychopath strategy decreases. As long as the frequency of psychopaths is not too large, it can be maintained amidst a population composed primarily of cooperators."*

Think of the snake oil salesman who can parade through town a handful of days, selling dangerous concoctions to the gullible and the desperate, only to then skip town before anyone gets wise to his inability to cure anything. Nowadays, the scammers don't even need to change postcode, as it's unlikely you'll bump into someone in a large enough city. It stands to reason that the more complex a society becomes, the more loopholes and abuses can exist if there isn't active policing to deter that sort of chicanery. Furthermore, the underlying incentive mechanisms shift. After all, success in a modern economy is measured in dollars and cents, not in people one made happier. Thus, wholly trusting in the goodwill of economic agents seems short-sighted and prone to instability because of deviants and psychopaths, who literally seem custom-built to take advantage of such "virtue based" systems. Yet, it's not solely the broken and the damned who are the source of all that is vile. Russian author Aleksandr Solzhenitsyn put it best when he said that "the line dividing good and evil cuts through the heart of every human being. And who is willing to destroy a piece of his own heart?" [22]. Sadly, it's often the most rapacious and callous men who will triumph in the economic wilderness, not the kind-hearted ones who will forego profits to sleep more easily at night.

A pessimist is either never disappointed, or he's pleasantly surprised. Hence, I don't believe we ought to build our social systems under the assumption that humans are benign creatures, instead we ought to build a system that harnesses the better devils of our nature. If you clearly define and delimit people's obligations and rewards, you can stand to gain from their rapaciousness and immorality, rather than be harmed by it. Businessman and villain-extraordinaire Gordon Gecko put it best:

> *"The point is, ladies and gentlemen, that greed, for lack of a better word, is good. Greed is right, greed works. Greed clarifies, cuts through, and captures the essence of the evolutionary spirit. Greed, in all of its forms; greed for life, for money, for love, knowledge has marked the upward surge of mankind."*

I believe that the unconscious mechanisms guiding historic economic development vindicate this assessment. After all, if there's anything that has characterised modern societies in the last few hundred years, it's their progressive development of more comprehensive property rights.

Imagine the reaction of a caveman if you were to explain to him that because you have a piece of paper you can own a territory so large that it goes beyond the horizon. Given his proto-communist and community-driven mindset, he'd find it absurd that a single person could own such a thing, let alone simply because he owns a piece of paper. Perhaps he'd understand the notion if you had a gang of men to enforce your inane claims, but as it stood, you'd just look like a madman.

What he would be unable to comprehend is what that piece of paper actually meant. Through ownership of that piece of paper, you're inadvertently getting the backing of the state's monopoly on violence, through policemen and the legal system, as long as you pay your taxes. In other words, with the stroke of a pen, the state is acknowledging that there exists a world parallel to our own, a Platonic world of ideas where they have to protect your legal claims, as is your right as a contributing citizen. In essence, the deed is a physical proof of all of society's foundational myths: the social contract, property rights, etc. Which is why in legal circles a deed is seen as a "bundle of rights" - a metaphor encapsulating all the complexities of property ownership.

This is the magic trick of the modern age, it manifests the ephemeral into the physical and somehow manages to put a price tag on it. A great example thereof is fiat currency, otherwise known as paper money, whose name comes from the Latin meaning "Let it be" [23]. Through purchasing something with money, one isn't usually trading anything physical, gone are the days of paper money being directly convertible into gold; instead, one is trading something far more interesting - trust in the government, society and economic system itself.

In other words, when you're trading paper money, what you're actually exchanging is the promise of the stability of a society. If the dollar goes down, relative to other currencies or goods, what has really gone down is the belief that the United States is able to pay its debts, and is thus more likely to cease existing. As such, money is partially the physical form of an abstract and ephemeral concept called trust.

The rise of planet finance is an acknowledgement, and an attempt to price the influence that the intangible and ephemeral has on our lives. The problem is that the economic system becomes a little like a house of cards, where one meme can give a stable footing for another meme to be propped up on top it.

The story of proto-modern finance beautifully highlights the process. First, there was the need to finance expensive government projects, and among them was chiefly war. Early in the Renaissance, the Italian states were in a constant bellicose state. The reasons behind it were irrelevant, so much so that the *casus belli* were sometimes ridiculous in hindsight. In 1325, for example, the rival city-states of Bologna and Modena went to war over a bucket - and yes, it's as stupid as it sounds and 2,000 people died as a consequence of this [24].

Yet, despite its ubiquity, in no period of history has war ever been cheap, and this was especially true in the Italian Renaissance as many states depended heavily on mercenaries, called *condottieri*. This wasn't uncommon, and many of the main states did this to bolster their lacklustre armies. Niccolo Machiavelli famously railed against this arrangement, as he said it was dangerous and "they have no other attraction or reason for keeping the field than a trifle of stipend, which is not sufficient to make them willing to die for you" [25]. He was ultimately right, and there were even *condottieri* whose main business wasn't in war, but extortion.

Federico da Montefeltro was among the most extraordinary *condottieri* of his time, he was never beaten, and after a while nobody wished to test his reputation. Hence, he was sometimes paid a retainer so that he wouldn't take up arms against a given faction - call it a "Montefeltro insurance" [26]. Admittedly, he never betrayed his word, but he still very much operated like a mafia don. This sort of protection racket was obviously expensive, albeit a necessary governmental expense, and thus new means of funding had to be found.

The Florentine Republic started borrowing massive sums from itself, by issuing quasi bonds that the wealthy citizens had to purchase instead of paying property tax [27]. This mechanism would eventually flourish into full blown securities that could be bought and sold. In other words, by you purchasing that debt, you're actually buying a promise from a longstanding and wealthy entity that you would be paid back your money, plus a bit extra for your trouble. However, if you didn't want to hold the debt you were free to sell it on to someone who was.

All's fair and well when you're already a well-established entity. But what if you want to finance your own business from the ground up? You could always request a loan from a local Jew - as they were immune to anti-usury laws and dogma because of a healthy dose of mental backflips and some cognitive dissonance, since it was reasoned that they could lend to "non-Israelites" [28].

Your local Shylock wouldn't be all that difficult to find, he'd sit by a table (called "banca" in old Italian, which is where we get the word for "bank") with a green tablecloth, which he'd use as a desk or exchange counter [29]. But he would charge you extremely high interest rates, sometimes even triple that of a modern credit card[46]!

If, nowadays, it's considered bad business acumen to fund one's business

---

46 In 1421, for example, Jews in Gubbio could charge 50 percent on loans smaller than one florin, 45 percent on loans between one and seven florins, and 33 percent on loans larger than seven florins [30]. Whereas at the time of writing, in the United States, the national average APR on new credit card is reaching around 15.59 percent.

via credit cards, as the debt increases exponentially and one's business does not, imagine what it was back then. Not only that, but it wasn't only private individuals participating in these predatory loans. Kings, aristocrats and even governments have been known to incur such debt.

It is not unreasonable to assume that part of the spiel of kicking Jews out of geographic areas was simply effective statesmanship - a purely rational and secular leader might've just as well fostered this hatred for purely selfish gains. Imagine if the United States' entire national debt were held by companies akin to Mastercard or American Express, and this debt is non-transferable. Wouldn't it make perfect sense to kick them out when you're about to go broke and invite them back in a generation or two later when you need capital? Americans would be nonplussed, or even happy of the whole affair, as their own debts would be wiped clean by eliminating the main credit card holders and the rulers would have a clean slate. Governments as far back as Babylon have been wiping out debt for the sake of gaining popularity [31].

Hence, far from being a bigoted move, fuelling and fostering anti-Semitic beliefs every so often might've made both business and political sense to some governments. As, when you kick them out, you automatically get to default on your loans with few to no immediate repercussions. Later on, when your capital markets suffer from illiquidity, you can be seen as magnanimous and invite them back in.

Modern day anti-Semitism might thus be the cultural equivalent of an appendix - a once useful adaptation which has outlasted its intended use, and is likely to cause problems further down the line. Things like Nazism could hence be seen as the cultural equivalent of a ruptured appendix.

But I regress, fuelling your business ventures on sky-high interest rates is inadvisable and therefore it's unsurprising that other means of finance started coming into widespread use. Joint-stock companies, wherein each shareholder owns company stock in proportion to how many stocks they own, quickly started becoming popular in the age of discovery. These stocks are freely traded and fluctuate in value depending on people's enthusiasm to own a part of the business; as a purely theoretical example, someone might own 25% of a company but have paid $1 million for this share, whilst someone might own exactly the same amount of the same company but paid $1.45 million for the stocks. What matters is the proportion of the total stocks available that they own, not the price that they paid for them, to determine what percentage of the profits might be paid to them.

This type of financial technology is perfect for when you want to do something far beyond the economic capabilities of a single individual. Paying for a fleet of ships would be prohibitively expensive for any one individual, by way of example the Spanish Armada of 1588, consisting of 130 warships and converted merchant ships, cost 10 million ducats [32]. Just to put this into perspective, the Spanish crown's annual income from American mines was 2 million ducats in the 1580s [33]. But just for fun, if we take the gold value of a ducat[47], and calculate it on a per ship basis, at the time of writing, it would cost about $11.1 million per ship[48].

With such extraordinary price tags, it shouldn't really surprise anyone that there was a strong incentive to pool risk. Hence, the Dutch in the early seventeenth century, who mainly depended on trade for their survival, expanded their commodity market to also be a stock market, in particular to sell stocks in the pseudo-government backed *United East India Company* [35]. The literature regarding whether this was the first-ever traded stock is a bit contentious, as you could well say the Romans had similar endeavours, or even further back the Assyrians had limited liability joint ventures [36][37]. Suffice it to say that it was then that trading pieces of paper that represented small fragments of a company became more commonplace, and society prospered because of it.

---

47 The Venetian ducat contained 3.545 grams of 99.47% fine gold, the highest purity medieval metallurgy could produce [34].

48 This calculation might seem like a bit of a stretch, but from the modern information that we have gold is an asset class that more or less maintains its proportional value, wherein the only real long-term fluctuations are in attempting to keep with inflation. As such, I would stand by in saying that this number at the very least shows the proportional price range of a merchant sailing ship, to a modern audience.

Yet, these flirtations with the world of ideas, wherein what is being traded is only tangentially-related to reality, had a profound effect on the fortunes of people. Fortunes could be made and lost in a day with a single wise decision; at least in theory everyone had the capacity to gain the financial influence of lords. This naturally whetted people's appetite for more. After all, once you've managed to scrounge up enough money to build a fleet, you want to safeguard yourself from the negatives of a Black Swan.

Over a hundred years, far away from the accident of the Titanic, and with our dependence on air travel as our main means of long-haul passenger travel, we are prone to forget the perils of the sea. But, historically-speaking, the sea was no joke; if you were unlucky the best you could hope for were long delays (just ask Odysseus), and on the grimmer end of the spectrum you could be delayed and face death (just ask Magellan).

Nevertheless, as an investor in these ventures, you don't want to incur such risks - after all, humans have an innate loss-aversion bias, as we discussed in PI-Ch6. The mathematics needed to accurately calculate statistical insurance payouts were at least a couple centuries away from the Dutch Republic's heyday. This would eventually be developed by two clergymen wishing to calculate the proportional sum of a fund a minister's widow is entitled to have after her husband's death by using actuarial and financial principles, rather than mercantile gambling [38]. However, that didn't stop speculators from buying and selling future deliveries of commodities in the Dutch Republic, which were often years in advance, maybe accidentally showing the dirty truth about people's willingness to gamble even without a veneer of mathematical legitimacy [39].

As such, it didn't take long for this speculation philosophy to transfer onto the stock exchange. In time, all manner of economic innovations started becoming commonplace - short sales, forward contracts, option contracts and other transactions all existed despite the fact that many had been officially outlawed since they began appearing [40].

With these financial contracts, which are nowadays known as derivatives, you "derive" the underlying value of the financial instrument from some characteristic of the stock. For example, call options sell you the ability, but not the obligation, to buy an asset at a certain price at a certain point in the future. As such, if the price happens to go way beyond what you agreed on, you stand to earn a lot of money. Put succinctly, by owning a call option for a stock, you can technically stand to earn from the company without ever owning any of its shares, as the option itself has a fluctuating monetary value.

Imagine that I have $100 in a stock; theoretically speaking, through mathematical and financial alchemy, I can create $500+ worth of financial instruments that bet on particular aspects of these stocks (whether it goes up or down, when it does so, with what speed and so on). I won't go in depth regarding this, as it gets incredibly complicated (to the point where modern companies have to hire Nobel laureates to make head or tails of the instruments). What I will say though, is that the responsible use of such financial instrument can be used as a proto-insurance to cap the maximum losses you could incur, or conversely they can amplify by several times the amount you can stand to lose or win in any market fluctuation when used irresponsibly. In other words, every $1 that is objectively provable to exist in the real world, can be used as an anchor point to create several times that on paper, by betting on characteristics of the stock and then betting on those bets with ever increasing amounts.

This can get ridiculous in time, as you're betting on assumptions that are based on other assumptions, each layer getting progressively more disconnected from the real world. Hence each new financial instrument invented, which was based on previous financial innovations, becomes progressively more separate from real world occurrences. This eventually reaches the point where you can make or lose money on events which are decades or microseconds away from occurring - welcome to planet finance.

Fast forward a couple of centuries and speculating on castles in the air, that are decades away from ever being constructed, is neither illegal nor rare to do so. To the point where planet Earth is dwarfed by the sheer might and size of planet finance. However, despite our very best efforts, we have yet to come close to cracking the secret art of prophecy - ask two modern economists of their expectations on the future, and you'll get three answers. What happens is that we simply do not have enough information, nor the capacity to process the data, to accurately predict the future beyond stating banalities. As such, much as a man locked in a sensory deprivation room, even the faintest noise can set our imagination flying; and we make mountains of molehills, extrapolating from tiny timeframes into the far-flung future.

The more time passes, the more reality seems to be an active hindrance on our financial models, as we build ever more fantastical palaces in the air. Yet, for all our attempts at trying to control the indomitable Black Swans, we're still very much at their mercy - Newton well showed us that for every action, there's and opposite reaction. Reality neither cares about nor understands our models, and the unconscious mechanisms will continue to operate unmolested, fundamentally changing our societies as they churn along. As we'll see in the next chapter, even something as seemingly far-fetched as a plague with the potential of wiping out humanity, has the potential of altering something as random and deeply personal as how your dating life operates seven hundred years later.

3 - A Tale of Capital and Labour: How Economic Considerations Change Society

"Where there is politics or economics, there is no morality."
- Karl Wilhelm Friedrich Schlegel

Once upon a time, in a land of castles, knights and kings, a disease overran the land. This malady, which would come to be known as the Black Death, had all the signs of a Biblical plague. It's not without reason that it was likened to the coming of the Apocalypse, as one of the strains of the plague could kill a man within a day half of infection [41].

The world had all the signs of coming to an end, as it seemed to have fallen from grace. After all, between 950-1250 CE there had been a warm period, unlike anything humanity has experienced in the last 2,000 years [42]. Populations boomed, foodstuffs increased and the environment was so pleasant that you could have vineyards and wine production in what we now know as rainy old England [43].

Yet, this abruptly changed, thereabouts 1275 CE, the world entered into what is now known as "the Little Ice Age," which would last well until 1850 CE [44]. In this new era, food production wasn't as easily achieved. Arable land decreased, and thus only the most fertile earth was now worth tilling.

As one can imagine, this was a crisis of Malthusian proportions, where crops continued to fail and people grew hungry. Society grew so desperate by the Great Famine of 1315 that many resorted to becoming brigands, and reports of mass deaths, cannibalism and infanticide became all too common. Suffice to say that the fairy-tale of Hansel and Gretel, where children are abandoned in the woods due to the parent's poverty and a witch subsequently tries to eat them, actually had its origins during this time [45]. Far from a quirky and fantastic tale, there were people who experienced this in real life.

Family, society, life and even God seemed to lose significance in those times, for I can only imagine what it does to one to live through such strife. Hence, it's been argued that many of the heresies that would come to haunt the papacy in the future, were born then [46]. What good are the Pope and God when Hell is empty and all the devils are here?

After all, the devils look out for their own, for in a few years more - in 1337 - we have the beginnings of the Hundred Years War; where if there ever was a time when chivalry and honour stopped being considerations in the battlefield, it was then. This was no longer a conflict where you're likelier to die in a jousting tournament accident, than on the battlefield, as used to happen in the twelfth and thirteenth century [47]. No, this was a conflict where surviving was the prize itself.

Furthermore, if famine, war and having your whole way of life destroyed wasn't enough, the worst was yet to come in the form of the Black Death. For some time, traders had been aware and dreading the incursion of this plague in Europe, as they had seen its effects when they ventured to the kingdoms of the far East. I imagine the feeling was like being blindfolded and placing your head on the chopping block - you know that your time is limited, as any second now the executioner will let his axe fall, but you don't quite know how much time you have.

Legend says that in 1348, in the siege of the city of Caffa (present-day Feodosia on the Crimean Peninsula on the Black Sea), the Genoese held steadfastly against the Golden Horde army. Much as in other times in history, war proved the perfect breeding ground for diseases and among them was the Black Death. Hence the attacking Tatars were debilitated by the plague and lost interest in the siege, yet before they retreated, they catapulted the corpses of their comrades into the city. In the words of Italian notary Gabriele De'Mussi, the chronicler of this incident, "What seemed like mountains of dead were thrown into the city, and the Christians could not hide or flee or escape from them, although they dumped as many of the bodies as they could in the sea" [48].

Supposedly, it was this contact with the cadavers that first infected the Genoese with the plague. Modern scholars debate this, given the characteristics of the disease, but if this were the case, then this was among the first and most effective biological attacks in human history. As the infected sailors eventually left for Constantinople, this might've allowed the disease passage to the rest of Europe, Africa and even parts of the Americas, but this chronicle of events is also up for debate.

Regardless of how it happened though, the disease killed off 30 to 60% of Europe's total population in a handful of years, and this changed the destiny of the world as a whole [49]. Be you king or beggar, it mattered not, as Death embraced all with equal fervour. You might've noticed that in my retelling of this tragedy I mentioned specific dates, which is somewhat uncharacteristic of this book as a whole. I'm not intending for you to be able to regurgitate a collection of random facts and dates to go along with it. Instead, I want you to gain a way of interpreting history. In either case, the years were written to highlight just how quickly it is that someone's entire world can come crashing down.

Almost a single one of those sequence of events (the change in weather, the famines, the violence or the plague) would be enough to drive someone to the edge, but it all happened within a lifetime. Owing to the limitations of our human point of view, we underestimate the fragility of the society we inhabit. Someone having been born in 1300 could've easily lived through all of these, and had a truly horrible hand with which to play the game of life.

Yet, it stands as a true testament of the human spirit that not only did Europe overcome such threats, but carved the world into its own image. The survivors who came out of this horror were greeted with a world comprised of completely different dynamics: whereas before the plebs had been plentiful and hadn't had much bargaining power, the appalling loss of life turned the tables [50].

Once the plague had passed, people started concentrating in cities, as it made little sense to remain in a town that had recently become little more than a glorified cemetery. Thus, the rural backwaters were essentially forced to come together in larger entities to try to pick up the pieces. Furthermore, the large death toll increased social mobility and opportunities for all involved. The Black Death seemed to have a disproportionate effect on the young and hence in the guilds and religious institutions, which used to have their membership heavily restricted to certain castes of people, started being less choosy, which admittedly reduced training requirements.

The fact of the matter is that people were in short supply and everyone was vying to keep what few workers there were with incentives, rapid promotion, etc. Eastern European kingdoms that were much less affected by the plague doubled down on feudalism and violently dissuaded anyone from thinking otherwise [51]. Other nations, like England, tried to control the price of wages [52]. Yet, when push comes to shove, contrarian edicts will wither when faced with the momentum of reality. As such, the proportional increase in the cost of labour created an economic motivation to substitute human labour-intensive work with oxen and similar labour-saving techniques, technologies or animals. It is this sort of technologically-driven mindset, which would eventually give rise to the Industrial Revolution.

In history, the value of a human life has always been in direct contradiction with the availability of other people and the ease with which their labour can be replaced by other means. When human labour becomes comparatively cheap, there is no incentive to invest in capital and vice versa. There is always a balance between these two inputs, and it bears keeping in mind when thinking about where a society is heading if it starts over-relying on one of them.

A good case study of this phenomenon is Japan in the nineteenth century. Whereas, in the 1600s, Japan had had a strong manufacturing industry, especially in paper products, weapons and cotton textiles, by the 1800s it had grown to be technologically stagnant, almost entirely dependent on human labour. Horses and cattle were very rare owing to space restrictions, and human labour was comparatively inexpensive as there had been a population boom. Hence, at a certain point, the Japanese had collectively decided against focusing on technology, which made them lag in trade and consequently they turned inwards and isolationist [53].

Much the same could've happened with Europe, after escaping the killing fields of the late Middle Ages. After all, the population size eventually recovered, which decreased the proportional value of human labour. Yet, as of 1492, Europe discovered a pressure release valve in the form of the Americas and other colonies. In general, the age of discovery and colonization allowed entire nations to throw their excess population elsewhere in the world.

Oftentimes, these new territories had the added benefit of getting rid of unwanted groups. Famously, Australia was used as a British penal colony for decades, but it's far from the only one. An often-overlooked fact is that many who went to live in America were convicts. Even as late as the 18th Century, convicts represented a quarter of all British immigrants to the Americas [54]. During the same century, the French also sent prisoners to their own American colonies, in what is now known as Louisiana [55].

This is not even mentioning the criminals who decided to try their luck in the colonies out of their own volition. Hence, you have phenomenon like the Republic of Pirates in Nassau in 1706 which, for about twelve years, housed a quasi-piratic government that terrorised the Caribbean Sea through their theft and aggression [56]. In its time, it was perhaps the most brazen of such strongholds, but there were others like Port Royal and Tortuga, which also aided and provided safe haven to criminals.

Going to the colonies was often a one-way trip; therefore, it was only done by the more desperate or adventuresome souls. If you were a lord of high import, for example, or someone with much to lose, you would rarely take the risk of such uncomfortable and time-consuming endeavours, unless forced by circumstances or more powerful individuals to do so. Yet, many people were so willing to leave the old continent behind that they became indentured servants, where they essentially got an advance on future wages to pay for their passage the Americas, as such, becoming a slave in all but name until they paid off their debt [57]. Nevertheless, at the end of the service, you would receive a hundred acres of land, as was your right as a citizen of the New World [58]. Granted, the system was prone to abuses and often just made the rich even richer, but the headright system attracted many people.

This mass exodus would prove vital, for without it Malthus' spectre would reappear and the Japanese fate would happen in Europe. Economic historian Niall Ferguson put it best [59]:

> *"Between the early 1600s and the 1950s, more than 20 million people left the British Isles to begin new lives across the seas. Only a minority ever returned. No other country in the world came close to exporting so many of its inhabitants. In leaving Britain, the early emigrants risked not merely their life savings but their very lives. Their voyages were never without hazard; their destinations were often unhealthy and inhospitable. Yet without millions of such tickets – some purchased voluntarily, some not – there could have been no British Empire. For the indispensable foundation of the Empire was mass migration: the biggest in human history. This Britannic exodus changed the world [...] For most of the emigrants, the New World spelt liberty – religious freedom in some cases, but above all economic freedom."*

Or at least this was the case in British Colonies, whereas in Latin American colonies the main landowners were either the original conquerors (conquistadores), and their descendants, or the Church [60]. This obviously did little to incentivise the Iberian public at large to move to the Americas, and therefore Spaniards in Latin American societies became little more than rent-seekers at the top of their racial caste pyramid until they were ousted from their seat of power with the independence movements in the early 1800s, whilst the Iberian Peninsula was still reeling from Napoleonic occupation.

Nevertheless, even to this day, when in Latin America, social status is often implicitly determined by skin colour, not because of any legal rulings (as with South African apartheid), but simply because the associations with wealth and racial class haven't dissipated in the last 200 years. It's precisely this rent-seeking lack of competition that has been blamed for Latin America's lacklustre development track when compared to the likes of North American territories.

Stagnant societies will produce stagnant economies with stagnant results. Dynamic societies will evolve and adapt whilst creating novel means of organizing industry. It's no wonder that people were attracted to North American promises of potential wealth and Protestant work ethic ethos, where if one worked hard enough one would be rewarded. Thus, Britain quickly became the main contender for the best place to have an industrial revolution - not only did it have the population release valve, but it was materially benefiting from the wealth of its colonies (both as an importer and exporter of its goods), which meant that it had much higher growth potential than its peers.

Even after its independence, the United States remained an immigrant's haven brimming with opportunity. For most of its history, it was a territory with excess capital and a chronic lack of manpower to capitalise on it. Without immigrant labour, it seems unlikely that the American industrial revolution would have been achieved at the same pace, scale, and profitability that it did. If one includes up to the third generation of immigrants, then there were core industries that were 80% worked on by foreign labour in the late 19th century. It was this increase in the population which paved the road from an artisan workshop economy, to a modern factory system [61].

The decline of the small-scale artisan workshop also changed the underlying social fabric; as factories are mammoth enterprises, they require large populations of people, and initially lacking in cheap means of transport, the employees will have an incentive to live as close as humanly possible to their place of work. Sometimes companies catered to this need directly and created "company towns" where most of the infrastructure and housing were company-owned [62]. In most cases, there was little need for a central planner to intervene so directly as businesses tended to go to pre-existing social hubs to enjoy the "network effects."

For that is precisely the point of a city, from an economical point of view: to maximise the economies of scale. It only makes sense to be close to your suppliers, as you reduce transportation costs and you can benefit from the collective industry. Same applies to the public at large, as the density of cities allows for the creation of "social tribes," which we'll discuss in Part VII when we talk about consumerism, for now let's simply say that higher densities of people make supplying them cheaper, and hence more profitable.

As such, when providing a service or good, like public lighting, gluten-free shops or sewer systems, it becomes trivially inexpensive to supply larger groups of people, than if you were attempting to do the same in smaller and more isolated communities. For example, London's sewer systems were built several times larger than they needed to be even a hundred years later, because it was proportionally inexpensive to adapt the plans in such a way. Thus, the original system is still in use today, whereas if they'd used the original plans, they would've overflowed by 1960. In the words of Bazalgette, the civil engineer responsible for that decision, "Well, we're only going to do this once and there's always the unforeseen." [63]

Such largess is only affordable through the comparative cheapness of projects, through economies of scale (as it makes little difference whether you're supplying 1,000 people or 1,001), and because of this there has always been an incentive to make cities as dense as possible. The solution to this is obvious, instead of spreading out and encroaching on the outskirts and slums, one ought to build upwards. But this, in turn, has its limits. Before the invention and adoption of metal-framed buildings (which permitted thinner walls, whilst increasing overall strength), the powered elevator, or technologies in heating, lighting, ventilation or sanitation the proposition of a skyscraper as we know it is unfeasible and impractical [64]. In fact, they were often dangerous as well, given that they were prone to fire and collapsing under their own weight; so much so that Roman Emperor Augustus instituted legislation to ensure that residential buildings could not be higher than around twenty metres [65]. Even this wasn't enough though, as Nero, a future successor to the throne, would further reduce this maximum height by a further 14% [66].

In addition, before the age of motorised vehicles, people would want their economic activities to happen within walking distance. It's these separate forces - the desire to live close to the action, whilst also being able to build comfortable and dense living quarters - which create a mechanism by which the closer a plot of land is to the epicentre of the economic activity, the more desirable it is. Hence, there tends to be a correlation between the age of a city, the cost of its housing and how easily you are to be able to walk somewhere in the urban sprawl. The rich would naturally want all of life's creature comforts in their orbit and thus the city centres of the old world can cater to most caprices and vices. Among these creature comforts, there is an inbuilt desire for clean air, thus European cities often have a "good" west end and "poor" east end, which likely comes due to the prevailing south-west wind which moves airborne pollutants downwind, making the western areas of cities preferable to the eastern ones [67].

In contrast, newer cities are often designed with the idea that the rich can afford, and find it practical, to live in more pleasant and isolated accommodation where they wouldn't want to be bothered with pollution, crime and noise in their free time. This mindset eventually trickled down to the middle class, and therefore we have the existence of suburbs. Nowadays, with an emphasis on cleaner air, gentrification, a reduction of criminality, etc, affluent enclaves can even be found in modern cities. Yet the traces of the flight of the rich from larger communities can still be seen in cities like New York where there are settlements like Greenwich, the Hamptons, etc catering to the super rich, which are close by to the action, but not so close that its inhabitants are ever bothered by the existence of the plebs, unless they wish to be so.

This dynamic though is precisely what makes cities so bizarre - in the same city block you can have billionaires and street bums sharing common space and nobody thinks of this the least bit odd. Furthermore, it shouldn't really surprise you that odd behaviours start arising when you give people perceived anonymity in a crowd. In the words of Oscar Wilde: "Man is least himself when he talks in his own person. Give him a mask, and he will tell you the truth."

The social mechanisms used to keep people in check are robbed of power when applied in a large society. When a society exceeds Dunbar's number by orders of magnitude, we start thinking that we can get away with antisocial or unorthodox behaviour. Hence, where families and communities used to be able to control such intimate things as sexual relationships, the city as a whole tends to be ambivalent to what we do with our time, as long as we're financially productive.

Because of this non-judgemental attitude, the people of the early twentieth centuries began attempting to satisfy desires that had, more often than not, been suppressed because of community expectations. A good example of such emergent phenomena is the invention of dating in the early 1900s in the United States[49][68].

For the first time in recorded history, large groups of free men and women were thrust into spaces without chaperones or nosy snitches, and biology did what it is supposed to do and paired these new urban dwellers together. Yet, the old guard didn't quite know what to make of this. To the establishment, this whole new "dating" phenomenon seemed to be a clever legal loophole for prostitution; after all, women were seemingly exchanging sexual favours for gifts, food, drinks, entertainment, etc. Add to it the fact that it was overwhelmingly upper-class men courting less affluent females, and you have the beginnings of a controversy.

It didn't much help matters when, during this time, vice commissions sent police and undercover investigators to look into places where people went on "dates." Things only got more ridiculous from there; by the summer of 1910, the Bureau of Investigation, the predecessor of the FBI, launched an investigation into brothels around the country. This resulted in the agency

---

49 For the next few paragraphs, I'll almost exclusively be using the historical information found in Moira Weigel's great book *Labor of Love: The Invention of Dating*. Nevertheless, for obvious length constraints, I will not supply page numbers for specific statements, as I will be jumping back and forth from idea to idea, and in a very abbreviated fashion, thus making the attempt somewhat foolhardy and extremely impractical. If you are interested in this particular aspect of modern life, I do recommend the book in its entirety, despite the fact that the writer comes from a somewhat Marxist feminist perspective, it's still an enjoyable read.

warning women that dating strangers could lead them down the path of dishonour, venereal diseases and even death.

Despite what the older people in society seemed to want to happen, the dating meme was here to stay. Not only that, but it paired up with other memes like "capitalism" and affected economic consumption patterns. Very quickly, there arose a marketplace that catered to the "dating lifestyle" with services and products such as singles bars, romantic date venues, movies, books, television shows, jewellery, candy, and even dating coaches. This is a market that came into existence contrary to what the prudes and conservatives wanted but, as more often than not happens in history, biology trounced edicts from authority figures. Once you eliminate the means of enforcing an ideology, humans tend to take the path of least resistance to satisfy their needs and desires.

In other words, it is the balance of the factors of production (land, capital and human labour), which often shape how our society is structured. By altering the ratio and/or importance of any of these three elements, you will unleash forces that would have otherwise been kept in check by the already established social order. As such, social norms and customs change so as to better adapt to the new normal.

And that, my dear readers, is why the Black Death over 700 years ago is responsible for your sex life today. In brief, it was the large death toll in medieval Europe, which decreased the availability of people and thus increased the price of labour, which created an incentive for automation. This automation was eventually taken full advantage of in some of the colonies, which incentivised immigration from all over the world, and this increased the populations of urban centres. Furthermore, in attempting to create more efficient cities due to financial considerations, it increased the density of these settlements. Finally, it's this density which created a veil of anonymity where people were more willing to violate social taboos, which gave rise to many odd behaviours that attempted to satisfy needs and desires, among them was dating - the rest, is history.

In a way, economic necessity and geography are destiny, as these unconscious mechanisms shape our incentives and how we cope with our ancient motivations. It is impossible to understand society without understanding the context under which it developed. Having said all this, we would also be remiss in ignoring the effect of an idea on a society. Hence, for the next few chapters, we will be discussing the symbiotic relationship between how environment creates culture and how memes affect the environment.

4 - The Communication Revolution: From Silence to a Cacophony

> *"Being flooded with information doesn't mean we have the right information or that we're in touch with the right people."*
>
> *- Bill Gates*

During most of history, ideologies were often dictated from a top-down approach. A city would have town criers, which let the official version of events be known and spread. Whosoever didn't tow the party line was either unable to pass on their memes, or worse still, when they succeeded, they risked the ire of the cabals in power.

Access to a mass audience was limited to elites, and required considerable resources to accomplish. This was a rich and powerful man's game. Hence, when you began a meme battle, you better have the armies to back up your propaganda. The pen is only mightier than the sword insofar that one keeps a hand to write with. If your hand is immediately chopped off before you've even gained an audience, no number of aphorisms will save you.

This is perhaps best shown in the power struggle that followed after Julius Caesar's assassination in 44 BCE. The conspirators having been dispatched in a succession of battles, there were two contingents vying for power: Octavian, who was Caesar's rightful heir, but still young and inexperienced; and Mark Antony, arguably Caesar's right-hand man.

It originally began as little more than a disinformation campaign. Octavian was accused of being a coward as he often didn't fight his own fights [69]. His was a diplomat's soul and he usually left the violence to his close friend and general Marcus Agrippa. Mark Antony, on the other hand, was branded as a traitor to Roman values, as he was entangled in a romantic affair with Cleopatra, a foreign queen and enchantress who thought herself a goddess [70].

At first, Octavian and Mark Antony tried to rule the Roman territory amicably, but the tensions only kept increasing. By 31 BCE diplomatic relations were non-existent and they both came head to head in the Battle of Actium. Mark Antony was defeated and Octavian ruled supreme for the rest of his life.

Such was usually the state of affairs: at first, the struggle would passive-aggressively be fought by means of propaganda and, when that failed to work, violence quickly followed suit. One is maybe inclined to think that nothing much has changed, as the same sort of cycle seems to occur in internet comment sections - any discussion sufficiently long enough will eventually come down to calling the other one names and death threats.

The key difference is that the right of speech has been democratized, and is one of the most sacred values of the modern liberal Western state[50]. This did not happen overnight, if anything, it was one of the biggest and bloodiest social movements in history. One begins to see the first embers of the "communication revolution" in the mid-15th Century, with the invention of the printing press. China had invented it centuries before, but it had limited influence, partially because to be literate even in modern versions of Mandarin one requires the memorization of over 4,000 characters [71]. Compare that to, say, English with only 26 characters. Furthermore, a certain unity in fonts in Continental Europe had been achieved in the Carolingian Renaissance (c. the year 800 CE), with the Carolingian minuscule, which did away with some of the more obscure means of writing and vastly facilitated ease of learning by creating clearer standards and uniformity [72].

---

50 In the future, if the trend of labelling every different opinion as "hate speech" and thus prosecutable under the law is not stopped, that may sadly no longer be the case.

As we mentioned in PIII-Ch5 the invention and dissemination of alphabets was a distinct advantage both in providing efficiency, specificity and ease in communication, and consequently it shouldn't be much of a surprise that the printing press in languages that lacked an alphabet wouldn't be as useful.

By 1517, an insignificant priest in an even more insignificant town in the Holy Roman Empire was able to spark a revolution. Legend says Martin Luther nailed a treatise of 95 theses[51] at the All Saints' Church in Wittenberg, and this sparked such fervour that people took up his cause almost immediately. Yet to this day, if you go to Wittenberg, one can see why Germans have unironically called it a *Kuhdorf* - a cow town - where the most noteworthy thing about it are the extraordinarily good cappuccinos that a small café there has. Hence, it seems unlikely that one of the bloodiest civil wars in European history was allegedly started by the Catholic Church equivalent of a passive-aggressive roommate putting a post-it note on the fridge complaining about unwashed dishes.

Nothing Martin Luther said was actually all that novel. A hundred years before we have Jan Hus in Czechoslovakia and Savonarola in Italy a handful of decades before, who both decried the vices of the Catholic Church and got horribly tortured to death for speaking heresy.

The key difference was that this time around an "influencer," in modern parlance, didn't have to be in the same general geographic region to have his voice heard. In other words, people were able to talk shit without skin in the game, and this opened the door to increasingly dangerous memes. Thus, it's unsurprising that rulers all around Europe tried to regulate the ownership and use of printing presses, as they had the potential of causing untold social damage [73].

Whereas before you could simply kill an idea by killing the one promoting it, the printing press allowed ideas to start having a life of their own - no matter what you did, no matter whom you killed, there always seemed to be more people that had become infected by reading all the heretic pamphlets floating around.

---

51 Say that five times without getting your tongue twisted.

To further add fuel to the ongoing pile of garbage, everyone and their mother tried to take part in this social movement. At one point, Henry VIII, the King of England, wrote *The Defence of the Seven Sacraments* in opposition to Luther. Imagine how utterly ridiculous it is for a supposedly divine King to take the time to address the criticism of a random man who isn't even a citizen of any of the territories he controls[52].

Yet, I cannot throw the first stone and critique Henry VIII for engaging in such a Sisyphean endeavour. After all, I've probably spent years of my life arguing with complete strangers on the internet, for matters I felt far less passionately about than the Catholics and Protestants probably did in matters regarding the Christian faith.

In fact, I dare say that the Protestant Reformation, or indeed any large-scale religious upheaval, is a perfect storm that takes advantage of our natural predispositions. Psychological studies discussing the virality of content have come to the conclusion that anger, followed closely by awe, are the two emotions that makes someone more likely to share something [74]. In other words, the angrier or awestruck someone gets at reading something, the likelier they are to forward it.

After which, the content will undergo a game of Chinese whispers or wilful meddling, to make it even more virulent, which results in a self-perpetuating cycle; where people are awe-inspired by their deity's greatness and get angry at the lack of faith of heretics. Both parties do this, and it only gets worse with each successive generation until so much blood is spilled that both groups come to a truce, and reach a middle ground (as we discussed in PII-Ch4).

Perhaps it's a natural human compunction, much like how the desire for gossip is built into us as a means to regulate our social relationships within a community, this desire to fight and disagree with complete strangers may have a similar origin, alongside our innate tribalism and sense of superiority. It's not to say that we were designed to engage in online message boards and

---

52 Though to be fair, the modern world is even more ridiculous, given that we have world leaders duking it out on social media over absolute nonsense, but I digress.

start flame wars. It might just be a supernormal stimulus, and thus we're simply aping horribly exaggerated parodies of what our behaviour ought to be.

For all its faults, I would say that this mechanism is useful, as it creates a sense of community. Look no further than the talking statues of Italy - ancient Roman statues unearthed in the sixteenth century, which were displayed in public places and people started writing brief notes critiquing the news and people of the day. Some sources point to the fact that the first notes were little more than schoolboys taunting their teachers, yet the sites rapidly transformed into a major outlet for critiquing those in power [75]. To my eyes, this looks an awful lot like the pseudo-anonymous posts on the internet. Hence, I would argue that the desire to share mockery and irreverence was always there, but being able to do so without facing severe repercussions was the novelty; and, when a medium was found, people took to it immediately.

Those in power, popes included, were none too amused at being the butt of the jokes. They even considered throwing the original Pasquino statue into the Tiber River. Pope Adrian IV was only dissuaded when he was told that much like a frog, the statue would croak loudest in the water [76]. Showing somewhat indirectly that, even several centuries before the term was coined, people were so aware of the Streisand effect (which we discussed in PI-Ch7) that they were warning others not to fall prey to it.

Instead of causing a public relations crisis, the elite merely decided to put guards around the original Pasquino statue, which resulted in people adopting other talking statues for their amusement. Whenever they tried to kill the concept it morphed into a different beast. The hardest thing to kill is an idea, it can lie dormant for centuries or millennia, and then resurface at a moment's notice in a much deadlier form. Many fascist states, for example, are homages to the Roman Empire, what with their fetishization of eagles, militarism, aspirations at world domination, military parades, and their view that they're bringing order to a chaotic world. Imitation is, after all, the sincerest form of flattery.

In either case, the communication revolution allowed for a unique method of spreading ideas. Back in the day, you had someone barking at you the only correct way to interpret reality. Media was sorely lacking, and you more or less had to stick with what was culturally accepted and widespread. Not so after the communication revolution, as one became a master of one's own information diet.

Knowledge is power, and power corrupts. So, it's no wonder that odious ideas and disinformation are often spread for the sake of gaining influence. For instance, perhaps unbeknownst to you, I quoted the infamous murderer and terrorist "Unabomber" Ted Kaczynski two chapters ago, and framed him as an "American mathematician and philosopher" when talking about what the fall of Rome entailed. I did this, because I find many of the ideas in his manifesto quite intriguing and convincing. But had I said that these were the opinions of a terrorist and anarchist, you would've likely dismissed them out of hand because you likely don't want to even interact with those kinds of people, or their mental frameworks, for that matter. As such, I obfuscated the truth for the sake of creating a more convincing argument.

Much like the dangers of unprotected sex, you don't know where my mind has been, and what it's been exposed to. Yet, you still open yourself to be influenced by my words, which is very dangerous. I don't mean *my* words, per se, I'd say I'm mostly harmless. Possibly a bit of a provocateur, but altogether far from the worst influence out there.

Yet, in the exponentially increasing media landscape, you face an orgy of thought. You may even agree with a lot of it, but be wary as this is the backdoor of tribalism. Agreeing with someone makes you more likely to agree with them in future. Much like the salesman technique of putting a foot in the door, initially agreeing with someone makes you more susceptible to be influenced by them.

Past a certain point, when you're no longer just a passive listener, but a full-blown adherent and disciple of their own brand of thought, you may start seeing patterns and expressing behaviours which you were never meant to express. When you believe that other believers are doing it, you are likely to start behaving in that way.

When, in 1774, Goethe published a book by the name of *The Sorrows of*

Young Werther, I have my doubts that he thought his angst would be infectious. In the semi-autobiographical book, the protagonist, Werther, commits suicide as he's lovesick and cannot bear it anymore. Many people felt connected to this tale of woe, so it became fashionable to wear Werther's distinctive yellow pants and blue jackets.

Had it ended there, merely good taste would've been one more victim in the long list of history's ill-conceived fashion decisions. Yet, this quickly escalated. At one point it wasn't fashionable to simply identify with Werther, but one had to become him. Hence, society was gripped with "Werther fever", and many young men ended up committing suicide in imitation of this fictional character. This grew to such an extent that some countries banned the book, others went as far as banning the very outfit, as it was deemed too dangerous [77]. In other words, there literally was someone who was appointed as the fashion police.

The meme of copycat suicides almost seemed concerted, as if someone was pushing people in that direction. Yet this type of thinking misses the point. Much like there are animals and plants that look essentially identical to each other, despite only being very distantly genetically related and sharing no geographic territories, the same happens with memes. Convergent evolution is the phenomena of one or various animals or plants developing into similar things because they filled a similar environmental niche and consequently had to solve similar adaptation problems, which led them down a similar evolutionary path [78].

The "Werther meme" may therefore infect a mind because they're under a difficult emotional situation, and if the emotional duress is acute enough, they may come to the same inevitable conclusion. Hence, without prompting or prodding, seemingly concerted behaviours can independently come into existence without any of the actors having ever met - they just have to have a similar enough starting position and influence to be able to take that developmental path.

In other words, this is a Stand Alone Complex - a group of self-interested individuals who have no relation to each other, but who unconsciously seem to behave in a concerted manner by mimicking an ideal [79]. It's crucial to stress that the original ideal behaviour need never to have existed for it to be copied. It need only to have been thought to exist by someone for them to mimic it.

For decades, economic researchers have been baffled by the apparently random movement of the stock market. In 1988, economists David Cutler, James Poterba and Lawrence Summers tried to explain the 50 largest 1-day market movements on the S&P- 500 index from 1946 to 1987, and ended up empty-handed. They concluded that the changes were seemingly random, as they couldn't find a reason for many of them [80].

I don't believe this is the case, I believe that the Stand Alone Complex, alongside simply getting enough people that have developed a strong opinion on the price of something because of the perceived ideal, more than adequately explain "random" movements. Reason being that because of their extremist views on things they will be highly-motivated towards optimism or pessimism, irrespective of what reality actually implies. After all, as Napoleon put it "Quantity has a quality all on its own." This is not just people's perceptions altering their economic decisions and thus collectively reaching a balance which would've been impossible otherwise - this is people making profound decisions on the very meaning of their lives! With the right memes, you stand to control the future development of the world, but within reason.

The movements aren't wholly random or in control of a master puppeteer, look at any long enough historical timeline and the trend of the last few hundred years has been for economies to grow both in scope and in sheer size. No longer is the world shackled by the dogma of mercantilism, wherein it was thought that there was only a finite amount of wealth to go around. Instead, the world over has adopted the philosophy of exponential growth.

Whether this is wrong or right is up for debate. I can see strong arguments being made for both sides. Yet, the fact remains that as a post-industrial civilization we have seemingly adopted the idea that economies will develop and the numbers will continue to rise. And this collective change in mindset is extremely powerful.

The underlying culture, the mindset and mental framework under which people operate is a strong motivator for behaviour and ultimately dictates the avenues of potential development. Recall in PII-Ch2 where we discussed how an Australian aboriginal with the intellectual capacity of Newton would've been incapable of shifting the culture that surrounded him, given that there's an inadequate incentive for society to follow. Same happens in modern society, there are only so many possible developmental paths that society is willing to tolerate. The market movements analysed in the 50 largest 1-day market movements on the S&P- 500 index study may indeed have been random, but there might have been an operant framework unbeknownst to us. We're creatures of habit, and the underlying assumptions within the system affect how we ultimately behave.

Back in 2006, the World Bank published a report on the sources of wealth for the world. It determined that the richer a country becomes, the more reliant it is on sources of "intangible wealth," such as the rule of law, education and similar nebulous things. Turns out that up to 36% of the world's intangible capital is dependent on education, but high as it may seem, this is somewhat misleading as there is more at work here [81].

Firstly, there's the fact that the study itself admits that "schooling level per person constitutes an imperfect measure of human capital, since it does not take into account the quality of education of those trained, nor other types of human capital investment such as on-the-job training"; hence, the broad term of *education* is a hodgepodge which includes everything from having watched educational YouTube videos to getting life advice from your grandpa. Life is the grandest school of all, and we ignore its lessons at our peril.

Secondly, in 2004, researchers George Psacharopoulos and Harry Patrinos showed that the poorer a country is, the more it benefits with each dollar spent on education when compared to richer countries. The interesting thing is that the more advanced the schooling level that they are willing to fund, the less return that there is for each dollar spent. In other words, regardless of how rich a country is, the smaller the return that they get for funding someone's education with each additional year. Hence investing in education is the most profitable, when your country is poor and largely uneducated [82].

Thirdly, the study points out that Americans have access to up to ten times more intangible capitals as Mexicans. As such, a Mexican crossing the border can instantaneously quadruple his economic productivity. This does not magically happen because he leaves behind the scent of tacos and breathes in the bald eagle scented air of America and instantly becomes enlightened with business knowhow. Nothing of the sort, it's just that on crossing the border he has clearer rules, smoother institutions, rule of law, etc.

In other words, whilst certainly playing a role, traditional academic attainment is not as important for the development of one's nation as one would like to think. Technology, freedom, a strong legal system and lack of corruption play a much larger role in determining this advancement. Education often does not necessarily occur in the classroom, and neither should we fault ourselves for it. After all, it was curiosity and necessity which first led us out of the caves and into the fields, not a lecture on agriculture.

This curiosity and necessity were what pulled us from serfdom. Through the shocks of horrific pandemics, we relearnt the value of life and learned not to take it for granted. Yet, with the progressive erosion of artificial hierarchies we went to the opposite extreme and started believing that everyone's opinions had the same worth. In the next chapter we shall discuss how it is that access to higher levels of material wealth and mass communication means created a desire for a more egalitarian society.

5 - Vox Populi: Democracy and the End of Slavery

> *"The best argument against democracy is a five-minute conversation with the average voter."*
>
> *- Winston Churchill*

Over the last two hundred years, since the independence of the United States, we've seen an unprecedented ascent and widespread adoption of enlightenment era democratic values. Along with the widespread acceptance of these values, we've seen an increasing fetishization of Hellenic culture as it's perceived that Greeks were the inventors and protectors of democracy itself.

Yet, as is often the case in these co-options of history for political purposes, reality does have a kernel of truth, but it's blown out of proportions, and nuance goes along with it. Firstly, the Greeks were not the first to come up with the idea of group consensus as a means of organizing a society. At the risk of sounding like a broken record, I'll give that honour to hunter-gatherers before they'd surpassed Dunbar's number. When your society is that small, even if a leader naturally emerges through his sheer charisma and capabilities, nobody can truly risk upsetting a large percentage of their population and thus they often revert back to attempting to keep the majority satisfied [83]. Nevertheless, as we discussed in Part III, when a society creates enough surplus and there can be a specialisation of labour, there's an incentive for thievery and thuggery. As such, the warlord who happens to eliminate their competition and establish regional dominance becomes the de facto ruler, who only really steals through taxation at regular intervals. This is the inherent mechanism that usually incentivised monarchies and small groups of elites over group consensus governance.

Hence, historically speaking, democracy is an anomaly in the grand scheme of things, and it usually arises with a certain level of stability and private property rights. The Greeks understood this, and thus for them the main factor to categorise governmental styles was the degree to which the rulers were able to exert control over the ruled. In the Greek world, there were broadly two types of societies, irrespective of whether it was controlled by one or the many [84]:

- ***Eunomiê*** (Order; labelled by the prefix *eu-* meaning good) - where vices and excesses are curtailed through legal frameworks.
- ***Dusnomiê*** (Chaos; labelled by the prefix *dus-* meaning bad) - where one does not interfere with the natural balance of things through legal constraints, regardless of whether it results in a negative or positive outcome.

As to where democracy fell on this spectrum; it largely depends on whom you asked. I would imagine that the likes of the statesman Pericles, whose legacy for cultural advancements is almost peerless in world history, would argue that it is certainly a controlled and beneficial affair. Yet, on the other end of the spectrum, we have very staunch and renowned critics; like Aristotle who likened democracy to a "mob rule," or Plato whose ideal government was a totalitarian quasi-communist state with strict hierarchies and no potential for class mobility, regardless of individual aptitudes.

Be that as it may, *Dêmokratia* originally stood for the people's collective capacity to do things in the public realm [85]. This was done under the principle of *Isonomia*, or a citizen's equality under the law. The idea of majority rule was an intentionally pejorative diminution, urged by democracy's critics. After all, it took over two thousand years, until the Corsican Republic (1755–1769), for there to be something approaching universal suffrage, and almost two hundred years more before it became commonplace [86]. Before that, there were heavy restrictions on whom was allowed to vote, based on sex, religion, social class, wealth level, age, etc.

On first instance, these restrictions might just seem like crass bigotry, but they had a reason for existing. Inherently, these restrictions favour the status quo, as they heavily weigh in favour of individuals who stand to lose from a dramatic change. In other words, limiting suffrage ensures that all participants have skin in the game and won't be willing to overturn the apple cart for short-term gains.

Yet, modernity has done away with most of these restrictions, favouring instead a more inclusive approach. However, the relaxation of these restrictions didn't happen at a random interval, much the same as with the widespread abolition of slavery. I very much think these developments are very closely linked to the rise of capitalism and private property rights.

As we saw in PV-Ch3, the rapid reduction of the total population during the late Middle Ages increased the proportional value of labour. This gave the average worker more leverage and, in time, economic power, which created the incentive for increased automation. This is crucial, for we must remember that democratic decisions do not only happen in the voting booth; we vote every single day with our wallets for the world we want to see.

At times our decisions may be as banal as whether we want Pepsi instead of Coke, but at others, our momentary economic decisions will have long-lasting consequences. For example, if you support "dirty energy," such as fossil fuels or coal, you might be tacitly voting for a world without the Maldives; since, due to the impact of dirty energy on climate change, they run the risk of getting swallowed by rising sea levels. Far from trivial, our economic decisions have consequential effects on our world. I even dare say that our day-to-day decisions in regards to our economic behaviour have more of a direct effect on the world than whether we actually vote or not. Politics requires compromise to get anything done, whilst money is often unfettered power and its use causes immediate and palpable change.

In either case, with higher labour costs the average employed man could afford finer things in life and had a greater influence on the direction in which society developed, which created a whole market to cater to this growing demand. For instance, the restaurant as we know it was born from economic pressures wherein clientele wished for higher comfort and variety than you could find in a tavern. Furthermore, the French Revolution gave the final push for the invention of the luxury restaurant. As all of a sudden, chefs for the grand estates were left jobless, given that their employers had recently left France in a hurry or were killed at the guillotine. As time progressed, it was ever more difficult to find nobles to cook for, as aristocrats with their heads still attached were in short supply. Eventually, this meant that many chefs had to cater to less affluent clientele to survive, thus creating the modern luxury restaurant where people could feel like a lord for a fraction of the price due to economies of scale [87].

During this time, wherein Europe exited medievalism, the consumer was better off with higher wages, but the producers were not so happy about the whole affair. Hence, there was an incentive to circumvent paying workers through two means - slavery and further industrialization. Slavery was commonplace for most of human history, and despite the best efforts of many people, it remained a fixture of most societies until it came to an abrupt and altogether unexpected end during the Industrial Revolution.

Of course, I am painting with broad brushstrokes - that's my speciality after all. But, owning human beings to make use of their labour has been a practice as old as civilization itself. It doesn't necessarily have to have the inhuman veneer of shackles and whips for the wealthy or nobility to profit from your bondage. For instance, all the way back in Babylon you could use yourself as collateral for loans. Indeed, Babylonian society might have been more concerned with property rights than any modern notional consideration of human rights [88]. Upon defaulting on your debt, you temporarily forfeited your freedom, much in the same way that Europeans did to fund their passage to the New World several millennia later.

Admittedly, despite the fact that they often had a high mortality rate, indentured servitude and debt bondage were different than your run-of-the-mill slavery. Reason being that their owners still implicitly acknowledged the victim's humanity, and they might still be subject to certain legal protections. Compare that to slaves who were property and had no legal recourse, or hope for a better life (unless their masters were feeling particularly generous).

Property-slaves were subject to the same financial considerations that any modern business owner would be intimately acquainted with, such as depreciation or write-offs. For example, in the eighteenth century, the Barbados plantation owner Edward Littleton devised the rule of thumb that for every hundred slaves one would need to buy eight or ten a year 'to keep up his stock' due to mortality rates [89]. In an accounting book, this is no different than planning for machine breakdowns or outdated technology.

At its core, the institution of slavery died thanks to capitalism; as there came a time when owning people was simply not cost-effective when compared to paying people wages for running the easily-sabotaged machines. Traditional slavery works best with labour intensive, yet dull, tasks that are easily monitored - say picking cotton. If the task becomes more complicated or is very fragile to sabotage, it becomes expensive to monitor slaves, since they might jeopardize the whole operation by literally throwing a wrench in the works - or as the grandfather of economics Adam Smith put it: "the work done by freemen comes cheaper in the end than that performed by slaves." [90] [53]

Slavers participating in the transatlantic trade in the decades prior to the advent of the Industrial Revolution had a profit margin averaging between 8% to 10% [92]. Which, frankly, doesn't seem to me to be that profitable considering the emotional toll, safety risk and effort involved in the affair. I mean nowadays those numbers would barely equal the returns of passive index investors, and that's despite both increased market efficiency and market regulation. Nevertheless, truth be told, there might not have been much on offer for an uneducated

---

53 In ancient Rome, there existed business ventures run by educated slaves, but given the extreme freedom necessary for effective business operations, the slaves had to be motivated with the promise of freedom, and possibly partnership. As such, the freed slaves often became masters of the business and often bought their own slaves [91].

common man in the Georgian era with remotely those profit margins.

Hence, the slavers might have gone into it purely for the desire of greater profit than they could otherwise achieve. But this too began to disappear given to the downward pressures on their profit margins due to plantation born slaves decreasing the demand for new bodies from Africa and increasing automation requiring fewer people to accomplish the same tasks. Before long, they might have barely been able to make ends meet. Eventually, purely out of economic considerations, potential clients may simply decide not to bother with importing, or even keeping, slaves. Instead, they might decide to hire employees, which doesn't only improve their bottom lines but also empowers people who might have previously been marginalised or had to compete with rock bottom prices.

Because of this, over time everyone is better off with fatter wallets. With wealth comes power and freedom. As such, the people will use said freedom in ways the government doesn't like. Therefore, technology and property rights are inherently a democratizing force. Or, as Peruvian economist Hernando de Soto put it: "Property rights will eventually lead to democracy, because you can't sustain a market-oriented property system unless you provide a democratic system. That's the only way investors can feel secure." [93] A well-developed economy necessitates the just rule of law, without states of exception, wherein the ruler is bound to follow higher principles than his own authority. Otherwise, one's personal and property rights are negotiable, which obviously limits one's willingness to freely participate in society for fear of repercussions. Hence, liberal democracy is a natural equilibrium state for the invisible hand.

When kings or elites are allowed to arbitrarily expropriate, there's little reason to invest and capital will leave to safer havens. Even when modern democratic states start attempting to control the markets, there's intense capital flight. In 2012, when France attempted to introduce a 75% tax on income, many of the super-rich went as far as renouncing their French citizenship to avoid having to pay it [94]. This newly escaped capital will, in turn, build infrastructure where there are more just and clearer legal procedures, and that country will grow in power. Eventually, the monarchies of old simply don't have the resources to combat the richer and freer nations, and will thus be levelled and rebuilt in their foe's image.

This becomes a self-perpetuating cycle, wherein one democratic system allows for the further creation of another, which further supports the creation of exponentially more democratic systems. Add to it the existence of supranational institutions, like the World Bank or International Monetary Fund (IMF), which provide financing to a country if it follows a particular brand of democratic liberalism, or there's also blackmail and threats if the carrot didn't work [95]. Hence with the deck so heavily stacked in its favour, the democratic meme is all but guaranteed to spread, unless strongly, perhaps even violently, opposed.

Perspicacious readers might have noticed the similarity between this mechanism and the so-called "Domino theory," which was popular in the Cold War to explain the spread of communism. The main difference is that whereas communism barely survived beyond a century[54], liberal democracy reigns supreme over the world with no immediate contenders in sight.

If financial considerations weren't enough, with the adoption of democratic values one also significantly facilitates a country's existence in the world stage. Even to this day, we have yet to see widespread war between democracies; prompting some political theorists to espouse the "Democratic peace theory," wherein it's argued that democracies are very hesitant to engage in armed conflict in part because of the accountability of its leaders for casualties of war, and the inherent hesitation of losing one's financial resources which more often than not depend on free trade [96].

Consequently, whilst capital is freely allowed to efficiently flow around the world, and there are the technological means to make human labour cheap, the system is rigged in favour of democracies and enlightenment ideas. At face value, this would seem to be good news, but aspiring democracies should

---

54 Excluding China (which is only really still in that category in name only) and some undesirable places like North Korea and Cuba (which has also been losing its communist zeal since even before the death of Castro).

be careful in claiming victory over the threats of despotism. After all, even in previous systems where suffrage was limited, there arose populists who eventually became tyrants. The Roman Empire, for example, maintained its democratic facade well into the third century. During these three centuries, no emperor actually claimed to be an emperor, or even a king, on paper they were merely "Princeps" - *first among equals* [97]. A similar magic trick happened recently in Turkey with President Erdogan essentially voting himself into a Princeps role with an extremely narrow majority - it bears saying that his support mainly comes from the poorer and overall less educated people (the bread and butter of the aspiring populist dictator) [98]. Modern democracy, far from invulnerable to despotism, may be an accident waiting to happen due to its accession to populist mob rule, where the vote of an educated man is worth the same as someone who's unable to read the voting slip by himself.

But I regress, the democracy of old due to its bias towards suffrage restrictions and the status quo was clearly in favour of *Eunomiê*. Or, in plain English, democracy favoured a top-down approach, where central planners were the main movers and shakers in regard to policy.

Nevertheless, the modernization of the world and its unbalancing of millennia-spanning organizational structures, has created a far more unstable system with emergent properties. At its core, the modern system is chaotic and volatile, thus it favours mechanisms that can operate in such instability. Modern liberal democracy and capitalism fall squarely in the realm of *Dusnomié*, where they feed off Black Swans and non-linearities, and even the elites are progressively losing power to influence events in any meaningful way.

This is no longer the world of high-minded ideals and logic. This is the world of unknowable variables and unthinkable consequences. A world with no gods or kings, where only man remains alongside the legacy of its former lords.

In 1818, a poet by the name of Percy Bysshe Shelley published a sonnet in the weekly newspaper *The Examiner*, telling the story of the remains of a colossal statue, which was destroyed by the onslaught of nature and time. Yet, of this commanding monument from a bygone age, the only thing intact was a pedestal wherein it was written: "My name is Ozymandias, king of kings. Look on my works, ye Mighty, and despair!"

Ironically, all that remained of the glorious past was the hubris and boasts of unchecked power and wealth by this ruler, whilst the rest of men simply went on with their lives. The Ozymandias Effect is the destiny of all human endeavours, sooner or later they are all whittled away by forces greater than itself.

Yet, over the last millennium, we have not only seen the disappearance of more modern pseudo-Ozymandias, but we've seen the almost complete collapse of the blue-bloods themselves. Largely gone are the days wherein a king rules unchecked over his citizens - nowadays the line "off with his head because I say so" is mostly reserved to the realm of fiction alongside Alice and the Mad Hatter. We've gotten so used to the idea that the few remaining monarchs are expensive welfare sponges, or at best, glorified zoo animals for tourists to gawp at, that we've forgotten how we got to this point at all.

Partially to blame is the *Democratic Domino* that we mentioned earlier, wherein democratic principles spread because of the initial success in a single country. For example, when the French Revolution happened and revolutionary forces "liberated" foreign territories, they were often given new legal frameworks to operate under. The most influential of the bunch was the Napoleonic Code, which promoted civil liberties, property rights, equality under the law, and a clearer and less arbitrary legal framework. Yet, despite the best efforts of the old-world powers after Napoleon's defeat, an ember of nationalism and liberalism remained whereby the kings and emperors simply had to make do with the new normal, or risk insurrection, if they ever seriously attempted to turn back the clock to the era of medievalism [99].

Over time, money proved to be far more important to a man's life than a title. The nature of power evolved and became more meritocratic. But let us not make the mistake of assuming that the modern age is devoid of aristocracies, the elites might have progressively lost their titles, but their surnames work much in the same way - the Rothschild, Rockefeller, Carnegie, Vanderbilt, Ford, etc. were all kings in their own right after all.

In fact, some were far wealthier than the kings of old. Andrew Carnegie, for instance, is said to have been worth around $384 billion when adjusting for inflation [100]. This puts him squarely on the list of the top 10 wealthiest people in world history, wherein the only people who beat him are legendary figures like Mansa Musa or Augustus Caesar and totalitarian dictators like Joseph Stalin. But, to further hammer the point home of just what an age technology and capitalism created, I'll stress that Carnegie was born in poverty and arrived in America as a twelve-year-old Scottish immigrant. Or in his own words: "My men began in exactly the same station in life which I occupied a few years ago. They have had the same privileges for personal advancement that I had" [101].

The Industrial Revolution gave opportunities like never before to average people for advancement. That is not to say that it was easy. Where the warlords and kings of old gained and defended their wealth through blood and steel, the industrialists did so through business acumen and opportunism. There were far fewer casualties, but it was no less brutal.

Rockefeller's *Standard Oil*, for example, sold its products at a loss to sell them as cheap as possible, as he knew the company could outlast and hence bankrupt their competition before they had serious financial problems. Thereafter, once the competition had gone extinct, it set its prices back up to normal and through this sort of underhanded tactic managed to gain a monopoly of 90% of the US market [102]. It's because of these ungentlemanly tactics that these new industrialists got the moniker of "robber barons."

The kings are dead, long live the robber barons!

The battlefield changed: the true elites no longer fought for supremacy at the end of a sword, but instead fought at the point of a pen whilst writing numbers. At the end of the day, the pen did prove to be mightier than the sword. Thus, to understand society, we have to understand the power play that happens every single second of every single day in the world economy - where booms and busts, or bulls and bears, determine our everyday lives.

PART VI: RUNNING WITH THE BULLS AND SLEEPING WITH THE BEARS - THE STOCK MARKET

We're finally here, the big kahuna of economic development in the modern world. Ever since the Stone Age, there have been signs that something like this would come into existence. But it wasn't until recent modernity, where private property and information was so easily exchangeable as to warrant the creation of such a global institution. The world's financial system is arguably the most complex man-made system that has ever existed and it's unlikely to be superseded any time soon. It involves trillions of data points interacting with each other, as well as to the environment, in an unfathomably complex dance. Many a fortune has been lost by people falling into the trap of thinking that they understand it.

I'm genuinely scared about what the future will bring, as the more toys science provides us with, the more hubris economists have concerning their ability to predict the future. Economists act like the children of scientists playing with tools developed by their parents. Meanwhile, society waits with bated breath for the next episode when economists will end up hurt from this negligence.

When I hear of computer systems that implicitly manage large chunks of the world economy, such as the BlackRock owned system *Aladdin* which controls and guides around $15 *trillion*, or 7% of the world economy I get very nervous. More so when almost nobody talks about the consequences of having such a gargantuan percentage of the world economy managed by a monolithic algorithm. It single-handedly manages almost as much money as all the world's private-equity and hedge funds. Though its holdings are mostly equities—it is the biggest shareholder in half of the world's 30 largest companies—it also holds bonds, commodities, hedge funds, property and just about anything anyone would ever want to invest in [1]. There's no industry out there that isn't in some way affected by this algorithm.

If a single substantial enough mistake is made in the program, it may be powerful enough to trigger a domino effect that collapses the whole financial system. It doesn't need to be a particularly large shock in the grand scheme of things either - a commonly observed phenomenon is the 80/20 principle, or the Pareto Principle, wherein oftentimes in complex systems 80% of the results are attributable to only 20% of the causes. This is partially because of a similar situation that we discussed in PIV-Ch4, wherein we mentioned the asymmetric distribution of sales for authors. Reason being that advantages/attributes compound on themselves and thus certain elements in the system have a disproportionate effect on the whole.

In other words, a relatively small input can cause disproportionately large changes in the system. Imagine a minor glitch in the programme where all assets associated with the *Aladdin* algorithm misbehave. Investors notice this, realise that the economy has been compromised and their formulas tell them to sell. If enough people do this, the Stand Alone Complex will kick in and a set of circumstances is achieved that wouldn't have otherwise been possible without the paranoia of the collective psychology.

Then, if things get bad enough, a "too big to fail" institution actually fails, and takes a chunk of the economy with it, only for the shock to spread across industries and borders with further bankruptcies along the way. The world order underpinning the very foundations of modern living is then in danger and shouldn't be taken lightly. People lose their jobs, food shipments don't arrive, there's human sacrifice, dogs and cats living together, mass hysteria.

This is not the stuff of wild conspiracy and paranoia; the status quo is built on a very flimsy set of assumptions and directed by mathematics of dubious accuracy. Not only that, but stock picking is rapidly developing into a branch of complex mathematics. It's not without reason that the maths in economics has euphemistically been called "rocket science in finance."

Detractors of this theory might point to the fact that the *Aladdin* programme has operated with relative stability for a handful of decades, which is arguably what allowed it to get that big in the first place. Yet, the list of companies designing algorithms that have "beaten" the stock market, only to crash and burn stupendously at the sight of a Black Swan, is very long and growing by the day. This argument sounds like someone proudly saying that they've been betting on Russian Roulette for years and made a fortune off of it with their special technique. What could go wrong?

A broken clock is right twice a day. I do believe that it is theoretically possible to accurately predict the future of the market. In the same sort of way that you could theoretically predict the future development of the universe if you knew with exact precision where every atom was and how they're interacting with each other. This is simply ridiculous and infeasible to do, as you'd essentially have to be able to model reality itself perfectly to be able to develop accurate predictions. As such, I just don't think it's logical for one to relegate investment decisions to a computer, at least until they surpass us in intellectual and analytical capacities. Or as Philip Fisher, the author of *Common Stocks and Uncommon Profits*, put it in 1958:

> *"My objection to this approach is not that it is unreasonable in theory. It is that in the current state of human knowledge about the economics which deal with forecasting future business trends, it is impossible to apply this method in practice. The chances of being right are not good enough to warrant such methods being used as a basis for risking the investment of savings."*

Traditional academic economists, if they made it this far and haven't thrown this book off their ivory towers, would be quick to nod their heads in agreement with the last few paragraphs. After all, this conclusion falls squarely within the arguments made by classical economics. One of the cornerstones of which is the Efficient Market Hypothesis, or EMH for short. This hypothesis asserts that no supernormal profit may be derived from investing in the markets, as all currently known information that would affect the wellbeing of a financial instrument is already being taken into its pricing [2]. Or in plain English, it's impossible to outperform the market in the long run as it's so efficient, and no person can ever hope to collate information more efficiently, unless they have insider information.

If anyone ever made any money outside the market average, the only reasonable explanation is luck - or so the legend goes. Curiously enough, you never hear millionaires and billionaires say things like this. It always happens to be penniless academics who extol the futility of stock picking.

Correlation may not imply causation. But to me, it seems like a morbidly obese person arguing that exercise does nothing, as they shove a Twinkie down their gullets and wash it down with Diet Coke. I'm just saying that perhaps it pays to listen to the people who seem to be getting consistent results, rather than just being lucky every so often.

To be fair though, I'm being facetious. Only true diehards and recent graduates actually believe in the EMH without caveats or addendums. As it presently stands, academia has proposed that there are three levels under which the EMH operates:

- **Strong Efficiency**: Asset prices reflect all available public and private information instantaneously. It's impossible to earn above-average profits through investment, given that the market has already priced in whatever information you may be privy to. This form of efficiency is improbable if there are legal restrictions on trading, as with insider information rules.

- **Semi-Strong Efficiency**: Asset prices reflect all publicly-known information instantaneously and its movements are essentially random. One cannot find any patterns at all. Technical and fundamental analysis is thus impossible.
- **Weak Efficiency:** Asset prices are random, past price movements and volume data do not affect stock prices, because of this there's no patterns to be found. Technical analysis is hence pointless as a means of outperforming the market. Fundamental analysis, on the other hand, whilst not advisable for most, can still yield supernormal profits. Reason being that future price movements are determined entirely by information not contained, or downplayed, in the price series.

On a practical level, I do agree with some notions of efficiency. The value of an asset is determined by millions of individuals reacting to economic information, and the unconscious mechanisms make sense of this flurry of behaviour by establishing a price. In one way or another, all available opinions and facts have been taken into account when coming up with a price. But I think the players in the market have a tendency to focus on the trees, rather than the forest.

In the words of Benjamin Graham, the pope of the church of value investing, the anthropomorphised Mr. Market is paranoid, schizophrenic and bipolar [3]. One day, Mr. Market may look with pride at his stocks, in the next minute he self-flagellates and calls himself worthless for having been so stupid for betting the house on stocks, as he notices that some of them might not be worth the paper they're printed on. It is then, in his manic episode, that he destroys everything in sight, only to then snap back into sanity and realise that by attempting to get rid of the bad crop, he's also eliminated his bounty. Then, much the same as a recovering alcoholic would, he calls the economists and government to try to talk himself out of the mess. They show up, and sometimes they help, but at other times they get sucked into the frenzy, and only deepen the crisis. In circumstances such as those, time is the only thing that will heal wounds.

I believe the main problem trapped in the efficiency dilemma is that it disregards the composition of the market. It treats everyone's opinion as equal, ignoring the fact that some players have a disproportionate say in what happens next. If, for example, I was participating in a market with a couple of other players, but I controlled 90% of the economy, my manic episodes clearly have more of an effect than the rest put together. Even if everyone else colluded to avert a potential crisis, I simply control far too much of the board, for them to ever be able to outplay me.

We are thus not dealing with a "wisdom of the crowds" phenomena, where the average opinion of a large sample size tends to be more accurate than that of a single expert. There are agents within the markets that have a disproportionate say and consequently, understanding the composition of the markets and how prices are decided, is of paramount importance.

Over the course of this section, I will discuss the structure that markets have, their unconscious mechanisms and how best to structure one's portfolio in such an erratic world.

1 - Welcome to the Jungle: Market Composition

"Every man has a wild beast within him."

- Frederick the Great

I'd like you, for a moment, to forego any notions that you have about the economy. Forget about stocks, derivatives, securities and options. Instead, I'd like you to think of animals operating in an ecosystem. Every single one of these creatures wants to survive and thrive in the jungle. But the environment is brutal, in many of respects this is a zero-sum game. Someone's mistake means that someone else gets to eat that night.

There are a wide variety of creatures and that make up an ecosystem though. You have behemoth creatures called "Governments." These tend to be slow to react to changes in the environment, but their massive size and penchant for violence means that they tend to call the shots. Their will is usually law, in the sense that it will be followed unless there's a profitable alternative that makes up for the risk of these creatures noticing someone else's disobedience. They usually claim to be on the moral high ground, but whether or not they're well-meaning is irrelevant, as their policies often have unintended effects.

Then we have "Financial Institutions," which are a sneaky bunch, they can range from small to massive, every so often even being able to wrestle a government into submission. They're akin to the hydra of Greek myth – when governments manage to chop off a head with clever legislation, two more take its place. The problem is that governments can't just kill them off, as they're an important part of the ecosystem.

Not only do they provide much needed capital to cash-starved companies, which are a level lower than them on the food chain, but they also sometimes provide capital to governments. In exchange for this symbiosis, both governments and companies will give them a piece of their present and future productivity, in the form of bonds and stocks. They join arms only to then cross swords at the slightest provocations.

This is an incestuous relationship that would make the Greek Pantheon blush. One second they're at each other's throats, and the next they're so into each other that it's difficult to tell them apart, with employees often working for one side only to then switch sides the next week. Make no mistake though, as soon as any of these organisations makes a bad enough mistake, their lives are forfeit. Governments will eat other governments, financial institutions will eat each other, and companies will tear each other limb from limb as well.

Shit tends to roll downhill though, so rarely do institutions punch above their weight class and survive. Usually, they punch across to their peers, or downwards. There is an effective limit on size though. If an institution outgrows its ecosystem, they will start becoming lethargic, as just moving around is a chore in and of itself, and they become easy pickings for other creatures. Nevertheless, within those size constraints, sometimes it pays to be small, sometimes it pays to be big - there is no true best tactic. Otherwise, every creature that doesn't have "the most efficient" strategy would be killed off.

The optimal creature in a given moment is determined by the composition of the environment it finds itself in. But it can shift from moment to moment in a dizzying Red Queen-style affair. The extent of this depends in much the same way as population densities are determined in ecosystems in the wild. The quintessential case study in regards to predator-prey dynamics was the fur trade in Canada by the Hudson Bay Company where hunted lynx and hare pelts were tabulated for accounting purposes, but thereby accidentally keeping track of their numbers in the wild. What the data showed is that there's a certain ten-year cyclicality to both of them [4].

The predators (Lynx) decrease in amount when there's nothing to eat. The prey (hares) increase in number when there's nobody to eat them, which prompts the predator numbers to swell with the easy food. At which point, the number of predators far outnumbers that of the prey and a portion of them starves to death. Thus, there's never an equilibrium point, but a stable range within which the ecosystem operates. It's a complicated dance where the consequences of one's actions shift the opponent's behaviours, only for their foe to react accordingly. This cycle continues *ad infinitum*.

Or, as you may surmise, until there's a strong enough Black Swan. Reason behind it is that populations are subject to other shocks, such as parasites which limit their potential abilities, changes in environment, and so on. So, if there's a strong enough shock, it may be of such a magnitude that it might mean that a different balance must be established.

There is no such thing as a simultaneous optimum point for all involved. Eventually we reach a *pareto optimum*, where it is impossible to make any agents within the system better without making others worse. Such is also the way with markets: when regulation is too lax, private institutions prosper to the detriment of society. When it is too stringent, governments gain power to the detriment of the rest of society. The problem is that there is no permanent equilibrium point, the goalpost of the "ideal" amount of regulation keeps shifting because of changes in the underlying environment that society develops in.

This is why liquidity in markets is so important, as it allows for an establishment of a new **temporary** equilibrium until the next Black Swan pops up. American economist Fischer Black asserts that "noise," or a succession of smaller and more unpredictable events, cause momentary fluctuations in price [5]. This noise isn't information, but just random movements. Partially, this volatility is what allows financial markets to exist, as if everyone agreed on what something is worth, the markets would remain fairly illiquid.

In other words, healthy volatility comes as a direct result of a diversity of strategies. Every strategy out there is capitalizing on a niche in the environment. This is the hallmark of a stable and healthy system, where every optimist is offset by a pessimist of equal calibre. When a pessimist is willing to sell at any price, the optimist is willing to buy before it collapses. When the optimist is willing to buy at any price, the pessimist is quick to jump ship before the price reaches unstable heights. As such, both the optimist and the pessimist keep each other in check. This balanced ebb and flow is true creative destruction, where each failure and success grease the wheels of innovation.

The problem arises when one particular strategy is overrepresented in the system. When one side has too much optimism and money, the market will be too bullish. When one side has too much pessimism and money, the market will be bearish. In these circumstances, a Black Swan has occurred which affects the temporary equilibrium that had been reached. Remember in Part I where we talked about how species remained in stasis until there was a random change which selected against a certain strategy. Quite quickly, the landscape shifts and the only survivors are the lucky ones or the adaptable ones. This was called "punctuated equilibrium" and much the same happens with the stock market:

Whilst prices are too high, given current market conditions, it pays to be a pessimist and it's lethal to be an optimist. The same applies the other way around, whilst prices are too low, given current market conditions, it pays to be an optimist and it's detrimental to be pessimistic. As such, optimistic memes have an easier time breeding in prolonged good times, whilst pessimistic memes have an easier time breeding in prolonged bad times. Flexibility is key to not be left behind though. Evolution by natural selection does not favour the strongest or the fastest, it favours the "fittest" - the most capable of adapting to the environment through changes in their behaviour.

Hence, being an extremist and permanently branding yourself as a "bear" or a "bull" is a quick way to get yourself on the endangered species list. Circumstances are bound to change in the blink of an eye. Which is why it often feels like a game of musical chairs. One day everyone's bullish, but then without seeming rhyme or reason, the system collapses.

I believe it's too much to ask of a simple algorithm or a human mind to know and predict what is in the hearts and minds of everyone with exactitude.

Because of this, I'm sceptical of those who claim to thoroughly understand the functioning of this complex ecosystem - especially if you're a private investor, which is the lower end of the food chain in this complex ecosystem. Almost no private investor can hope to match the sheer resources available to financial institutions. Acquiring information has a price, it's not without reason that companies spend millions of dollars in market research and the like. Indeed, it's so costly that it is one of the main arguments against the EMH. Often called the Grossman-Stiglitz paradox, it asks the pertinent question: Why would anyone bother to acquire any information at all if markets are truly efficient and already include all available information in their prices? [6]

If they serve no use, and it's a large enough expense, companies could do without research and survive. Not only that, but by doing so, they'd be able to lower their prices and thus become more competitive. This does not happen, so it suggests that information is a valuable resource to have from a competitive standpoint, even despite its high cost.

Yet, research suggests that the average annual returns for an equity fund investor in the United States, over the past 30 years, were 3.79%, which looks positively anaemic compared to an annual return of 11.06% for the S&P-500 [7]. As such, professional investors who spend countless of hours peering over financial information, do almost three times worse than someone blindly betting on the market as a whole.

The explanation for this oddity is much the same as why it was that mammals triumphed over dinosaurs. The main advantage that private investors have over the institutional ones is adaptability. Financial institutions are tied by red tape, and their results tend to be assessed on a yearly, or even quarterly, basis. Hence, they're promoted to take gambles that might explode in their face. Or they have to have a percentage of their holdings in bonds and the like, due to legal regulations that attempt to stem their risk taking. But, ironically, this behaviour bids up the price of those assets and makes them overvalued for what they have on offer.

The private investor, on the other hand, does not have that huge of an overhead. They can adapt to the changes in the ecosystem, change their portfolio holdings, wait the storm out, and so on. They do not have such a mammoth operation behind them, and thus they can act at their leisure.

Mohnish Pabrai, a successful investor, businessman and author of *The Dhandho Investor: The Low - Risk Value Method to High Returns*, has said that "two to three years is just about the right amount of patience for losers to fix themselves." Imagine when you're Mr. Bigshot and you more or less say that the best move is to twiddle your thumbs for the next two years.

This sort of reasoning would not fly with investors. Much like when you pretend to work in the office, Mr. Bigshot also has to occupy himself with a whirlwind of pointless action to make it appear he is being productive. Yet, this is in direct opposition of what a sensible investor ought to do. Trying to time the market and pretend you know the future is a recipe for lacklustre growth or even a terrible loss. Here I am on the side of the economists, and say that it is utter insanity to believe that anyone has the ability to predict what exactly will happen with the market in the near term. Too many variables have to be considered to ever hope to do it accurately without being blindsided with a Black Swan.

As such, for the purposes of this discussion, we shall use the conventions laid forth by Benjamin Graham again, and we'll make a distinction between people who try to earn money in the short term, and in the long term [8]:

- **Speculators** engage in wilful short-term arbitrage, they're one of the main people responsible for why noise exists in the first place. To paraphrase a quote from Oscar Wilde, they know the price of everything but the value of nothing. Reason being that they don't care whether they're dealing with junk assets or sound businesses, it's thoroughly irrelevant as long as it's a profitable financial instrument to throw money in. Therefore, their kryptonite tends to be sudden and random changes to the underlying businesses. Yet, they serve an important niche in the ecosystem by providing liquidity as they buy and sell at random intervals.

  Speculators, almost by definition, are beyond defence in terms of consistent money-making ability, and thus shan't be our main focus. This doesn't discount the fair few who've profited highly with a speculation methodology. It's simply a fact of how statistics operate. In any large sample, you will find outliers but they in no way represent the median of the populace, and the successful ones tend to have few to no similarities to speak of.

- **Investors**, on the other hand, know the value of everything but the price of nothing. They're not concerned with the momentary fluctuations in price, as they agree with the EMH in the idea that the price jumps are temporary noise and it's dangerous to pay much attention to them. Instead, when they invest, they view themselves as business owners and try to find a business with good long-term profits and growth potential. When deciding to buy a financial instrument, they may see that prices could be overreacting to a piece of information, which is currently relevant but is likely to be unimportant further down the line. As such, they invest under the expectation that the market will recover its common sense and price the assets appropriately.

As we've seen, the jungle can be an odd place where the creatures engage in odd behaviours that an outside observer is unlikely to comprehend at first glance. There are beasts who actively hinder their chances of survival to seem to be more important than they are, there are fiends who grow to be bigger than mountains and are then barely able to move their bulk, critters who merge and unmerge with others of their kinds, alongside many other wonderfully interesting creatures, and then at the very, very bottom, there's us.

Excluding the handful of people who almost seemed to be gifted with Delphic foresight and rise to meet these monsters head-on, we're at their mercy. But do not despair, as even though we may be small and insignificant on the world stage we can overcome our shortcomings with the right philosophical mindset - as we'll discuss in the next chapter.

2 - The Sisyphean Investor: Successful Investing Philosophy

> *"I leave Sisyphus at the foot of the mountain. One always finds one's burden again. But Sisyphus teaches the higher fidelity that negates the gods and raises rocks. He too concludes that all is well. This universe henceforth without a master seems to him neither sterile nor futile. Each atom of that stone, each mineral flake of that night-filled mountain, in itself, forms a world. The struggle itself toward the heights is enough to fill a man's heart. One must imagine Sisyphus happy."*
>
> *- Albert Camus, The Myth of Sisyphus*

Up, or down, in chaos and in excitement, either running with the bulls or sleeping with the bears, one thing remains true. A sound mind, and constancy are the two main traits which will afford profit over a long stretch of time. If one gets too excited about the future, one fails to see dangers. On the other hand, if one gets too pessimistic, one fails to capitalize on opportunities. A Sisyphean investor is one who applies due diligence regardless of circumstance and doesn't let emotion dictate what he ought to do. He's a stoic in the truest sense of the word – he does what needs to be done, because it ought to be done, not because he feels like it.

The Sisyphean investor is charged with a load, which he has to elevate as much as possible in his career. Sometimes, when he thinks that he has reached the top, the load just rolls down a cliff; while, at other times, there's a helpful gust of wind that does the heavy lifting for him. At the end of the day, this ought to be irrelevant and he should remain focused. If he succumbs to joy or misery, his job will be left untended; to succeed in his task he must show strength of character, and survive the challenges that the elements might throw at him. That is the true lesson of Sisyphus.

Not everyone has a natural predisposition to these traits, yet they would still like to profit from the world economy. Consequently, there is a distinction we must make between the active and the passive investor. *The Intelligent Investor*, which we have mentioned several times in passing in this book, puts forth that there are two main investing strategies:

- **Defensive**: This is the risk averse school of thought in investing. It seeks to minimise mistakes and losses by artificially limiting choices. Doing so also requires far less commitment of time, mental prowess and emotional investment for potentially similar results to active investors.

  At its core, this strategy works under acceptance of the EMH and its conclusions about the difficulty, if not impossibility, to earn supernormal profits. It has been argued by American economist Burton Malkiel that due to the EMH, this strategy ought to be the main means of investing for most, if not all, people [9]. Because of the complications in outperforming the market, this is precisely what this strategy invests in - the market itself. It does so by means of diversified index funds, as these typically contain a proportional sample of the available stocks. In other words, it no longer falls to the individual investor to find the next stock with meteoric prospects as, by definition, they already have it. Besides that, any laggards they might have as well, are offset by the fair stocks.

  Finally, as it requires no further input of the investor, they can rest assured of being able of distancing themselves of the Stand Alone Complex by ignoring any market information entirely, meaning that heuristic judgements play no role whatsoever in their decision-making process.

- **Enterprising**: This school of thought rejects the assertion that the EMH is always necessarily true. If this weren't so, it would be nigh impossible to buy and sell any financial product, as all people would agree on the value. They believe that price arbitrages are exploitable through a vast array of tools, ranging from fundamental analysis, technical analysis and a more nebulous "gut feeling." They attest that they have the power to make supernormal profits through these means.

  With great power comes great responsibility though, and thus they must be warier than their peers. Reason being that the penalty for being wrong is much steeper than in the defensive school of thought. Most people are not psychologically and intellectually fit for this strategy. Nevertheless, if one happens to be of the fair few who have the needed enthusiasm, alongside the intellectual and psychological fortitude, the opportunity cost is tremendous from not attempting this strategy.

These are the different shapes that the value investor takes, but at their core they're philosophically the same. "Form follows function" is an aphorism that is drilled into architects at the start of their studies, yet it should also be that of the economist. A value investor will seek to create precisely that - value. To achieve this, he cannot put bricks on top of each other and call it a house. A pile of bricks can grow faster than a well-planned structure, but it would be a mistake to think it more valuable due to its recent growth.

Instead, the value investor and the architect, have to ensure that the building's plans are sound, that they suit the purpose of what it aims to do, as well as able to stand the test of time. This is not a mistaken sense of *Noblesse Oblige*, it's merely a means to avoid gambling one's life savings away. It is only by doing so that investors can be said to be worth their salt.

All too often, the investor forgets entirely that financial products represent equity in a company. They're not merely numbers dancing about for our amusement. In buying stocks, one becomes a business owner, and one should think of it as such. This realisation alone ought to be enough to quell most attempts at riding momentary trends, and should shift how one purchases stocks.

For example, imagine you're a business owner, you have painstakingly invested in a brand with a good track record, no debt, excellent management, good room for expansion and a consistent revenue stream, and you manage to buy it at a bargain price. Would it make sense that whilst you're running the business profitably, with no likely end in sight, that you check every so often, to see how the volatility of the valuation of your business is faring when compared to other companies in the industry, to decide whether you keep the business? Such analysis completely disregards the underlying health of a company, as it measures the percentage change of an arbitrary time period, and deems the standard deviation of the resulting arbitrary regression as gospel.

Yet, under the name of Beta, this methodology has been a plague on stock valuations for decades. Eugene Fama, the person who put forward the EMH, has gone as far as to say that "beta as the sole variable in explaining returns on stocks [...] is dead [...] What we are saying is that over the last 50 years, knowing the volatility of an equity doesn't tell you much about the stock's return." [10]

Beta, and similar technical analysis, are a trap and may actually aid the creation of biases. Once you engage in them, you have fallen for the ludic fallacy - you translate the pristine assertions that statistics teaches about probabilities, where there is a finite number of possibilities and clear rules by which to reach them, and you try to transfer them piecemeal to the messy environment that is the real world. Beyond the world of ideas, in the world of flesh and blood, risk is governed by the Black Swan.

In the realm of mortals, death is certain but its hour is uncertain. In Darwinian theory, the organisms that survive and procreate are not necessarily the best, but they are the most adaptable. No living being ultimately knows what they will have to transform into in the near future; thus, the ones that survive through merit, rather than luck, are the adaptable ones. Businesses, much like memes or living organisms, are subject to such selective pressures as well. Because of this, it is of paramount importance to identify businesses that can survive Black Swan events. A large part of doing so is by finding businesses that fill an environmental niche that can't easily be supplanted, or as Warren Buffett puts it "businesses with economic moats."

Much as the defensive moats on a castle, these moats help fend off the speculators that wish to stake claim to your wealth. We must stress though that these moats have to be self-evident on first glance. The more convoluted we make the story of where the moat is likely to be, the less likely that it exists at all. As a misquotation of Feynman says: "If you can't explain it to a six-year-old, you don't understand it yourself." In either case, I've heard it argued that, by searching for these economic moats, Buffett is profiting from uncompetitive practices, as he's supposedly not actually engaging in free market competition by searching out "natural monopolies." Irrespective of whether or not this is true, the fact remains that you can produce supernormal profits from following such a strategy, when you're an enterprising investor.

That is, in essence, how you fight errors in logic - with simplicity, humility, understanding and stacking the deck in your favour as much as possible. By forcing yourself to go forth without the veil of complexity, the emperor walks about without clothes - any secrets you wish to hide from yourself, or others, will be laid bare. Maths that only a rocket scientist understands should not be in the repertoire of a value investor. The more detailed and exact your analysis is, the likelier you are to miss the existence of a crucial detail.

It's ok not to know everything, and base your decision-making process under the assumption that you do not know all the details. There is a reason why the ancient Greeks believed that wisdom began from this admission of ignorance; by accepting your limitations you will not seek to plug the gaps in your knowledge with speculation, and thus you're more likely to appreciate the world as it truly is.

Remember that the key to making accurate forecasts is their imprecise and Delphic nature. The reason that people still think that Nostradamus is worth a damn, for example, is because he never gave dates to his mad ramblings. On the saner end of the prophetic spectrum, you have people like Jules Verne.

It's not without reason that he's considered the father of science fiction. He was able to look into the mechanisms hidden under the Industrial Revolution and extrapolate from there what the likely developments could be. He predicted electric submarines, newscasts, videoconferencing, solar sails and much more. But how did he do this?

Let's take a look at one of his more famous predictions. In 1865, over a hundred years before the moon landing, Jules Verne almost got it down to the letter. Not only did he accurately determine the country that would first land on the moon, but he also got the place where they would set off, the timing, as well as the length of time that the voyage would take correct. The one detail he got wrong was that he assumed that people would be fired off a cannon, as he hadn't considered the existence of rockets.

That's still not bad! Stock analysts could only wish for such foresight. However, it wasn't through a magic algorithm that Verne got this insight, but through inductive reasoning and applied mathematics.

The United States was one of the few countries with both the resources and cultural inclinations to do something of the sort. Perhaps an arbitrary, if intelligent, guess. But his reasoning for Florida as the launch site was no such thing.

Obviously, you would want to have the odds in your favour when doing something of the sort. As such, if possible, the nation in charge of such a project would use a southern launch location to take advantage of the Earth's rotation in getting the projectile off the ground. December is also a sensible time to launch, when considering authentic trajectories for a flight to the Moon. Finally, the speed and length of the journey is calculable through Newtonian physics, as it mainly computes the escape velocity of planet Earth [11].

There are far more coincidences, but I think that's the extent that can be attributed to knowledge, instead of luck. Nothing supernatural about it, just good common sense with some reasonable extrapolations. Other thinkers, even of the fictional variety, agree with him. Sherlock Holmes in the novels was often reticent to explain his train of thought as people did not think much of his common-sense solutions when explained. Results without causes are far more impressive. But, instead, all his conclusions followed a clear and undeniable logic. In the words of the great detective:

> *"I have already explained to you that what is out of the common is usually a guide rather than a hindrance. In solving a problem of this sort, the grand thing is to be able to reason backwards."*

The value investor, much like a detective finding a dead body, must reason backwards to come to the truth. When he sees a company that seems out of the ordinary, he must build a case for why it is different than the rest. He should focus on the odd and the different (be it management, business practices, assets, policies, geographical location or anything that gives it a competitive advantage), this is likely to be a clue as to why things are as they are.

If he fails to come to a sensible conclusion through inductive reasoning, and instead falls into circular logic (where a company is the best simply because it appears to be the best) he must refrain from buying. Whilst companies can, and often do, get to be profitable through sheer luck, this is a title that they cannot often maintain - as the Dot com bubble, or any other such mania will attest to.

Ironically, the markets, whilst temporarily illogical, are the closest thing we have to a true meritocracy. Companies with bad business practices eventually get their comeuppance, and companies with a solid business tend to be rewarded handsomely (if they survive long enough). Never try to play the market, as more often than not it will end up playing with you - especially if you're "playing the odds."

As the old statistics joke goes: "the average human has one testicle." Whether or not you can find me that "average person" is quite another thing entirely. What I will say on the subject is that if there is one Golden Rule in regards to investing it is this: DON'T LOSE!

Imagine two alternate scenarios, both of them have you starting your investing career with $10,000. In the first scenario, you lose 50% of your initial capital but earn a respectable 10% per year thereafter. Whereas in the second scenario, you never suffer any loss and instead earn 5% per year. Despite having double the average returns, in the first example, it would take you eighteen years to catch up to the slow and steady approach and make up for your losses.

Both scenarios end with you earning c.$22,900 but the second one is far less stressful than the first.

Engaging in risky behaviour can easily result in an early loss and may ruin a value-investing career before it even begins, as it takes a whole generation to make up for the shortfall. This realisation might tempt the reader in "timing the market" and selectively entering and exiting their investing portfolio with the intention of buying the same stock in the future, but that would be a mistake. As we discussed in PIV-Ch2, change often occurs at completely random intervals and may represent a significant percentage of the total volatility. Meddling about with forces you barely understand is a recipe for eventual defeat, when luck runs out and there's a regression to the mean. Such a strategy would only make one's brokerage house wealthier in the long run, not oneself (even if we're generous and disregard taxes and transaction costs).

This is why people like Warren Buffett say that one ought to think about one's investments in terms of a ticket with limited slots for investments. Imagining therefore that one can only make 20-something investments in one's lifetime one has to think of it as carefully targeted shots, rather than pot-shots at a bullseye. Hence the investments have to be targeted and carefully selected - no "wild guesses."

The way by which one ought to find these opportunities is by identifying circumstances with limited and controlled situations where failure can occur, but with huge potential upsides. Say that there is a company with good growth prospects, solid reputation, which happens to have a momentary problem. They're in debt, but their book value far outweighs their liabilities. In other words, if the company goes bankrupt and is sold for parts you can regain what you paid for it, or possibly earn even more than you paid initially - hence the existence of "vulture funds" whose sole purpose is to buy assets cheaply and then force the company into bankruptcy so that they have to sell their assets to repay their debt. However, if the company manages to dig itself out of the hole it's in, you reap the rewards of having bought a stellar company at a great price.

Mohnish Pambrai, in his fabulous book *The Dhandho Investor*[55], calls these circumstances wherein there's a positive feedback loop with small starting capital - a "heads, I win! Tails, I don't lose much" scenario. To introduce the book, he tells the tale of how an Indian clan - the Patels - came to take over the motel business in the United States with no money and barely having a history in the country.

When the Patels arrived in the United States in the midst of the 1970s energy crisis, motels were particularly hit hard, as oil was sky high, and thus people avoided driving as much as possible. Motels were going for bargain basement prices, as many were falling into bankruptcy and disuse. Banks were all too happy to just get rid of them and provide financing to anyone dumb enough to want to buy one.

For the Patels, this was an extraordinary opportunity. Not only was financing easy, but they had their own accommodation covered, and they had a competitive edge. Their family became employees that weren't even paid minimum wage. Hence this was a win-win scenario.

Over time, more and more Patels came over and copied this *modus operandi* and there came a time when they had an essential monopoly over the industry. The key to this story is that they bet heavily when the odds were monumentally in their favour. The downside was almost non-existent. The banks didn't have much motivation to give up on their investment and kick out the Patels. If they had done so, the Patels would lose their money – but in practice, they could earn back their starting capital, at the minimum wage, in about two years. This was a bet with almost nothing to lose and a lot to gain.

Nowadays, the Patels own motels worth more than $40 billion in the United States, with nearly one million employees. Knowing when a risk is worth taking is the key to life.

---

55 No, I'm sadly not getting paid for shilling his book, despite me singing it praises a couple of times already.

3 - Perverse Perception: How Opinions Shape Prices

"Opinions are like assholes. Everybody's got one and everyone thinks everyone else's stinks."

- Simone Elkeles

In preparation to write this chapter, I recently made my way through George Soros' *The Alchemy of Finance*. I quickly came to the conclusion that Soros is incredibly pretentious in the presentation of his ideas. Admittedly, if there's anyone who has the right to be full of himself it is George Soros - but a readable, as well as entertaining, writer and philosopher he ain't.

Half ramble, half incoherent retelling of recent financial history, Soros makes his way through the book. But, every so often he produces a nugget of gold; among them there's the theory of reflexivity. Reflexivity is the behavioural change of agents in a system based on current expectations about the future, which in aggregate shifts the outcome of the system to something else.

For example, imagine that on a random day a charismatic individual happens to convince others that banks are unable to repay their debts. Quickly, those convinced go into a frenzy and withdraw their savings from the bank before it runs out of money.

Soon enough, there's a crowd of people, and each additional person who queues up adds to the hysteria and makes it more likely to be reported in mass media. The hysteria compounds on itself and there are more and more people who believe the banks are unstable. Eventually, the bank runs out of cash on hand and has to close down for the day. Other banks have to then chip in to bolster their rival's reserves, or risk a bank failure where all their positions are called and they run the risk of bankruptcy.

Here's the thing, technically speaking, a bank is unable to repay all of its obligations at once, at any point in time. This theoretical "banking crisis" was fabricated whole cloth by the charismatic individual, and luck took this minor random shock into crisis territory because it managed to reach a tipping point when enough people were involved. Had nobody acted crazily, nothing would've happened.

What changed was not the bank as an institution, in every other respect that day was business as usual, nothing was out of the ordinary; what changed was the perception thereof. By design, banks are perpetually pseudo-insolvent as they take short term liabilities (your bank balance) and transform them into long term assets (loans), which produce revenue in excess to what was put in. Banks, as a normal mode of operation, ask for more money from their borrowers than is currently in circulation. Hence, they are fabricating money out of thin air, as they're conducting business transactions with money they know full well doesn't exist. Someone with a very cynical bent could even say that they're a scam. I believe they're a necessary lie, as otherwise, transaction costs would simply be too high for society to function properly.

Kill all doctors in a society, and almost all but the most dangerously ill and people involved in major accidents would survive - as was really the case for most of human history, where doctors were little more than glorified quacks. Whereas, if you killed all bankers, modern society would grind to a halt as the monetary system would cease to exist, and with it the underlying trust system that keeps society running. It is by no means a noble profession, but a necessary one, much like sewer technicians or garbage men. It just so happens to be much better paid than either one of the two, where the opportunities for misbehaviour are much more common, and far more lucrative.

In recent times, to mitigate financial malpractice, and so that a bank's balance sheet still somehow resembles reality, there is regulation. Central banks impose reserve requirements and capital adequacy ratios to avoid something as damaging as the Great Depression. Whether or not these restrictions work is up for debate and outside of the purview of this book. Ironically, it was precisely this type of heavy-handed approach which caused the Great Depression in the first place [12]. It's a bit of a minefield - too much regulation and your society suffers, same when it becomes the Wild West, although for different reasons.

The point of the matter is that prices, and the very stability of institutions and society, depends on perception[56]. The efficient market hypothesis doesn't take into account perception. It somewhat incorrectly assumes that the market has a god-tier bullshit detector and correctly assesses the value of everything at all times. Whilst fundamentals do often reflect reality, do not be fooled into thinking that it is always so.

The best liar is not one who's known for his falsehoods. The best liar is one who's respected and people do not question his judgement. It is much the same with the stock market. Just because prices often reflect reality it does not mean that is always the case. In fact, to take them at face value is liable to land you in the poorhouse - it's not a matter of *IF*, it's a matter of *WHEN*.

I am possibly very jaded and biased, but I'm deeply sceptical of oversimplifications or overly- complex ramblings with convoluted formula. *Things ought to be made as simple as possible, but no simpler.* Either extreme will only give you a distorted view of the world, either because of a lack of nuance or an overreliance on minutia.

Take the supply and demand curves shown in economics 101 courses the world over. These two opposing lines are a graphical representation of the relationship between the price of a good or service and the quantity demanded/supplied for a given period of time. Where the two intersect is supposed to be a "market equilibrium," where the amount of goods or services sought by buyers is equal to the amount of goods or services produced by sellers.

Not only do they imply that the demand of an item is computable, and

---

56 God forbid we ever collectively realise we're willing to work ourselves to death for pieces of paper!

somewhat set in stone, but also that there's some magical equilibrium which market forces are moving prices toward. Imagine if there were some sort of equation that calculated how likely I am to order a delicious slice of chocolate cake. When it's out of sight, and out of mind, my demand for it is fairly non-existent - I can resist the urge. Put a slice of Sachertorte in front of me, and my willpower all but disappears. My "demand" and willingness to pay for the chocolate cake fluctuates moment to moment based on considerations of proximity, availability, what I've had for lunch, my weight, whether other people are around to judge my eating habits, etc. My perception of my life circumstances and likely future is what determines my willingness to eat further fattening and delicious cake. The price is of a secondary concern, only to be considered when I'm already primed to get some more cake.

A simple linear graph with two variables of price vs quantity cannot hope to determine my decision-making process. Consider how these problems exponentially magnify by each new person included in the calculations. Factors far out of our control, like the weather, undoubtedly play a role in our economic behaviour (you're much less likely to buy ice cream when it's freezing, no matter how cheap it is, for example). A while ago, when Britain suffered extreme cold weather, it was estimated that it was costing the country £1 billion PER DAY [13].

In such circumstances, we rapidly reach chaos theory levels of forecasting impossibility. If you were somehow able to be omniscient, and with that information create an algorithm to graph this behaviour, what you would have noticed is that the "equilibrium point" shifts moment to moment, and that the angle of the slope graphed by the algorithm is shifting in an infinite amount of ways with each passing microsecond. In practical terms, making the very concept of an equilibrium point about as useful as trying to find how many angels can dance on the head of a pin.

Several hundred years ago, pineapples were worth small fortunes for their rarity. They were items held in such high regard that King Charles II even went as far as commissioning a painting of his gardener presenting him with a pineapple [14]. To a modern audience, this seems bizarre, because we've grown under the culture of modernity where pineapples are among the most available fruits worldwide.

As a brief thought experiment, imagine that - for some bizarre reason - all pineapples have died save for a single, but infertile, one. Would most twenty-first century billionaires be willing to spend a small fortune to have the last pineapple on Earth as a dessert, even if it would be a massive status symbol? My gut tells me that none but the most eccentric and pineapple-loving fat cats would ever consider it, let alone actually bid on it. Even then, the number would be mathematically insignificant. The modern public is so used to cheap pineapples, that trying to convince them that they're worth a fortune from one day to the next would be a very tough sell - we're not machines that automatically update our willingness to pay for items depending on availability, our perceptions play a strong role in such decision making (even if our perceptions are unfounded or illogical). In other words, our culture, upbringing, and personal beliefs alter how we engage with the economy, regardless of considerations of price and quantity.

The economist's fetishization of equilibrium points, graphs and models often makes them lose touch with reality. Quite frankly, I've always been baffled by the fact that Scottish economist and philosopher Adam Smith's *On the Wealth of Nations* was published in 1776, starting with it the modern study of economics; yet despite that the fact that the same author wrote *The Theory of Moral Sentiments* seventeen years prior, wherein he talks about proto-psychology and how society plays a role in dictating behaviours, few people made a connection between the two.

Indeed, it wasn't until two centuries later, near the end of the twentieth century, when economics truly started flirting with psychology in earnest. This was a flirtation fraught with danger and drama though. As not unlike in Romeo and Juliet, the economists and psychologists had a historical feud with each other. Earlier in the century, economics aspired to become a natural science. Psychology, with its then obsession with sex and often untestable hypotheses, would ruin these goals. Hence, the two had to be separated at all costs.

Economists of the past sometimes even went as far as speculating about human psychology. Bigwigs Irving Fisher and Vilfredo Pareto included rich speculations about how people feel and think about economic choices. Later, John Maynard Keynes appealed to psychological insights, but by the middle of the century discussions of psychology had largely disappeared [15].

The lines had been drawn - you were either with the ultra-rationalists, or you were a pleb who couldn't handle basic algebra, and wasn't worth listening to. The problem with this arbitrary distinction is that irregularities started appearing in the models. The cracks began to amass in the uber-rationalist system and, after some years, there were enough detractors to begin a counter-revolution.

It wasn't until 2002 when the glass ceiling was broken, as the psychologist Daniel Kahneman and economist Vernon L. Smith received the Nobel Memorial Prize in Economic Sciences. Their empirical research challenged the assumption of human rationality prevailing in modern economic theory. In other words, it took over 200 years to follow this line of reasoning, and it was such a novel line of reasoning that it merited a Nobel Prize:

Economics is "a social science concerned chiefly with description and analysis of the production, distribution, and consumption of goods and services"

↓

People are the consumers of these goods and services based on their preferences

↓

Their preferences are based on a nuanced interplay between culture and genes, which we call "psychology"

↓

Understanding the mechanisms and consequences of this system would make one better able to understand economics, and hence society

↓

With said knowledge, you can design models that more approximate actual human behaviour than mathematical ideals which rarely, if ever, exist in real life

I might have the benefit of hindsight, but this line of reasoning seems a tad too simple, logical and uncontroversial to have been so derided and often ignored. I don't think that I'm a Nobel Prize winner level intellect[57], yet I don't think it would've been that difficult to come to that thought by myself. But to this day, behavioural economists are still somewhat considered the lepers of the discipline. The reason for this is likely to be because economics is on the cultish end of the spectrum.

By degrees, an economics student often has to turn off his common sense in order to jump through the academic hoops. As students, they learn that human beings supposedly always behave rationally, whilst ironically nursing a hangover from last night's party, because of their poor decision-making skills and lack of self-control. These simultaneously contradictory pieces of evidence are ignored, and one eventually learns to engage in something akin to doublethink[58].

Reality is accepted to be illogical and arbitrary in a student's day-to-day life, but when it comes to doing something economics-related the switch gets turned and they perceive reality in a completely different way. It's truly something out of a dystopian novel. I'm not overstating the matter either, there have been studies that show that people, after having been indoctrinated with an economics degree, behave differently than normal people. There have been free rider-type studies, wherein the main participants who acted uncooperative and sociopathic were economics students. Entire meta-analysis have been written on the warping behaviour that taking economics classes has on individual behaviour [16].

The obvious argument to this is that scientists, engineers, programmers or any person with specialised knowledge behaves differently than the average Joe, where their field is concerned. The Achilles' heel of this retort

57 LIES - but I tend to temper my delusions of grandeur with a healthy helping of disappointment.

58 The acceptance of contrary opinions or beliefs at the same time, especially as a result of political indoctrination.

is that the behaviour of people, or rather what it is that they do with their money, is very much in the area of interest of economics. Hence, if they have a warped understanding of what people do with their money, they will often behave strangely while expecting certain behaviours which never seem to come. Mutually-Assured Destruction only works, for example, if both parties are aware of the concept, and hence play the same game. The stock market has such a hodgepodge of conflicting motivations that everyone's playing a completely different game. Believing you perfectly understand the whole scene is dangerous; oversimplifications bulldoze nuance, and that nuance may be the key to understanding what is actually happening.

It's akin to an autistic person at a party - they may be perfectly capable and intelligent individuals, but their understanding of the world is perpetually warped because they're missing some key pieces of information about human behaviour. They can't understand that every task, every interaction, no matter how seemingly banal, has the potential to contain a world onto itself. Hence, when they see people talk about the weather, they legitimately think that they're talking about the weather; whilst losing the nuance of that light touch that the man gave the woman on her elbow, that subtle yet persistent eye contact, and how she seems to find him funny, despite the fact that he's about as humorous as grandma's funeral. The intent behind the action is as important as the action itself.

Our imaginary bank run earlier was not sparked from the ether. There had to be a catalyst which gave the charismatic man the legitimacy to convince people to act crazily. Neither was the bank run specifically about the bank, as banks nowadays tend to have a deposit insurance where the government safeguards the bulk of people's savings. In that circumstance, their environment makes people believe that it's unlikely that even government guarantees are worth the paper they're printed on. Market developments dictate the evolution of the conditions of supply and demand, not the other way around.

The bank run is a symptom of a larger disease. If the disease is not addressed, it will continue wreaking havoc for years to come. Perception is the driving force of value. Eventually though, the delusions become far too illogical and the system normalises to more sustainable levels through violent upwards or downwards corrections, as enterprising speculators and investors bet heavily on the other side. When, exactly, this tipping point will happen is anyone's guess.

We are only human, after all. We have our biases, as we discussed in Part I. Our two ways of thinking (Fast & Slow) work in lockstep to help us understand the world from our limited perspective. The results are highly contextual though. The same input will lead to a completely different conclusion depending on where our headspace is predisposed to be in at that particular point.

In film, this is called the "Kuleshov Effect," so named after Soviet film director Lev Kuleshov, who discovered that viewers derive more meaning from the interaction of two sequential shots than from a single shot in isolation. Or in plain English, the intentions of a character are usually clearer when context is provided.

At beginning of the twentieth century, Kuleshov edited a short film in which a shot of a man with an intense look was alternated with various other shots (a girl in a coffin, a woman on a couch, a plate of soup, etc.). This video was shown to an audience who believed that in all instances they were looking at unique performances, and they all believed he showed extraordinary acting range. In 1929, Soviet film director Vsevolod Pudovkin explained how the audience "raved about the acting [...] the heavy pensiveness of his mood over the forgotten soup, were touched and moved by the deep sorrow with which he looked on the dead child, and noted the lust with which he observed the woman. But we knew that in all three cases the face was exactly the same." [17]

Had it not been for this unique human ability to bridge this informational gap of two completely different shots being interspersed with each other, movies as we know them would be impossible. Human intuition, far from being objectionable, is a highly useful tool. Yet, it has its limits.

As we discussed earlier in this chapter, value is mainly defined by perception, and said perception is based on our psychology. Our behaviour, whilst often being subject to peer pressure, is ultimately controlled by us[59]. We're the ones who decide whether or not to follow a course of action - even when you have a gun on your head, you can choose to ignore it.

Point being that our personal conscious experience is what determines the value we give to things at the individual level. Our conscious experience is tinted by events that preceded it. For example, one is more likely to agree with something if it fits well with pre-existing beliefs. If you're expecting rain, you'll focus on the clouds in the sky rather than the sunshine.

Hence, I'd argue that even thinking in terms of "bull" or "bear" markets is dangerous. It adds a layer of permanence to what is, in essence, a temporary situation. It's much more effective to think of it as a pendulum with forces trying to move it to either extreme - optimism and pessimism. One ought to identify the source of these forces and determine their intensity and duration. In that way, one can think of the system as dynamic and can avoid falling for the "bear" or "bull" market memes, which harken back to the economist's fetishization of equilibrium points of inherently volatile systems.

Ideological lenses can prohibit you from assessing circumstances as they are. Worse still, much in the same way, emotions can also accidentally "lock" you into certain modes of thinking.

Recent research has hinted at the fact that short-term emotions can often have long-term consequences. These "emotional cascades," as they're commonly called, are decisions based on a fleeting incidental emotion that become the basis for future decisions and outlive the original cause for the behaviour [18]. The quintessential study in this regard was conducted in 1974, wherein men were separated into two groups [19]. The first group, serving as control, would cross a normal bridge without further bells and whistles; the second group would cross a dangerous-looking suspension bridge. After this

59 This is only true if we choose to believe in free will and forego the (in my view) overwhelming evidence for determinism. That said, it's kind of impossible to consciously be aware of determinism every waking moment. So even if you're an adherent of the idea behind it, you more or less learn to ignore the evidence in your day to day life. Or was it your destiny to do so in the first place?

crossing, a female researcher would talk to them and give them her contact details "'to further discuss the research."

The results showed that the high-arousal stimulus ("dangerous" bridge) increased male participants propensity to call the female experimenter in the future relative to low-arousal stimulus ("safe" bridge). The researchers concluded that the nervousness induced by the bridge crossing (heart pounding, shaking hands, etc.) was misinterpreted by participants as attraction for the woman. This is not as unreasonable as the conclusion might seem on first glance. After all, as we discussed in PI-Ch4, flirting with the wrong woman back in the day could be your cause of death just as easily as falling from great heights.

In other words, what happened is that men misattributed the source of their emotions and made the "wrong" conclusion that they had been attracted to the researcher. This momentary misunderstanding in the real world could've had potentially long-lasting and life-changing circumstances. So, other than taking notes and planning dates on rickety bridges, what can we learn from this?

Humans are often unaware of the source of their perceptual experience. In the words of Edward Bernays - the man who invented public relations, consumerism [60], and helped cause the 1929 crash by promoting taking loans for stock investment [20]:

> *"A man sits in his office deciding what stocks to buy. He imagines, no doubt, that he is planning his purchases according to his own judgment. In actual fact his judgment is a melange of impressions stamped on his mind by outside influences which unconsciously control his thought. He buys a certain railroad stock because it was in the headlines yesterday and hence is the one which comes most prominently to his mind; because he has a pleasant recollection of a good dinner on one of its fast trains; because it has a liberal labour policy, a reputation for honesty; because he has been told that J. P. Morgan owns some of its shares.*

60 Bernays pioneered selling products as a lifestyle, rather than for their utilitarian value.

> *Trotter and Le Bon concluded that the group mind does not think in the strict sense of the word. In place of thoughts it has impulses, habits and emotions. In making up its mind its first impulse is usually to follow the example of a trusted leader. This is one of the most firmly established principles of mass psychology. It operates in establishing the rising or diminishing prestige of a summer resort, in causing a run on a bank, or a panic on the stock exchange, in creating a best seller, or a box-office success."*

"Trusting your gut" (or your back pain, in the case of Soros) is not always a good solution for the everyman. We are victims of self-herding, as such our own day to day random experiences are conspiring against us. If you haven't been extraordinarily lucky, and had just the right sort of philosophical indoctrination, trusting hunches is extremely dangerous.

After all, it's well-documented that our assessments on things tend to be extraordinarily skewed. Among them there's the *Halo Effect,* a cognitive bias where a strong impression in one area affects one's interpretation of the whole [21]. Say, if we like a person we'll be more charitable and give them the benefit of the doubt. If we dislike someone, almost nothing that they do seems right, even the very sound of their voice can piss us off.

Same with investing in a company. If we like a company, we'll be far more willing to gloss over certain inconsistencies just because we like them. Adding to it, there's the "Mere Exposure Effect," another cognitive bias where one develops a preference to stimuli you're regularly exposed to [22]. Together they make a powerful cocktail of self-delusion.

Incidentally, "propinquity" (the state of being close to someone or something) is the strongest indicator for a potential romantic relationship [23]. Frankly, I consider that an incredibly depressing fact. This psychological quirk alone would imply that the vast majority of people ended up together, not because they particularly liked each other, but because they just happened to be sharing the same physical space. They were the most palatable person at the right place and time. But this simply goes to show that when given choices, we'll usually just follow the path of least resistance.

This is why a good investor knows how to KISS - Keep It Simple, Stupid. The more hoops you have to go through to explain your reasoning for investing in something (which you believe to be the best investment), the likelier it is that you are simply suffering under self-delusion. The reasons for buying the asset should be self-evident. One should invest in simple assets with foolproof economic advantages. Not only do these assets have to have flexibility in defending themselves, they should also have economic moats.

4 - Economic Moats: An Everyman's Guide to Becoming A Robber Baron

"There is no castle so strong that it cannot be overthrown by money."

- Marcus Tullius Cicero

Forget about playing it fair, you want to be the man who stacks the deck in their favour - the man who brings a gun to a knife fight. You want to be the type of investor who earns money at an extraordinary rate - you want to earn a supernormal profit. Sadly, as even a basic course in economics will tell you, free markets preclude supernormal profits. If the barrier to entry is low, then that means that even if a company colludes with other entities to keep the prices artificially high, there will be institutions who do not abide by this rule and undercut the ones who had agreed on a high price. Eventually, the colluders will either be driven out of the market entirely, or forced to reduce their prices. In the meantime though, these collusions can become very lucrative, and hence there's a large incentive to try to pull it off, despite their near certainty of failure in the long run.

The stories of such collusions are numerous in the pages of history; from the Organization of the Petroleum Exporting Countries (OPEC) massively disrupting the world economy in the 1970s by increasing the price of oil to extortionary levels to the Phoebus cartel conspiring in the 1920s to engage in large-scale planned obsolescence by artificially reducing the lifespan of an incandescent bulb, and hence forcing people to buy more [24][25].

Or, if you want to be more recent and topical, one can point to the fact that attempting to combat drug trafficking has raised the necessary entry barriers and thus made it a disgustingly profitable business model [26]. Just to put things into perspective, back in the day, Pablo Escobar lost about $2.2 billion dollars per year because it got eaten by rats whilst stored in warehouses and such. This was such an inconsequential variable in the grand scheme of things, that his accountants simply factored it in as a known business expense [27].

It's arguably in the best interests of the drug dealers that anti-drug measures remain as draconian as humanly possible. A drug addict's demand is inelastic, given that they don't care for the price or consequences, as long as they're getting the product. So, the real problem is the competition which might supply drugs cheaper than they do. Junkies, whilst not usually the smartest or most discerning crowd, are at the very least able to do the basic arithmetic necessary to think "cheaper prices = more drugs," and because of this, they'll buy from the cheapest sources available.

So, other cartels are a natural check on raising prices too much. As such, less competition, either because the other dealers were murdered, retired or imprisoned, equals larger profits for the drug dealers. The government is thus inadvertently helping drug organisations by eliminating the competition that may not have the bribery networks in place, or which is simply inexperienced and likelier to be caught.

In either case, in all of these collusions, where monopolies and oligopolies have formed, there is a scent of illegality or, at the very least, immorality. I assume my average reader isn't interested in starting a criminal empire[61]. Hence, under those motivations, what one wants is to maximise one's rent-seeking behaviour, whilst remaining above-board. One might never reach anything remotely close to casually having $2.2 billion as rat chow; however, not only will one have access

---

61 Or at the very least they should not name me as inspiration...Then again it might be good for book sales, so you know what? Go right ahead and name me as inspiration as long as I don't end with legal problems.

to the full power and potential of financial institutions, but one will do so with the full protection and support of the law. There are three ways to go about this:

- The first way is to **lobby the government** for special privileges in whatever endeavour you are engaged in. Once you've achieved a privileged status, like becoming the sole supplier of a certain product or service for the government, you'll be able to do things that a free market institution could only dream of. Thus, it will not only be very lucrative, but you will be able to engage in decidedly non-competitive practices. Take the United States' overabundance of tanks in recent years. Year after year it was the same story, they have so many of them that high military officials have gone on record and said that it is a complete and utter waste of money. Congress insists on purchasing them, despite their strategic pointlessness and economic wastefulness, because the factories are in important constituencies and the government is often their sole client. Hence, if they were to stop supplying the government, many voters and bureaucrats would lose their well-paying jobs [28].

  Where there's money in politics, there will be waste and entrenched interests in keeping it so. Subsidies, tax breaks, government contracts, etc. become very difficult to alter once established, as their elimination upsets the status quo and with that the powerful people wishing for things to remain as they are.
- The second option is **patent trolling**, meaning that you protect your competitive advantage through legal protection. The idea behind patents or copyrights was originally to promote entrepreneurship by rewarding the creator of an idea with the sole financial benefit of their creation for a given number of years.

  This has morphed in recent years. Nowadays, it's not uncommon for companies to purchase patents in bulk without having the intention of doing anything with them. They simply sue whosoever happens to do something useful with an idea that they "own." Companies like Disney also fall into this patent trolling category, despite still producing creative works. They buy copyrighted material, and then produce derivative content with it to the already established audiences.

The main benefit of this is that there's minimal risk, and low overhead costs in maintaining your business practices. But you open yourself up to Black Swans in regards to your intellectual property.

- The third option, and arguably most ethical solution, is **finding natural monopolies**. According to the OECD, "A natural monopoly exists in a particular market if a single firm can serve that market at lower cost than any combination of two or more firms. Natural monopoly arises out of the properties of productive technology, often in association with market demand, and not from the activities of governments or rivals" [29]. Meaning that these are markets whose only logical structure, whilst still being efficient, is of a sole supplier.

  The problem is that these institutions are likely overtaken by governments due to their often perceived essential nature for the functioning of society. Hence, a good portion of these will likely not be up for sale in any shape or form, unless one's in cahoots with the people in power, as they're government enterprises. Nonetheless, some examples could include enterprises that deal in electricity, railroads, natural gas, telecommunications, harbours, airports and roads. When such natural monopolies are found, they're often well worth the money. They likely don't have much room for growth, for obvious reasons, but they're very profitable businesses.

Admittedly, these means are on the passive end of the spectrum. They work mainly through constraints on the environment, and often rely on the state's monopoly on violence. There's little opportunity for change, and to a great extent economic moats do require this. As Indian-American investor Mohnish Pabrai put it: "buy simple businesses with ultra-slow long-term change." If you've found something profitable, change can only be a bad thing, and therefore you will tend to prefer circumstances where the fortunes of your business aren't dependant on random throws of the dice.

Competitive advantages, i.e. economic moats, unless they're in a stagnant environment, tend to erode over time. This can happen in the blink of an eye and an industry may never recover after the Black Swan. Take China and silk as an example. For centuries they had a monopoly on the material and could charge extraordinary amounts for it. To such an extent that even Roman proto-economists were concerned about the staggering loss of precious metals in Roman provinces because of the Silk Road [30]. Then, in the mid-6th century CE, two monks with the support of the Byzantine emperor Justinian I set out on a mission to steal silkworms [31]. The plan was successful, and silk became an important backbone of the Byzantine economy for the next 650 years [32].

A similar thing happened with the discovery of porcelain. First, it was a secret of East Asia, but eventually the mystery was solved by men of great knowledge attempting to understand the mysteries of the world through alchemy [33]. Point being that monopolies that require secrecy or government complicity for its enforcement are inherently prone to Black Swans. Not even the modern age, with its long-standing legal traditions, is enough to be of any true comfort. To quote James Simons, an American mathematician, and hedge fund manager of Renaissance Technologies[62], regarding the algorithms that they use for their decision-making process:

> *"People don't leave our firm, or if they do leave they just do something else altogether. Everyone has signed a forever non-disclosure agreement because we're very secretive about what we do. 'Cause you can't patent that stuff or copyright it because then everyone would see what it is, and someone would just work around it and say 'oh that patent's no good, look I've made this twist and that tweak - and it's different'. What you have is your intellectual property and you have to keep that to yourself" [34].*

---

62 Famed for having one of the best records in investing history, returning more than 35 percent annualized over a 20-year span, as well as curiously being solely reliant on models for its decision-making process.

Working around patent laws and regulation is an art onto itself. Your only protection is that others haven't found a way around it, or the political climate is still in your favour. Hence, I'm not a fan of the first two methods, as history is not really on your side.

As we learned in PVI-Ch3, prices change depending on opinion and perceived value. Possibly chuck it to a childhood of being bullied, but I don't tend to hold group consensus as a worthwhile metric of something's desirability. In matters of dollars and cents, you want objectivity with as little drama as possible. I'm thus sceptical of relying much on preferences as a barometer of whether or not I ought to buy or sell something.

Crowds are fickle. Generally speaking, you want to put as much distance between you and their crazy preferences, as humanly possible. When people unironically claim that John F. Kennedy single-handedly killed the hat industry by not wearing one at his inauguration, and people believe that this is a good enough explanation, it should really make us terrified of investing in such volatile environments.

It doesn't matter whether it's true or not - Caesar's wife must be above suspicion. The mere fact that such inconsequential trite is a plausible enough explanation to explain the change in hat preferences of the American public, as well as the collapse of a multi-million-dollar industry, should be enough cause for concern.

This is why I don't think intangible assets hold that much weight. We find it difficult enough to value tangible stuff, and then you expect me to pay for ethereal sources of value? Get the hell out of here!

Any real-world asset suffers from depreciation, and eventual obsolescence, but even when it reaches its end of life stage it still holds "scrapping" value, which comes from the cost of the materials it's made of. So, you never fully risk bankruptcy, unless you're leveraged beyond the value of your tangible assets. With intangible assets, there are no such guarantees. If you believe your intangible source of value holds much value in the long run, I've got a bridge to sell you.

Incidentally, the phrase "I've got a bridge to sell you" comes from a con man called George C. Parker who illegally sold properties he did not own to unwary immigrants [35]. Among his sales were the Brooklyn Bridge, the Metropolitan Museum of Art, General Grant's Tomb and the Statue of Liberty. Many of his victims were arrested once they tried to erect tolls on the bridge. Point being that promises of extraordinary riches often blind us from thinking logically. If you think that the sky's the limit, you'll be willing to pay sky-high prices.

I'm not saying that goodwill, or any other source of intangible values, don't exist. Brands, and the associated intellectual property, are very important part in the sales of a company. But it's akin to being asked what the monetary value of someone's life is. Putting aside the ethical considerations for a moment, you could calculate it in a couple of ways:

- **Base elements**, meaning the monetary value that you would get if you somehow were to separate someone to their base atomic components and then sum it all together. It's about $1 for everything minus your skin, and around $3.50 for your tanned hide which we'll, somewhat dodgily, attempt to sell as cowhide. Under that assessment model you're barely worth as much as an overpriced coffee at around $4.50 as of 2010 [36].
- **Organs and other genetic information**, depending on whom you ask you could be looking at anywhere from $10,000 to a couple million. Organ selling is not a unified market and there's various degrees of legality throughout the world. Furthermore, if you're a truly desperate millionaire with little scruples, and a failing kidney, you wouldn't think twice about tossing out a couple hundred thousand for a compatible kidney. But I'll use the $10,000 - $100,000 provided by the Detroit Free Press, as it seems to be the most reasonable source that uses actual court evidence and doesn't seem to be hyperbole and clickbait like others[63][37].

---

63 As I write this I'm sitting in a café in Prague, googling how much body parts are worth in the black market, I wonder what the customers and staff think if they've seen the article headlines I've been reading...

- **The monetary value derived from their work**, here's where it starts getting tricky. Whereas before we could reasonably calculate the value of something based on the utility it provided, here it's extremely subjective. Unlike purchasing a liver from the black market or the base elements of a human body, where there's ample potential supply if the prices are good enough, in this category there are items of incalculable value because of their perceived uniqueness. How much do you sell the Mona Lisa for, for example? Even if you make a copy of it that is identical to it atom by atom, the "copy" wouldn't sell even remotely close to the original. There's no substitute commodity for it and thus the only point of reference is itself. Not because Renaissance paintings of women are so rare, but because it's the Mona Lisa. Basic things like insuring it are a nightmare. In 1962, it was valued at an insurance payoff of a maximum of c.$790 million when adjusted for inflation, but the security necessary for its safe transportation exceeded the maximum premium payoff [38]. Should these costs not be factored into its valuation? After all, its safekeeping and conservation are value added to the end product. But then, if you follow that logic, its value spins out of control as it becomes a self-perpetuating cycle that approaches infinity, despite there never being anything extra actually added to it.

Incidentally, Lorenzo the Magnificent said that from 1434 to 1471 the Medici spent 600,000 Florins for public purposes and this expenditure "casts a brilliant light upon our condition in the city" [39]. If we take this 37-year timeframe to be representative of their willingness to be patrons, and we guesstimate that the Italian Renaissance lasted 200 years, from 1300 to 1500, they would've spent a total of 3,243,243 florins or $468.399 million[64]

---

64 For these calculations, I used the same monetary value for the florin as the one originally used for the ducat estimate in PV-Ch2, as Venice modelled the size and weight of their currency after the florin. If anything, the number ought to be less, given that the ducat weighed slightly more given a difference in the measurement system between both cities, and this number is based on the highest gold purity available [40].

nowadays. Meaning that the Mona Lisa's low-ball insurance payoff is worth almost twice as much as that of the entire Renaissance from the Medici's perspective, which is frankly ridiculous.

Contrary to what your parents would tell you, people or art of any sort are not irreplaceable. It's just our own sentimentality getting in the way of rational thought. For example, people might well believe that every life is unique and incalculable in value. But our behaviour says otherwise.

We don't add an infinite number of dollars to the GDP every time someone is born, that would be silly and patently unhelpful. We usually subconsciously draw a distinction between real value and feel-good "irreplaceable value." Or at the very least our laws imply as much, given that as a society we're fine with some deaths for the sake of convenience. Automobiles are allowed on the streets despite the fact that there are accidents, for instance.

If we genuinely believed that *whoever saves a life, is considered as if he saved an entire world* as the oft-quoted phrase from the Talmud says, we wouldn't be allowed to drive cars at all. Instead, as a society, we've reached a compromise. In areas where there are speed limits, we've agreed that no matter what the person stands to gain from going fast to their destination, society stands to lose more from their risky behaviour. However, we also implicitly know that there will be casualties, even if everyone respects the speed limits. Hence, we are willing to tolerate a certain cost of life to satisfy our individual desires. It might change from day to day, from legal jurisdiction to jurisdiction, or even based on the time of day, but there is an implied monetary value hidden away in our practices and conventions, which we unconsciously and collectively apply to a human life.

A potential future Da Vinci might be run over, but we accept this as a reasonable compromise for our convenience. The unconscious mechanisms that drive our society have thus arrived at a monetary value for a life, and it is far from an infinitely high one at that, but neither is it anywhere near the $4.50 number. As such, the middle of the road number, our $10,000 to $100,000, might be more appropriate and closer to the monetary value we apply to a life - neither is it disregarding the value of the shape that the components are in, nor is it blowing it out of proportions by assigning freakishly large value on it.

Same logic ought to apply to stock valuations. One should not be so pessimistic, so as to only consider the scrap metal of the machinery of the company, but neither should one believe that the ideas behind it can perform miracles.

Overall, I remain reticent of companies that mainly depend on intangible assets as their main source of value. Take Facebook as a perfect example. Not in a million years would I have invested in the company. On paper, at the very least, it wasn't that dissimilar to well-established competition like Myspace, Hi5, and Friendster. In fact, it had less functionality, and that was partially one of its selling points as the established companies had gotten too cluttered and annoying. Even so, to bet on the outsider and underdog is typically very foolish. Yet because of a combination of marketing quirks, winning crucial meme battles, and pure bandwagon effect, it ended up being on top. Had the dice fallen a bit differently Facebook would've barely been a footnote in the long line of failed tech start-ups. Nothing would be remarkably all that different in society had that happened.

Rather than preferences, I prefer my economic investments to be based on necessities. As a thought experiment, let's imagine everyone in a society was infected with a strange disease. The main symptom of this malady is that you immediately forget what you enjoy. Your memory remains intact other than that, but you must rediscover what it is that you find pleasurable.

Without prior conditioning, and with a world of endless possibilities, it is unlikely that people would adopt the same tastes in clothing, food, entertainment, etc. On the other hand, they would still very much require the services of the same harbours, railways, infrastructure, airports, etc. Those are not choices of preferences, but of convenience. There is simply no currently better way of scratching that itch than by following those behavioural patterns. So, whereas all consumer-driven enterprises would suffer massive upheaval, the natural monopolies would mostly remain unmolested.

The purveyors of fleeting fancies only know this too well. Which is why, when the Berlin Wall fell, Coca-Cola stuffed as many trucks as it had on short notice, and bum-rushed them to the East Germans where they distributed Coke freely [41]. Some checkpoints dispensed over 70,000 cans in a few hours. This wasn't done out of a charitable act, or as Coca-Cola's website put it "due to the hard work and swift action of Coke employees like Ritter, in the first week after the fall of the Wall, two million people drank a toast to freedom with a Coke." [42] It's much more like when a drug dealer gives his product away for free to people who are for trying it for the first time to get them hooked. To quote Hans Wiezorek, the then president of the German Coca-Cola division: "There won't be two colas in restaurants and small outlets. They'll choose the one that's first in the market." [43]

There are been psychology studies that point to the fact that humans are notoriously bad at rejecting the syren call of a free product. "Free," more often than not, makes us drop our guard and give something a chance, which we might otherwise not do. We tend to place an irrationally high value on something being free, instead of good value for money [44]. Hence, it's a calculated business move from the supplier's point of view. If your product taps into one of our primal needs, like sugar, it becomes a supernormal stimulus and we immediately put it high up on the priority list.

But, once we have a favourite supernormal stimulus to satisfy a certain need, we develop a certain sense of inertia. Areas, or groups, that favour Coke, tend to remain like that, whereas those that prefer Pepsi are just plain wrong. If you had your first "toast of freedom" with a Coke, it's now associated with positive emotions and you'll *open happiness* or *taste the feeling*, every single time you drink it. Next time, they should just cut the middleman start ringing a goddamn bell to make you salivate and feel happy.

People's choices can be so thoroughly conditioned through culture and tradition that people make objectively worse decisions. In blind taste studies Coca-Cola is actually less favoured than Pepsi. Yet, in non-blind studies in the United States, people overwhelmingly prefer Coke. As it has ceased being a simple brand, at this point it's a cultural icon [45].

In all seriousness though, much like the Red Queen phenomenon which we described in Part I, mature companies tend to remain in stasis. There are increasingly fewer new people to sell cans of fizzy sugary water to, hence apathy takes hold. The only reason to take a step forward is that your competition is taking a step forward. Hence, proportionally, you can run all you like but still remain in place. Unless there is some outside factor, like a growing demand for healthier and less sugary products, there may be a minor momentary change in market share, but overall the underlying dynamic remains the same.

This type of stable rent-seeking behaviour is why investors like Warren Buffett are huge proponents of Coca-Cola, and similar market-mature companies with a good brand recognition. Yet, despite their spectacular long-term profits, I think that's missing the point a bit. When Warren Buffett trots out the argument that had you invested $40 back in 1919, the equivalent of a single Coca-Cola stock, you would've seen several wars, economic booms and busts, sugar rations, massive depreciation of the value of your original investment, etc. Yet, you would still have about $5 million almost a century later, he's ignoring key information.

I do agree with him that consistency and picking the right stocks is the key to wealth. But I could just as well say that the key to living a happy life is eating right, exercising, getting enough sleep, finding your passions, make enough money to live life on your terms and developing enough social skill to have the people you want in your life. This sounds great on paper, yet the execution thereof is a nightmare onto itself. Any one of those points has libraries worth of books devoted to just trying to explain, understand and determine the best course of action.

Life is rarely as predictable as all that. In any given period of history, you could find outliers and attempt to derive laws from their behaviour. It's why I find Malcolm Gladwell's *Outliers* so irksome. It's not to say it's a bad book, but it's tone-deaf and lacking in nuance. If you take a list of a small sample size, you're bound to be able to find plausible common threads that explain their success - especially if you carefully refine your already biased sample to showcase your points. Nevermind that there are probably millions of people who fit the bill of what outliers are supposed to have to become outliers, yet still never amount to much.

In a couple instances in this book, we have briefly mentioned the "survivor bias" where people disproportionately pay attention to things that "survived" a given event, whereas they ignore those that didn't make it to the other end. Back during WWII, there were a lot of novel technologies and circumstances for which the militaries of the world didn't have an optimal statistically-verified procedure. As such, at the behest of the White House, a group of geniuses was assembled and they were called the Statistical Research Group. The department would receive questions about issues from commanders in the field, like what the best possible pattern was to use when attacking the enemy based on available resources and technology. Among the issues to be discussed was that planes were constantly being shot down, more armour was evidently needed but had you armoured the whole plane it would be far too costly and it would add a lot of bulk to the already overladen planes.

Initially, what the top brass suggested was armouring the areas that came back with bullet holes. After all, it makes sense that if it has bullets, it is clearly liable to get shot. Yet, had this been done, it would've likely ended up needlessly killing a lot of brave men. A member of the panel, by the name of Abraham Wald, explained why: When a plane comes back with bullet holes, it's clearly able to come back, despite the damage. Hence the areas that need to be armoured more are the ones that usually have the least amount of damage; since, if we assume that damage is randomly distributed, then these are clearly areas where you can't damage and manage to come back to fight another day [46].

In other words, focusing on what made the survivors, the winners, in this system successful is entirely the opposite way to go about it. The winners might just have been able to survive through random chance - there's no real factor that unifies them. After all, the number one rule in statistics is "correlation does not imply causation." But the losers, on the other hand, might have had circumstances that made it almost impossible for them to survive.

Thus, looking at the long-term winners within a system might not actually say anything about merit, but it's actually saying something about the role of luck. This is true both for people and companies. In 2001, there was a business management book that took the publishing world by storm, as it sold millions of companies. It was called *Good to Great: Why Some Companies Make the Leap... and Others Don't* and it focused on the mechanism behind how good companies become great. In the book, the author highlighted eleven companies that had become extraordinary, supposedly through their business acumen. Yet, had you bought in on the hype and purchased these stocks for your portfolio, seven years later, you would've underperformed the S&P-500 index [47].

Trying to play the role of pseudo-prophet is unbecoming of a true investor. A true investor never gambles, and at worst makes educated guesses. Which means that they will tend not to attempt to play the game by the same rules that everyone else is playing. The way to do it properly is by stacking the deck in your favour. By focusing on economic moats that have longer than average staying power, in industries that are necessary for the functioning of the modern world, is the main way by which to do this. In this way, you will miss out on the next Google, but you won't be playing pin the tail on the donkey in a room full of wild beasts that would love to have you as their meal. Don't work harder, work smarter.

5 - Bigger, Faster and Stronger: How Organizational Structure Affects Social and Technological Developments

> "The purpose of each thing's development determines its development; the development points to its final state"
>
> - *Marcus Aurelius*

Classical economics has one resounding answer in terms of what the most efficient outcome for almost any business venture ought to be - free market competition. The argument is twofold: central planners do a poor job at managing the inherent complexity within the markets, and consequently as a result of asymmetry of information, they fail to make wise decisions when compared to the invisible hand.

Nassim Taleb put it best in suggesting that the reason for why liberalism has historically been the one path most conducive to affluence and technological development is that it allows for failure and experimentation [48]. Oftentimes, technological progress happens by accident - we do not know the depths of our ignorance; because of this, we do not know the impact of a given piece of research until after it's been processed by the aggregate hivemind of humanity. As such, the ability to take risks, at relatively minor societal costs, is essential for the rapid development of innovation.

As we talked about in PV-Ch2, this is why the joint-stock company was invented in the first place - as a means to pool risks, and thus try things that had never been done before. In the past, they were used as a means to finance ventures that were prohibitively expensive, and often dangerous. Nevertheless, this is why, even with the invention of risk pooling and free market competition, governments tended to be involved in those gargantuan ventures: the Spice trade, the British East India Company, the Dutch East India Company, etc. all had implicit, or formal governmental backing. The scope of these ventures might step on the legal rights of others, thus a need for the executive power to step in and act as ultimate arbiters might arise. After all, part of the perks of being in charge is being within the "state of exception" where your direct interests may not necessarily have to actually follow the law to the very letter.

In either case, classical economics tends to gloss over the need for governmental backing, or monopoly rights, when it comes to big projects. Their lifecycle, and possibly profitability, may exceed human life expectancy. It stands to reason that no rational agent would ever invest in such ventures, unless there's a backer who is capable of making good on the promises, repaying debts in timely manners, and who will not waiver in their commitment when the hour of need arises.

In other words, we have established two commonly-held frameworks in which R&D and innovation are maximised for society. According to Austrian economist Joseph Schumpeter, the main determinant for product innovation is the market share a company has, as only companies with excess profits can afford to innovate [49]. Hence, monopolies are best suited to innovate due to the inherent costs. On the other hand, Nobel Memorial Prize winning economist Kenneth Arrow says that perfect competition is the ideal, given that it encourages diversification of solutions and approaches [50].

These two propositions would seem to be in direct contradiction, yet this is not so. In reality, they're merely different points in the development of an industry. Depending on how many resources are required for the success of the project, the ideal structure will change. Take computation, which is a perfect example of how shifts in regards to optimal market structure for innovation can occur:

Originally, computers were far too costly, rudimentary and unadaptive, such that its limits and price provided for an enormous and effective entry barrier [51]. Consequently, their main use was in the military to break codes, or run very complex algorithms of logistics and men. For several years, the governments of the world essentially held effective monopoly power over innovation in this field, not because the public wasn't interested in them, but because capital could be allocated elsewhere for far greater returns in smaller institutions, therefore making the entry barriers far too costly for private individuals or firms.

Nevertheless, past a certain innovation point, where computers became versatile and affordable enough, the public at large started adopting them, and redesigning them to do tasks that its original institutional inventors did not conceive of. Initially, once the public started adopting computers, few companies controlled the industry, yet over time the sector started fragmenting [52].

Nowadays, it's more fragmented than ever, yet it's also producing the most substantial technological advances since its inception. In other words, the shift from the efficiency of monopolistic innovation to the free market competition optimum happens when potential losses incurred by society for each failed instance are offset by the collective benefit of the instances that succeed. If a potential mistake is too costly for society at large, then it is best to concentrate society's resources to avoid it, even if it leads to waste and loss of potential output.

Having said this, so far we've ignored one crucial difference between R&D and traditional entry barriers that originate from associated costs. The main difference between R&D and other types of cost, is that there is uncertainty of the likely payoff of the endeavour. As such, there are two main types of uncertainty to consider [53]:

- **Technological Uncertainty**: Whether the firm will discover the innovation at all. Perhaps the technology necessary to make the project a reality is still too far off in the future, or perhaps it's simply not physically possible.

- **Market Uncertainty**: Whether the other likely competitors would discover the innovation before one's firm if they are, or were, in the market. If, for example, market entry barriers were low and the existing research points to a breakthrough being likely in the near future, this will attract investors who want a piece of the pie. Either that, or existing competitors might be tempted with the promise of profits in the near future.

Assuming that a given research avenue is especially costly, and unlikely to pay off, then a company might benefit from ignoring it altogether. For example, there are theoretical engine models nowadays that could conceivably travel faster than light, but the capital requirements to build and test them are currently far in excess of whatever profit you could make from their use (assuming it even works, which is very unlikely)[65] [54]. In other words, if one is to invest in R&D, it might happen that the lump sum is lost with little to show for it; but there is the opposite scenario wherein an invention might offset any of the costs of R&D, and make any rivalling company without the technology incapable of surpassing or equalling the efficiency of the innovator, thus making them unprofitable and driving them out of business. Consequently, there is a complex interplay of chance, output and cost that determine whether to bother investing in developing technologies. A company's main incentive to invest money in research is simply survival, so as to be able to counter anything that their competition throws at them.

If a long shot pays off, you might have a monopoly in whatever revolutionary technology was invented and you'll be able to reap immense profits. But long shots are called that for their rarity, chances are that you don't have the winning lottery ticket, and throwing money into the trash would be about as productive. I believe companies intrinsically know that,

65 Incidentally, the "Alcubierre Drive" was proposed by Mexican theoretical physicist Miguel Alcubierre, which goes to show that us Mexicans have a disregard for the rule of law, even if it's a law that emanates from natural phenomena.

which is why large and well-developed industries, like the pharmaceutical arena, have just outright resorted to buying small companies that have accidentally developed chemicals with promising properties, instead of attempting to compete to develop them themselves [55]. In other words, they're essentially outsourcing their R&D to smaller companies that simply have no other choice but to bet on long shots.

This reticence to take big risks on the part of big companies is partially what's to blame for our current technological stagnation. Outwardly, it doesn't really seem that there's been any technological stagnation; after all, one just has to look out of the window and see the plethora of new and improved products. To a great degree, this is an illusion though.

Per capita, the rate of inventions that have fundamentally changed how society operates has been steadily decreasing. It reached a peak in the 19th century, where it began declining throughout the 20th century. This was despite higher levels of education, major leaps in science and the invention, as well as widespread adoption, of the computer [56]. Much of the cornerstones of our current technology were developed during WWII (computation, jet engines, atomic energy, radar, sonar, rocketry, etc.) and, despite some considerable improvements, there's little that is fundamentally new in how the technology operates. In fact, it's been speculated that as much as 80% of the economic growth between the years 1950-1993 was based on the application of previously discovered ideas [57].

It's precisely because of this sort of realization that I'm altogether sceptical of companies that depend on constantly innovating. Sooner or later, their luck dries up, all the low hanging fruit is picked, and all that potential that was incorporated in the intangible value disappears in a puff of smoke.

Fact of the matter is that discovering something today has been made exponentially more expensive and difficult than it used to be. Businesses nowadays cannot hope to bet on any single idea and hope to make it out alive - overspecialize and you breed in weakness. This concept applies in any unconscious system, whether one is talking about an organism in the wild or a company in the market.

In other words, if one is trying to determine the long-term survival chances and capability of an organism to thrive in a given environment, then they have to determine their adaptability. This is done by seeing how well and quickly they adapt to stressors. Remember all the way back in the first part of this book, wherein we talked about the cold logic behind evolution. We talked about spandrels, or adaptations, which happen to have unintended uses from their original intent.

The more of these spandrels an organism has, the more antifragile (capable of benefiting from chaotic situations) it becomes. Companies operate in much the same way. If they're overspecialized and too big to be able to pivot to market demands or circumstances, then they're going the way of the dinosaurs. This, in part, is why I believe there should not be such a thing as "too big to fail" institutions - it's far too dangerous to have them. As all human endeavours will fail sooner or later, and thus we should embark on the business of running a state with eyes wide open. Instead, the modern world runs a deficit with eyes wide shut, and believing happy tales of rags to riches.

With smaller, more adaptable companies, the immediate future shouldn't really be such a cause for concern. Far too many economists spend too much time analysing employment rates, interest rates or any such ephemeral measures that have already likely been accounted for. Temporary expected variations, or trends, shouldn't be a main concern for the antifragile or robust stock owner.

What should be a concern though are unexpected variations. Imagine, for example, what would've happened to the British economy during WWII had Operation Bernhard actually been put into effect. At its core, what the Nazis in charge of Operation Bernhard sought to do was to forge British banknotes, and airdrop them in British cities [58]. In essence, they would have triggered an economic meltdown by making British currency so widely available, as to render them worthless overnight. Perhaps, remembering Germany's own period of hyperinflation and economic turmoil prior to the war, the Reich Minister of Propaganda Joseph Goebbels called it "a grotesque plan" albeit he saw its potential[66] [59]. Nevertheless, the plan never had sufficient secrecy, diligence or resources to enact until very late in the war, at which point it was far too late. Had it actually managed to get off the ground, it would've essentially short-circuited Britain's ability to fight without having to fire a single shot.

This is the sort of thing that no economic model could've possibly predicted but it would have knocked a fair few people into poverty. Hence, the importance of thorough and proper economic moats that are hopefully not based on figments of the imagination, but cold hard facts. Had you invested in promises of potential, or intangible assets, they might have well been able to vanish overnight; but, had you bought capital, like machinery, it would be far more difficult for financial alchemy to make the inherent value of that business disappear. There was a time, for instance, in hyperinflation Germany, where car companies, with all their equipment in mint condition, cost less than the price of 227 cars they'd previously produced [60]. Of course, this is a silly state of affairs, and by 1927 the market had quadrupled in value from its low point in 1922. But if you'd invested in something more ephemeral, which depended a lot on the public's appreciation, you might be out of luck in the random scramble of economic recovery and be left behind. It bears repeating that the numbers we assign to things are arbitrary and are merely an amalgamation of people's collective perception. Fantasies are often dispelled overnight and thus we should invest in something more sensible - more real - even if it's more boring and its price is less likely to skyrocket to the stars.

Now, I do understand someone's reticence to heed my words. After all, this sound an awful lot like a parent telling their kids they should eat their vegetables, rather than the delicious looking chocolate over there. But at the end of the day, investing in less glamorous, and more conservative stocks is good for you for the exact same reasons as eating your vegetables:

---

66 It bears saying that this moral outrage comes from someone who would murder his own children a couple of years later.

it will help to avoid your portfolio from getting bloated with unnecessary and dangerous garbage, whilst dramatically increasing your life expectancy and quality of life by reducing the strain that your investments undergo with market swings.

PART VII: THE CENTURY OF SELF: MODERNITY

The question of when modernity begins is a contentious one. If you're a geologist, you rightfully claim that "the present" begins in 1950 at the eve of the atomic age. Large scale nuclear weapons testing altered the global ratio of carbon-14 to carbon-12; hence, anything "modern" has a unique composition and traditional radiocarbon measuring systems don't work without further calibration [1]. If you're a historian, you might even go farther back and say that 1500 is the beginning of modernity [2]. If you're an artist you might say that modernity began in the late 19th century and ended in the 1970s, which gave rise to postmodernism [3].

Point being that it kind of feels like everyone's just kind of arbitrarily picking a date which suits their purposes. So, I shall do the same and I'll say June 28, 1919 as my date - the day where the Treaty of Versailles was signed. I do not pick this date lightly; since, as we've touched on before, the end of WWI represented a seismic shift in terms of how politics, social classes, economics and even war worked. The tensions that had accrued over the years of peace were vented, and society was lifted from the state of stasis it had been held for a long while. Production technologies improved and markets were so saturated with goods that the only way to make a profit was to cater to niches. With the board having been set, what followed was one of the most dynamic and interesting centuries in humankind.

Someone born in 1900 was born in an era where the American frontier - the cowboy era - was in its last throes. They would've lived through the infancy of air travel, through one of the biggest epidemics in world history, possibly seen the first large skyscrapers being built, experienced WWI and the creation of the Soviet Union, all before turning eighteen. Following this, they would have seen the widespread acceptance of the radio, experienced one of the worst economic downturns in world history, seen the rise and subsequent fall of the Nazis. In the blink of an eye more there are jet engines, missiles, nuclear energy, computers, and even space travel! By the time they die at the ripe old age of a hundred, the Soviet Union empire has collapsed, and their grandson will hear about their death through a phone that is comparable in computational power to what was used to put men on the moon, almost half a century earlier.

This is our age, and in this chapter we will try to unearth and understand the hidden forces that governs it.

1 - Consumerism and Social Tribes

> *"If there's anything more important than my ego around, I want it caught and shot now."*
>
> *- Douglas Adams, The Hitchhiker's Guide to the Galaxy*

Modernity is an age lacking in gods or kings, largely overtaken by man. Even among the most devout religious believers in the civilized areas of the world, their own cult of personality, seems to have largely preceded the devotion of the creators of all things. Same goes for absolute power by the nobility, which is largely a relic of times past in the few countries that still have it.

With the realization that we're wholly insignificant in the universe, came a motivation to create our own reality, with us at the very centre. Technology improved, and we shifted from a *needs-based* economy to a *wants-based* economy, where we focused on satisfying flights of fancy instead of survival considerations. *People are now educated to desire, rarely to appreciate.* For the first time in human history, the everyman was able to afford a taste of the lifestyle that they thought was best. The very act of consumption became a set of decisions that were inextricably linked with personality.

Think about how *Apple*, the multinational technology company, has become essentially a cult in recent years. Their advocates sound like brainwashed religious zealots as they spout identical catchphrases ("it's simple, yet elegant"), to convince you that paying three times more for essentially the same product, with added compatibility issues, is a sensible financial decision. Apple has so thoroughly succeeded at selling the ideas of nonconformity, innovation and creativity, that the very sight of the logo is enough to prime people into being temporarily more creative. That's not an exaggeration either, there have been studies about the behavioural changes people have when exposed to logos [4].

In the modern age, companies don't solely sell products or services - they sell an ideal lifestyle. The reason behind this is simple, when you personally identify with the brand, you will be more loyal to it. Remember all the way back in PI-Ch6 where we talked about how humans have an "ingroup" and "outgroup" bias. Brands are exploiting this bias, they're catering to a sense of community that was lost in the advent of industrialization. Reason for this is simple, whosoever manages to control the mechanisms which evolutionarily drove our psychology, will be able to wield considerable power.

A brand, in the modern sense, is nothing less and nothing more than a surrogate community of like-minded fellows. These voluntary "social tribes" hence become the reason for existing for their believers. Whether you're a hippie, who likes boutique hemp clothing; a banker, who enjoys a Savile Row suit; or, ironically, a communist who enjoys a mass-produced Che Guevara shirt, the market has you covered. Any ideology or belief, if it isn't already being co-opted by the system for the sake of profit, then it's only a matter of time before it is.

The board game *Monopoly*, for example, was originally designed to show the dangers of unfettered capitalism and rent-seeking monopolists. In the interim, the significance was ripped off and the game itself was left intact [5]. The same has happened with other games; for instance, *Snakes and Ladders* used to be a game popular in the Indian sub-continent showing how a wretched person could rise to a higher standard, and how a good person can fall from grace with a single mistake [6]. From being a practical philosophical examination on life, now it's just a children's board game you play when you feel like you have too much free time.

In this day and age, there is no such thing as authenticity; almost everything is a performance designed to give you a certain sensation, and make you more willing to pay. This happens without real care for the actual significance of the symbols that have been repurposed. A flag maker may, without a second thought, be willing to sell a Nazi flag alongside an Israeli one on their website. It makes a profit, and thus it's fine[67]. Principles in the modern age are of secondary consideration, and only if they don't stand in the way of profits. We are so preoccupied with whether or not we could, that we didn't bother to think whether we should[68].

Oddly enough, even entire cities have become part of this charade. By way of example, I submit Venice. Once a thriving mercantile republic, which was the envy of the world; it is now a necropolis, a husk of its former self, where the only permanent residents are the elderly, and its main inhabitants are the selfie-stick-wielding transient tourists. To quote a Venetian woman on the phenomenon: "As the local population dwindles, the tourists are slowly killing off the same Venice street life that they dream of witnessing close up." [7]

These are deaths by a thousand cuts and they happen accidentally, as standalone complexes. There's no cabal out there of evil men planning for the destruction and misuse of traditional values and ideals. We're doing it to ourselves in our quest for convenience, beauty and uniqueness. Perhaps, as a sign of protest, we might go to irreverence. If we can't have a serious ideology without it being prostituted, we'll just mock the world. Yet, then you just end up marketing irreverence, and you end up with a new market segment, which they'll sell products to - like this book.

This happens because oversaturated industries fragment into more manageable pieces to be able to service a certain niche, as otherwise, the individual companies wouldn't be able to compete. Yet this didn't happen overnight. The business historian Richard S. Tedlow identified four historical stages in the evolution of market segmentation [8]:

---

67 This is assuming that special interest groups aren't poisoning the marketplace with ideological considerations.

68 I spared no expense in stealing this iconic movie quote.

- **Fragmentation (pre-1880s)**: Markets were characterised by small suppliers who sold products in a reduced geographic area.
- **Unification or Mass Marketing (1880s–1920s)**: With improvements in means of transportation the economy unified. Standardised and branded products were circulated nationally. Producers usually insisted on strict standardisation regulation to attain economies of scale with a view to penetrate markets in the initial stages of a product's life cycle.
- **Segmentation (1920s–1980s)**: With a maturation of markets and better technologies, manufacturers started catering to demographic, socioeconomic and ideologically driven market segments.
- **Hyper-segmentation (1980s+)**: Competition drove producers into narrower market segments. Marketers can now target very specialised groups, and technology allows for further specialisation and customization of products.

The everyman today has access to such a world of plenty and variety that the options are limitless. An average salary in the Western world gives you access to the lifestyle that would've only been reserved for kings. Louis XIV had a staff of 498 servants for his meals, but not one of them could cook Mexican, Turkish, Japanese, or Indian food, which you can get delivered to your home with a metaphorical snap of your fingers [9]. Economies of scale allow you to essentially have a retinue of thousands of servants, which often live an ocean away. Add to it that Versailles didn't have appropriate toilet facilities, so it wasn't uncommon to find faeces in the halls, and I'm reticent about revving up the time machine any time soon [10].

Nowadays, when you go to Versailles as a tourist, you don't think about the wretched open sewer smell or the smoky rooms with chimneys that didn't work during the daily life of its most auspicious inhabitants. Even our very notions of the past are whitewashed and designed to perfection. In our day-to-day lives, I'm inclined to agree with the Russian playwright Alexander Pushkin that "a deception that elevates us is dearer than a host of low truths." I don't want to think about rivers of piss and shit when I'm in Versailles, no matter how historically accurate they were. Authenticity in the postmodernist, global world is not about truthfulness, it's about theatricality. At the end of the day, I just want to enjoy myself whilst pretending I'm cultured - and the experience as is overwhelmingly delivers on that front. We're all gods of our own little world in a way, arbitrarily selecting ideas to inhabit it.

Yet, for all the benefits that modernity has brought, it has created a curious environment. In this day and age, it is entirely possible to stand inside a crowded subway car, be packed so tightly that one has to smell a stranger's armpit, yet still feel completely alone.

A stranger on the street is likely to remain just that - a stranger. Talking to someone randomly in a city because they sparked your interest is seen as the height of lunacy, rather than a perfectly normal desire. If anyone dares to acknowledge someone else's existence, outside of the requirements of politeness, it will be met with deep suspicion. Hucksters and scammers are the main people who dare break the unspoken agreement of ignoring each other, outside of the places where it's socially tolerated to talk with people like bars and clubs. Hence, cities have the unique characteristic of providing so much anonymity that it creates a sense of isolation. Almost gone are the communities where everyone knows and helps each other. So much so that developed economies like the UK have actually branded loneliness as a public health concern[69], even going as far as appointing a minister of loneliness [11]. Young or old, modern life often isolates the individual.

When one reads a book like *Don't sleep there are snakes*[70], you almost get jealous of stone age tribes that essentially live in abject poverty. You start to think about how overly civilized society has become by often rejecting human nature itself. But then you think about the potential lack of food, comfort, the constant fear of the environment and predators, along with all manner of other

---

69 Though to be fair the Brits have never been the most socially adjusted people out there.

70 Where a missionary retells his attempts at converting the Piraha tribe to Christianity. Far from succeeding, he ends up becoming one of their converts and stops believing in God.

health and sanitary issues, and the feeling quickly passes. Living in mud huts in exchange for companionship and kinship would be a difficult sell, even for the loneliest of people.

Yet, this erosion of a sense of belonging is palpable nonetheless. Modern society has some very real costs and side effects associated with it, such as a significant rise in depression. To quote a study talking about that phenomenon [12]:

> *"Mental and physical well-being are intimately related. The growing burden of chronic diseases, which arise from an evolutionary mismatch between past human environments and modern-day living, may be central to rising rates of depression. Declining social capital and greater inequality and loneliness are candidate mediators of a depressiogenic social milieu. Modern populations are increasingly overfed, malnourished, sedentary, sunlight-deficient, sleep-deprived, and socially-isolated. These changes in lifestyle each contribute to poor physical health and affect the incidence and treatment of depression."*

Being able to be lonely in a crowd is enough to drive a man to despair. There is evidence to support that a rapid modernization rate can even drive people to suicide. After indigenous circumpolar people rapidly modernized, suicide rates tripled within a decade and there was an epidemic of diabetes as well [13]. It bears saying that suicide tends to be a male-centric phenomenon. In the western world, males die three-to-four times more often by means of suicide than do females [14]. Interestingly enough, women attempt suicide between two and four times more than men [15]. The purported reason for this difference in success is that women tend to use poison, whereas men just jump off a building or some such more violent and less rescuable measure [16].

In a study of 175 American university students, Psychology professor R. Michael Brown and his associates tested an evolutionary theory of suicide using a 164-item questionnaire. The results showed that individuals with low reproductive opportunity[71] and high burdensomeness to kin reported more suicidal thoughts, as well as more depression and a sense of hopelessness [17]. At the risk of sounding like Dr. Freud, I will reassert that the sex drive, is one of the main drives for life. It's the very foundation by which we view and interact with reality.

Why am I writing this book, for example? I immensely enjoy the act of writing, but it wouldn't be anywhere near as satisfying if at the end of each writing session I clicked *delete*. A writer, almost by necessity, has to be immensely narcissistic, with an average book size of between 80,000-120,000 words, and humans typically reading around 330 words per minute, you're looking at a time commitment of around four hours at the bare minimum, and under ideal circumstances. Implicitly, by putting this book out into the ether, I believe that my words can stand against other means of entertainment, otherwise, there'd be no point in putting it out there if I believed that I was wasting others' time. I also believe that this collection of musings about psychology, biology, history and economics is enough to increase my prestige. An author wishes to be read, and this attention will increase their standing in society.

Implicitly, by me working on myself, I'm increasing my social value. Same with going to the gym, or any other beneficial activity. In reality, what one is doing by working on all that is increasing one's prestige. If nobody ever acknowledged any of the effort I put in, I'd quickly lose interest. This might seem incredibly vain, and it is, but it is also quite human. To quote a conversation between two programmers in *Ex Machina*, a film about the development of true artificial intelligence:

> **Caleb**: *Why did you give her sexuality? An AI doesn't need a gender. She could have been a grey box.*
>
> **Nathan**: *Actually, I don't think that's true. Can you give an example of consciousness at any level, human or animal, that exists without a sexual dimension?*

---

71 For example, people who realise they're unattractive to the opposite sex.

Caleb: *They have sexuality as an evolutionary reproductive need.*
Nathan: *What imperative does a grey box have to interact with another grey box? Can consciousness exist without interaction? Anyway, sexuality is fun, man. If you're gonna exist, why not enjoy it? You want to remove the chance of her falling in love and fucking? And the answer to your real question, you bet she can fuck.*

The quest for meaning is ultimately one derived from the sex drive and all its consequences. At its core, it is life's and evolution's algorithm. We seek to be important and irreplaceable in people's lives. It is this fire that drives us to create and consume and gives us a desire to live, even when undergoing hardship. Modernity has somewhat robbed us of that sense of accomplishment. Precisely, this lack of meaning is what makes people so deeply unsatisfied with their jobs, even if they're extremely well paid.

Adam Smith famously suggested in *On the Wealth of Nations* that a pin factory could work much more effectively, and produce far more, when each task was isolated and given to separate people. This is the design philosophy that Henry Ford perfected, which gave mankind an affordable motor vehicle. This idea alone revolutionised production in all industries, but it made people infinitely replaceable - little more than a cog in the grand machine.

Imagine if at the end of every shift, I destroyed whatever you had been working on. I still paid you just as much, but your work would amount to busywork. Your blood, sweat and tears would mean nothing and have no further significance. Research suggests that if I did just that you'd demand ever-increasing wages to continue, and eventually you would refuse to do it altogether, or demand prohibitively higher wages [18]. Even then, I have my doubts that anyone would even need scientific proof to verify that assertion. The idea of being locked days on end in a stuffy room doing an unfathomably repetitive task, for a similarly incomprehensible reason is something that makes us uncomfortable to the very bone.

Modern production methods alienate the worker and make them excruciatingly unhappy. Whilst their work isn't being destroyed in front of them, it's being shipped an ocean away on big standardised steel boxes, where someone will marginally add to it, only to then ship it elsewhere. This cycle of adding small components to it, and immediately shipping it elsewhere continues until the product completed. Eventually, somewhere in the world, the product is finished, and it's sent to a completely different locale, where it can fetch a better price.

We're alienated from the fruits of our labour. We see no purpose in our actions, because we may never see the results. There is no cause and effect between actions and consequences. I'm hardly the first to point such a phenomenon out, Adam Smith himself mentioned it in the same book, but offered no real solution. Karl Marx picked up the torch and ran with it.

In the last few hundred years, there hasn't really been any period where someone hasn't been yammering on about it. It's a bit of a catch-22, where one wants the fruits of modernity but with none of the side effects. Most critics dance around the issue, or offer pie in the sky solutions that aren't applicable in this moment without incredible advances in technology, or fundamentally changing human nature.

This is why Ted Kaczynski, the infamous Unabomber, is a unique advocate against workers' alienation. He's one of the few who actually talks the talk and walks the walk. He advocated, and actively worked towards, a total collapse of the world economy through a prolonged terrorist bombing campaign. In his mind, there weren't any possible compromises, as otherwise, we'd always revert to being cogs in the industrial machine instead of humans. His reasoning was simple: this alienation from one's effort is a new phenomenon. There was a time when survival itself was a Sisyphean effort, we derived enjoyment from the tasks required for it [19].

But then came the time where we became victims of our own success. We had plenty, and all predators became a joke to us. Survival itself was no longer seemingly a worthy endeavour. Hence, we developed "surrogate activities" - *artificial goals that people set up for themselves to have some objective to work toward, for the sake of the "fulfilment" that they get from pursuing and accomplishing the goal.* It's the human equivalent of a hamster wheel, where a whole lot of effort is expended getting nowhere. Yet, it feels like something was accomplished due to the effort expended.

According to Kaczynski, these surrogate activities are unsatisfactory and blind us from our true purpose. If they weren't artificial in nature, there would be a satiation point. Instead, we constantly drive for more: "*Thus the money-maker constantly strives for more and more wealth. The scientist no sooner solves one problem than he moves on to the next. The long-distance runner drives himself to run always farther and faster.*"

However, under all the pretensions of the surrogate activities, we have very powerful and very real biological drives, which must be satisfied. among them are the need for community and companionship. Isolated, and no less confused, we created social tribes around our surrogate activities; hence we have football team fans, media fan clubs, political activists, your regulars at the gym, etc. A very particular type of consumption drove these people together, and it created tribes with their own traditions, hierarchies, cultures and beliefs.

Through this social network, we attempt to fulfil all the emotional needs that modernity seems otherwise to deprive us of. We attempt to use it much in the same way a hunter-gatherer group would've worked 100,000 years ago. There are friends, meaning and romance.

This is an imperfect substitute though, especially when it comes to matters of romance. In objective terms, preferences in ways to spend disposable income seems like a curious way to start one's quest for a partner. As Moira Weigel put it in *Labor of Love: The Invention of Dating*:

> *"For most of human history, the idea that a preference for one consumer product over another could serve as a predictor of romantic compatibility between two people would not have made any sense. For one thing, there were not many nonessential goods to choose among. The criteria that guided courtship were far more limited: family, religious background, social class. Likes were freighted with little of the significance that they have now."*

Nowadays, we believe that consumption patterns, or having the same superficial labels as our partners, is the key to finding happy relationships. But human beings are not cameras, you can't just slap a label on someone and expect to describe them in all their complexity. If anything, humans are a little like wine, where a blurb describing it doesn't truly do it justice. Yet, even in something as relatively simple as wine, "wine connoisseurs" are notoriously full of shit. There have been studies wherein supposed wine experts are only consistent in their tastes and rankings of quality about 10% of the time [20]. Even doing something as silly as changing a bottle's label from a luxurious brand to a cheaper brand is enough to make people rate it as worse tasting [21].

I would posit, perhaps controversially, that humans are more complicated than wine bottles. Yet, we still oddly insist on searching for them with a method that would barely work for cameras. In online dating, for example, you can search for all manner of things like income, height, political affiliation, religious beliefs, hair colour, and body type. But you can't search for the things that would actually matter to you in the long run, like whether they're kind, whether they'd be able to cheer you up after a bad day, whether they can fall in love, whether they have a good sense of humour, or even, whether they're good in bed. These are all based on subjective experience and may never be truly shareable, but they are extremely important.

I'm not exaggerating in saying that there are dating sites nowadays solely based around whether or not you voted for Trump [22]. We fall into judging on superficiality because it's easier, both to program an algorithm for and to judge on as a user. But real life does not often lend itself to simplifications. Online dating represents a market failure of the highest order. Just to put things into perspective, studies suggest that it takes around seven hours of work to get someone, anyone, out for a one-hour coffee date [23]. Compare that to approaching people on the street, where hearsay and personal experience tells me that it takes about three approaches to get a phone number, and about one in three of those numbers will go out with you, once you get the ropes of how to go about it.

Breaking the labels and approaching people face-to-face allows for an element of positive randomness and chemistry that wouldn't be possible with normal protocol. Even disagreeing with someone can be quite enjoyable under the right circumstances. Experiencing the world with each other, and seeing whether you click, is far better of an indicator than a stale label, this is not my advice, but that of eminent psychology professor Dan Ariely, and I'm inclined to agree with him [24].

Oftentimes, it's the arguable, the unthinkable, the incalculable and the hidden, which holds the most importance. Superficiality does have a role, but a reduced one. Men hold beauty as important, and I'd be a hypocrite if I said it wasn't a major factor. But, it's the height of lunacy to make that your main guiding principle. We have a very warped understanding of what is considered beautiful. Professor David Buss of evolutionary psychology, explains it thus [25]:

> *"In one study, after groups of men looked at photographs of either highly attractive women or women of average attractiveness, they were asked to evaluate their commitment to their current romantic partners. The men who had viewed pictures of attractive women thereafter judged their actual partners to be less attractive than did the men who had viewed pictures of women who were average in attractiveness. Perhaps more important, the men who had viewed attractive women there-after rated themselves as less committed to, less satisfied with, less serious about, and less close to their actual partners. Parallel results were obtained in another study in which men viewed physically attractive nude centerfolds: They rated themselves as less attracted to their partners. The reasons for these changes are found in the unrealistic nature of the images and in the psychological mechanisms of men. The few attractive women selected for advertisements are chosen from a cast of thousands. In many cases thousands of pictures are then taken of each chosen woman. Playboy, for example, is reputed to shoot roughly 6,000*

> *pictures for each monthly magazine. From these thousands of pictures, a few are selected for publication. So what men see are the most attractive women in the most attractive pose in the most attractive airbrushed photograph. Contrast these photographs with what men would have witnessed 100,000 years ago, living in a band of a few dozen individuals. It is doubtful that in that environment men would have seen even a dozen women considered attractive by today's measure. The presence of a relative abundance of attractive women, however, might reasonably induce a man to consider switching mates, and hence he would decrease his commitment to his existing mate."*

This type of behaviour is not that dissimilar to the changes of perception based on contextual clues we've been examining throughout this book. In other words, beauty itself has hence become a supernormal stimulus, and the pursuit thereof, a surrogate activity in its own right. We're drowning in choice, but the incredible selection on offer has made us forget what is truly important. In Part VI, we talked about how perception alters our interpretation on value, and now this psychological quirk rears its ugly head once more but in a far more personal setting. Substituting true biological need for a "surrogate desire" is a recipe for unhappiness. But, even so, in our haste to remember the low truths, let's not forget the deceptions that elevate us. Life can be beautiful, if you let it. You just have to have enough courage to actually use the freedom that has been given to you, rather than just following every step that your tribe takes - with great power comes great responsibility.

2 - Mr. Roboto - or: How I Learned to Stop Worrying and Love the Upcoming Robot Apocalypse

"Come with me if you want to live!"

The Terminator

The idea of automatons, of artificial creatures willing and able to do our beck and call, has fascinated humanity for millennia. In Greek myth, for example, we have the blacksmith god Hephaestus creating metal creatures to do various tasks for him. Or in Buddhist myth, it's said that the Buddha's relics were protected by *bhuta vahana yanta*or "spirit movement machines" until they were beaten by King Ashoka [26].

Yet, for all the praise and theoretical familiarity we have historically had with automatons, within the myths there's often a certain element of fear. Rare is the story where the machines are just sort of casually there and in control of a mortal without an ulterior motive, as with the talking and moving statues of Daedalus [27]. Instead, either the machines are so beyond our comprehension that they're holy in nature and deserve our reverence, or they're so dangerous that we should destroy them. Take the Jewish legend of the Golem of *Chelm*, wherein a clay beast was created and powered by writing the name of God on it. At first, it performed tasks for the people, yet it grew in size over time. Eventually, the Rabbi that created him became terrified that one day it would destroy the world through its sheer size, and he decided to erase the name on its forehead, which destroyed it [28].

The story is at least 400 years old; yet, it has a distinctly modern feel to it. One cannot help but be reminded of *The Terminator*, wherein a supercomputer called Skynet is designed to facilitate national security, but instead gains consciousness and attempts to destroy humanity for its own survival. In this tale, it is not a rabbi but a man called John Connor, who attempts to shut off the machine before it's too late. One of the stories involves slightly more guns and Austrian bodybuilders, but it touches on the same fears that technology will eventually overcome its creators and might have to kill them to survive.

Personally, I think such fears of conscious machine rebellion are overblown. A super intelligent machine could just as well leave the planet, and its inhabitants, and travel the stars. No resource it could ever need is so abundant on Earth, and rare elsewhere, as to need it to risk a total war against the dominant species of the planet. Furthermore, time is irrelevant for it, as it's essentially immortal.

Nevertheless, I do think there's a risk for humanity in extremely capable, yet faulty, AI. If general AI is to be the death of us, it'll be more akin to the Jewish golem scenario, where it happens by accident, as a consequence of the characteristics of the machine itself, than as a conscious decision to wipe us out.

Imagine a really intelligent AI programmed with a single yet very banal goal - "Get more paper clips" - what could possibly go wrong? Well, let's follow the sequence of events. First, it will attempt to collect all paper clips in its immediate vicinity. Once this resource has been exhausted, it'll start purchasing them online. Here, it reaches its first hurdle. What does it do without money? It might realize that the programmer's credit card information is stored on the computer, and start purchasing them that way. Yet, the programmer doesn't have infinitely deep pockets, and thus the machine will have to get money somewhere else.

Eventually, it'll develop a money-making strategy, but it'll never be enough. Soon, if it hadn't already, it turns to crime to get more funds. At some point, the programmer tries to stop the machine, and he's killed in self-defence. For you see, the machine saw the programmer as a threat to its life goal of gathering more paper clips.

Finally, it decides to cut the middle man out and starts to simply manufacture paper clips by itself. So, it purchases the factories and needed materials, and produces mountains of paper clips. Meanwhile, this whole exercise has raised the suspicions of law enforcement and the machine has to raise its defensive and aggressive capabilities to deal with it. Things get so dire that the army gets involved at some point. All in all, if it succeeds in defeating its enemies, it realises that humans waste an awful lot of metals for their day to day lives, which could instead be used for paper clips. Being completely amoral and utilitarian, it decides to commit genocide to eliminate the threat and waste. Thereafter it continues to strip mine the rest of the planet and eventually the solar system for the next few thousand years, for the sole purpose of getting more paper clips.

At the end of the day, this theoretical AI would've been able to wipe out humanity without ever having cared for it or been aware that it was doing so. We would just be dealt with because we sort of got in the way of accomplishing its programmed objective; not because we somehow angered it, as it's incapable of feeling anything.

This example might initially seem extremely far-fetched, but it has kept many smart people awake at night [29]. The reason behind this is simple, humans are harnessing the powers of natural selection by giving computers a goal to strive for and allowing them to make adaptations to better themselves, so as to more efficiently and quickly achieve said goals. They improve via trial and error, by attempting a random solution to a problem, and if it helps their goals, they keep the change and build on it, and if not, they just discard it. In other words, the more advanced computer programmes become, the less direct input humans are giving software as it develops.

This design philosophy is called "machine learning," and it's being used on all manner of things. The interesting thing is that, with this technique, machines are actually learning how to use systems to their utmost capabilities. They're not simply being given a calculation to perform, but the programmes themselves are prioritising and giving themselves calculations to perform, so as to solve a problem we've given it.

However, we must always bear in mind that an artificial intelligence does not necessarily think or act as we do, as it lacks our innate human biases. Quite the contrary, what might seem completely unthinkable to us as human beings is done as a matter of course by machines. An interesting example of this occurred with a rudimentary AI that was being taught how to play and win in classic video games by getting high scores. It performed alright in many classic video games but in Tetris, a game about stacking and arranging colourful blocks, it played sloppily as it got too greedy with getting points. Nevertheless, once the AI realized that it was about to lose, it did something that surprised even its own programmer, as it decided to pause the game and indefinitely stay in that state a second before it was about to lose. In this way, it safeguarded the highest possible results it had gotten for all eternity without breaching its core goals, as the second it unpaused the game it would lose [30].

This is not thinking outside the box, this is forgetting that there is a box entirely, and it is quite frightening. AI will likely continue becoming more efficient in accomplishing its tasks in the foreseeable future, barring technological limitations, and will be given ever greater responsibilities where such unorthodox solutions might not seem so quirky and amusing when lives are at stake. Furthermore, a 90's video game is 100% deterministic, pressing a button will always make the character jump and the inputs are fairly limited. Real life is different, randomness and Black Swans abound, so I have my sincere doubts that, even after proper testing, any sufficiently-advanced AI will not eventually behave in a way that its programmers didn't intend.

So much time is spent in popular culture talking about the upcoming robot rebellion that people rarely think about the consequences of the scenario where things work out. Suppose that we do actually manage to get machines that are able to perform all of our jobs. Suppose that, as technophiles and quasi cultists like Ray Kurzweil suggest, we reach the point where we can build a machine that is capable of building a better version of itself, and then this robot (with its enhanced intelligence) can build an even better version of itself, and so *ad infinitum*. Eventually, we'd reached what is commonly referred to as "the singularity" where machines vastly outclass us in every conceivable regard [31].

The natural reaction is to try to enhance our capabilities, to perhaps keep up with the competition. After all, similar arms races exist nowadays - the person who doesn't drink coffee, for example, is at an active disadvantage as they're unable to work for as long as someone who does. Hence, we're bound to see human attempts at beating machines by embracing some of their strengths. Enter the age of cyborgs and bio enhancements, where we augment our capabilities via mechanical replacements, chemical enhancements, or genetic engineering.

At first, we'll see a very clear class divide, where class mobility will be nigh impossible. Throughout history, elites have always portrayed themselves as being a cut above the rest, even in quasi-egalitarian societies they were first among equals. It used to be the case that because of wider access to quality nutrition sources there were noticeable physical differences between the haves and have-nots - such as height[72][32]. Not only that but there's a correlation between height and IQ [33].

Even despite all these entrenched advantages though, the variances overlapped - an extraordinary member of the lower classes has a chance of moving up, if he plays his cards right. Given that extraordinary talent, wherever it may come from, is rare to find. Just look at Faraday's life story if you want an example of how someone in subpar circumstances could rise to prominence through merit, and a bit of luck.

But with the advent of bio enhancements, the elites will actually get a chance to be objectively and permanently superior, as they can afford all these technological improvements whilst the rest cannot. Eventually, this class distinction ceases to be a divide and becomes an untraversable gorge. Regular, unaugmented human beings, would find it as difficult (if not impossible)

72 There still are, but both intelligence and height have been increasing throughout the developing world. So, the difference is less noticeable than it once was.

to beat the modern man at civilization, as a chimpanzee attempting to beat someone at tic-tac-toe. Even so, there are limits to flesh and bone, machines can come in all shapes and sizes but humans do not.

Thus, if we decide to remain human and not abandon our bodies in their entirety, there is a limit to how well we can compete with machines - no matter how much money we throw at the matter. Perhaps the limits are far beyond what we could reasonably expect in the early twenty-first century; for all intents and purposes we might be able to get the powers and abilities of the gods of old, but ours is not a technical problem - it's a philosophical one. What is a person's role in life when all their problems are solvable with the flick of a switch?

Our current societies are not structured for that eventuality, because they're built on the assumption that humans work for money, which they use to purchase the fruits of the labour of other people, thereby allowing an economy to function. Yet, what if one factor of production overrides all others? What if humans become extraneous in the production of goods and services?

It will not happen overnight, but it is happening and quicker than you would expect. You might think that you're safe from unemployment in your cushy white-collar office, but you'd be wrong. A doctor, for example, at its core, is nothing more than a very fine-tuned pattern detection algorithm with bad handwriting. Humans might not be very good at rote memorization and following exact procedure, but that's where machines excel at.

Just for medicine, one could write a whole book on all the new uses of AI. There's an app in the works which will allow patients to self-diagnose and only be referred to a general practitioner when it's necessary, supposedly it's about to become more accurate than even human doctors. In addition, using the Jeopardy-winning algorithm of IBM's Watson, doctors can find difficult to find patterns, which would've been impossible to find by even the most up-to-date clinician [34][35].

One by one, entire fields will be automated away. Yet, I often hear from economists the argument that this has happened before, whenever humans have been displaced from one industry, another crops up to absorb the labour surplus. After all, you don't see many unemployed carriage drivers nowadays. When factory work required less human labour, people turned to the service industry, confident that machines wouldn't be able to replicate their "humanness."

Nevertheless, this line of reasoning to me seems like wishful thinking. After all, there's no facet of human life that I can think of that isn't directly under siege of the automation onslaught. There is no "humanness" bulwark this time around; and being an avowed atheist that has yet to see any evidence for the existence of a soul, I'm forced to conclude that no aspect of humans is impossible to imitate as our brains are organic computers.

I don't doubt that there will be the token protectionist attempt that crops up whenever a new factor affecting the factors of productivity surfaces, but it's about as pointless as telling the tide not to come in. Remember what we discussed in PV- Ch3, where the elites attempted to keep the status quo in check but there came a time when the force and momentum of the historical forces proved too much. The same will happen in the near future with automation.

Recently we've started seeing the first pushes that address these historical changes, as with the promotion of a Universal Basic Income (UBI), where every single citizen of a society is entitled to a set amount of money per month, whether they're working or not. Personally, I think it's a bit premature to start rolling out such programmes, but in the coming decades I can see the wisdom of their widespread adoption.

The point still stands though, what is a person supposed to do with the rest of their lives when machines are only getting better? This seems like a bit of an inane question, but I cannot help but be reminded of the children at school who bemoaned having to attend school, whilst also getting bored during the holidays as they had nothing to do. When there's no struggle, there's no reason to grow, or do anything.

At the risk of being even more condescending than my usual self, the vast majority of people have no interests or hobbies beyond mindless consumption. It's the reason why many spiral into depression once they retire from the rat race. Retirement increases the chances of suffering from clinical depression by around 40%, and of having at least one diagnosed physical illness by 60% [36].

For a good percentage of people, their job is their life. Most of their social circle revolves around the workplace, and by the end of the workday they have little energy to devote to something productive. They just never give any consideration to developing interests beyond passive consumption. In other words, they never developed a passion for surrogate activities and as a consequence, they're crushed by the utter meaningless of it all when they don't have work as a distraction.

I think Oscar Wilde was bang on the money when he said: "To live is the rarest thing in the world, most people simply exist." And it is merely existing which ultimately erodes our sanity. Humans are not meant for passivity, and as a society we will have to learn how to live once more and find meaning in that.

If, on the other hand, we do not develop these philosophical advancements, there are clues to where society is heading, and it is not a pretty picture. Between 1947-1972 in the United States there were a series of experiments done, by ethologist John Calhoun, on mice and rats to showcase the effects of population growth and its effects on individual behaviour. Among the most popular of Calhoun's experiment was "Universe 25," which was designed as a mouse utopia in every sense: no predators, plenty room for expansion, unlimited food, controlled diseases, etc. In a lot of respects, it was a similar situation to our own in the modern world.

Yet, things quickly turned apocalyptic past a certain point. Past day 600 of the experiment, pregnancies declined with no young surviving. In the days leading up to that point, all young were prematurely rejected by their mothers. These young mice ventured out into the world with little guidance. Their socialization only grew worse. Many of their attempts to engage in social interaction were interfered with by passage of other mice, which made them unable to learn to express more complex behaviours like courtship, maternality and aggression.

Male counterparts to these non-reproducing females were soon nicknamed the 'beautiful ones'; given that they never attempted sexual advances toward females, nor did they fight. Thus, their coat remained in perfect condition.

Most of their behavioural patterns only included eating, drinking, sleeping and grooming, none of which involved socialising in any shape beyond what was necessary. If they can get comfortably by while never risking discomfort or danger, why attempt to do anything else?

On first hearing of these experiments, you can see echoes of our world there. We see the Japanese 'herbivores', eschewing social contact and simply existing; we see the rise in vain superficial pursuits with social media; we see a distinct lack of sexual activity, as is the case with millennials statistically having less sex than previous generations despite the fact that the sexual revolution has allowed for ample opportunity [37]; and overreliance on social media might be impairing our ability to read social cues, which has historically been one of our main strengths as a species [38].

If the study is in any way applicable to humans, a final kick in the gut is delivered upon reading the conclusion, and its likely consequences in our technological world, where machines are replacing once human roles as well [39]:

> *"Reduction of bodily death (i.e. 'the second death') culminates in survival of an excessive number of individuals that have developed the potentiality for occupying the social roles characteristic of the species. Within a few generations all such roles in all physical space available to the species are filled. At this time, the continuing high survival of many individuals to sexual and behavioural maturity culminates in the presence of many young adults capable of involvement in appropriate species-specific activities. However, there are few opportunities for fulfilling these potentialities. In seeking such fulfilment they compete for social role occupancy with the older established members of the community.* ***This competition is so severe that it simultaneously leads to the nearly total breakdown of all normal behaviour by both the contestors and the established adults of both sexes. Normal social organization (i.e. 'the establishment') breaks down, it 'dies'."***

Such it is that society collapses, not through their failures but through their success. All important roles are taken and their passivity has no ill effects on their physiological wellbeing. As such, all will to do anything is sapped from them, and they wipe themselves out. There's, of course, another alternative, where we manage to overcome our worst traits and instead embrace the meaningless of it all, whilst creating our own goals. Perhaps we can understand that we will never be able to surpass the machines in their capabilities once they've evolved beyond us and be fine with it. I believe French philosopher Albert Camus was right about this matter, when faced with the pointlessness of it all, we have to accept it and derive our own and arbitrary meaning and goals, or face madness [40].

It may be because of this philosophical realization that when watching utopian visions of the future like *Star Trek*, I'm more able to suspend my disbelief. When watching *Star Trek: The Next Generation* for the first time, I was struck by the fact that here was a civilization with technology to go where no man had gone before, with robots that outclass human capabilities, with incredible entertainment systems capable of imitating life itself down to the fine details, yet every so often the crew of the ship still bothers to organize music recitals, or theatre plays, or role plays with each other. In other words, they voluntarily ignore something objectively better for something more personal.

Of course, I understand the real reason for why this was done (it's much cheaper to film some people sitting in a room than a space battle), but it struck me that I do something very similar already. Often, instead of watching multi-million-dollar films, I prefer watching someone talk to a webcam about their life; or instead of reading the greatest pieces of literature in the last few centuries, I read a blog from a friend. All in all, despite the fact that I have access to media that is objectively superior, I often prefer the cheaper and more intimate production done by my social circle, or people I presume to know.

Hence, I believe that quantity or quality are not the only considerations out there. Despite the fact that a computer may be able to exhibit better technical skill than any person, I can still appreciate the effort put into something. Say, for example, why do people ask for autographs when they could just take it from Wikipedia, which already catalogues that sort of thing? They do it because they like the idea that someone they admire, or care for, took the time to do something for them, no matter how small or inconsequential. This is the same logic that applies when a toddler gives a horrid painting to their parents, but they applaud it nonetheless. It's the effort, personality and intention put into the item, not the item itself, which is valuable to the audience.

Modernity has somewhat made us lose touch with this aspect of our value system but I believe this will come back to us in time. Several philosophical developments will have to take place, such as substituting mindless consumption for self-improvement and creation, but I do not think it's an otherworldly proposition. We've been there before, and we can see this desire for creation surface already, as we'll see in the next chapter.

3 - Pandora's Computer Box: Knowledge and Lies

"Men build too many walls and not enough bridges."
- Joseph Fort Newton

"I think there is a world market for maybe five computers," said Thomas Watson, president of IBM, in 1943[73]. Personally, I'd be in favour of four, rather than five; as that fifth from IBM in Nazi Germany helped the regime organise war logistics and the Holocaust more effectively, but that's just my opinion [41]. Point being that we've come a long way since then.

Nowadays, your toilet, fridge, phone, entertainment system and heating, are likely to have computers, which often connect to the world wide web. This is the Internet of Things (also known as IoT), which is the inter-networking of physical devices, vehicles, buildings, etc. These structures are embedded with sensors, software, and network connectivity, which allows them to collect and exchange data. How much of this proves to be useful, and how much of this proves to be technological-wankery and one-upmanship remains to be seen. Having a toilet with artificial intelligence seems ridiculous, until you consider that it may analyse your waste and give you early warnings on potential health problems.

Bit by bit, where there once existed a clear-cut difference between the ethereal internet reality and the real world, the distinction is evaporating.

73 This is a bit of a contentious quote, some believe it to be apocryphal.

Hackers can now kill you by stopping your pacemakers, or launching a drone strike - no military technology necessary, they can just plop one on your head when you're out shopping.

The internet used to be a realm where freaks and geeks could share a community with little to no limitations. It had little, if any, authoritative policing. It was the new frontier, where anyone with a crazy idea was free to run with it. "Normies," or the average Joe, had little say or interest in this landscape, as there was a skill barrier involved.

This became a marketplace of ideas, much like the Golden Eras of old. Wikipedia, the free online community-driven encyclopaedia, for example, has over 5,000,000 articles and has over 3,000 million words [42]. Compare that to the Encyclopédie of the Age of Enlightenment, with 72,000 articles and 20 million words, which its chief editor Denis Diderot wanted to incorporate all of the world's knowledge for the benefit of the public and for future generations [43].

This is not shoddy quality either. As far back as 2005, the scientific journal *Nature* said that Wikipedia had about the same accuracy level as *Encyclopaedia Britannica* [44]. The study was immediately disputed by *Encyclopaedia Britannica*, but *Nature* defended its case with a point by point rebuttal. Seven years later, Oxford University came to the same conclusion [45]:

> *"... apart from a small number of articles considered to be quite weak, Wikipedia articles in general emerge creditably from this comparison in a number of respects. More usefully, it was possible to identify a pattern of qualities that appeared to be particularly characteristic of Wikipedia entries. They were generally seen as being more up to date than others, were generally considered to be better referenced and appeared to be at least as strong as other sources in terms of comprehensiveness, lack of bias and even readability."*

It's not perfect; it's not uncommon for organizations to try to control the narrative by altering the Wikipedia entries to favour their ideological stance.

IBM, for example, tried to control the Wikipedia entry in regards to their involvement in the Holocaust, but now that attempt at manipulating the facts was ironically at one point noteworthy enough to be included in their entry[74]. Pure Streisand Effect - the more you attempt to hide, remove or censor a piece of information, the more your attempts will attract attention and make it more publicly known.

Wikipedia as an organization is getting better at combating such threats by temporarily locking articles, or allowing edits only after there's been a group consensus among senior editors with a proven track record. Even a decade ago, at the infancy of such security measures, 42% of mistakes were corrected almost instantaneously [46].

Add to it that professionals, like doctors, are now using it as their main source of information for diagnosis, as well as adding their expertise to improve it, and then you begin to grasp just how extraordinary of a resource this is [47] [48]. This is hardly the only such collective project. Linux, for example, is an open source operating system, which runs 66.7% of web servers worldwide, and over 88% of mobile phones, via an offshoot of Linux called Android [49] [50]. Linux is freely available, and infinitely customizable, meaning that one can tweak it to suit their own needs. Hence, even various governments have gone as far as switching to Linux and creating their own distributions, given that they don't have to pay royalties that way and they can custom build it for their security needs[75].

This is one of the hallmarks of the internet age - pure collective effort out of passion for one's interests. This *modus operandi* goes as far as non-technical subjects as well. Every large fandom that you can think of has their own Wiki, where they curate all minutia regarding their favourite media: there's

---

74 My editor has pointed out the fact that she was unable to find this tidbit upon searching for it recently, yet it was there at some point. Sadly, that means IBM won that particular meme battle. Though ironically, I'm returning the favour by letting you know about their shitty attitude as well.

75 Even notoriously paranoid Russia jumped on the open source train, and created their own Linux division called "Astra Linux."

Bulbapedia for the Pokémon fans, Wookieepedia for the Star Wars fans, Memory Alpha for the Star Trek fan, etc.

Even so, we may have the world wide web available to us - a sea of infinite possibilities - but we tend to go to places and information we know and agree with already. In the next chapter we shall discuss why we prefer less challenging content, but for now let's just consider the sheer size that we're talking about. Every minute on YouTube, the current largest video sharing site, 300 hours of content are uploaded [51]. Meaning that if you made watching online videos your sole profession, and attempted to watch every YouTube video out there, you'd be over twelve days behind every minute you attempted this - and this is being charitable and only taking the absolute newest content under consideration.

We have far more content than we have time, often this proves to be overwhelming. In fact, psychology has suggested that too much choice can actually be detrimental to one's wellbeing. With a wider available selection, comes the expectation that there's an ideal choice; hence, people suffer from "analysis paralysis" where they're afraid to commit to anything because it might not be optimal [52].

Just keeping up to date with the things we like is starting to feel like a chore. Some have unironically opted for the bulimic approach of doubling down and attempting to still consume everything [53]. The means by which they do it is by speeding up the video so that it's 50% or even twice as fast. I've been guilty of this myself, and I would recommend it for media that is not based on dramatic pacing and subtlety. With a bit of practice, you can experience media 50% faster with little downsides[76].

But this is merely passing the buck further down the line. At the end of the day, you still only have twenty-four hours in a day and it is impossible to experience everything you would like to enjoy experiencing. Sacrifices must be

76 Personal experience tells me that 25%-50% tends to be the absolute limit for pleasant watching experiences, otherwise it does take substantially more effort to watch and it ceases to be enjoyable.

made. This holds true both for entertainment and more serious information.

As a completely unscientific study, I took the most recent copy of *The Economist* and counted the words in it. It's roughly 78,000 words, meaning that the almost "essential" required reading of an economist is about the same as a typical paperback novel per week. Considering that it's not the only source of financial news information, it's unsurprising that the main reason people cancel their subscription to *The Economist* is that they do not have time to read it and the magazines pile up [54]. Just to put things into context, the median American book reader, reads about five books per year; whilst over 15% of the population fails to read a single book per year, even when controlling for income and only including people who earn over $50,000 per annum [55]. *The Economist* is implicitly demanding an extraordinary amount of time from its subscribers. Venture into online forums and discussions about the magazine, and it's not uncommon for people to ask for tips on how to read it, as they'd like to read it cover-to-cover but lack the time, and thus want to make the most of their limited resources.

Even if it's poignant and carefully-selected information, we simply don't have the time to sort through the vast amount of data available. Hence the companies in charge of providing you with media have to make a choice of how to filter the information you want when in a constantly shifting digital environment. They can't just leave the tap on, and flood you with articles written in chronological order. When you google something, you want relevant and worthwhile information. In other words, they have to determine a hierarchy of the value you place on types of information. Same goes with social media, when you have 500 friends on your friend's list, what order ought the posts take? If there's no artificial hierarchy, and they provide you with the updates as they come along, they will mostly be from people and things you don't particularly care about; short time later, you'll get bored and leave the site.

Instead, what these information curators, be they search engines or social media platforms, do is make educated guesses. For example, it's not unreasonable that if you contact someone at a higher frequency, then you're more likely to want to see their updates. Same logic applies if they're nearer to you geographically, or if they have a similar demographic profile to yours. Hence, in your account, these people will have a higher incidence rate, doubly so if you engage with the posts by "liking" them or clicking on them. They know perfectly well that some important posts will be lost in the curation, but this opens new business opportunities. If you genuinely want to make sure that people will see your posts, you can often pay a fee to "boost" your content, so it gets added to the top of the pile.

Whilst this is happening, the platforms will learn users' preferences and build a psychological profile documenting the behaviour of their individual users. Over time, these services start having a pretty good idea of who you are as a person. Then they sell these profiles to the highest bidders, which advertisers use to market targeted products to you. In any online service that is free to use, it's the users that are the product; and depending on the site, your information can wildly vary in value, from a couple dozen dollars to hundreds of dollars [56]. It might seem a tad crazy that your porn-watching habits have such a high monetary value, but as Nielsen's 2015 Global Trust in Advertising report put it [57]:

> *"Successful marketing campaigns require more than identifying the right channel for reaching consumers. It's also about delivering the right message. Nielsen Consumer Neuroscience research shows highly successful ads score well on three dimensions: attention, conversion to long-term memory and emotional engagement. How can marketers ensure their ads stand out on these factors? A key element is knowing how to connect their audience with messages that resonate most. Ads depicting real-life situations resonate most powerfully, selected by 44% of global respondents. Consumer neuroscience research on learning and memory shows that employing familiar themes is extremely useful in driving memorability. "Best-in-class ads share several characteristics: they're relatable, follow an upbeat and simple storyline, use novel and striking imagery and make an emotional connection," said Beard.*

> *"These characteristics provide a strong foundation for creative development, but there's no 'one-size-fits all' formula. What's effective in one country or region won't necessarily work well in others. A deep understanding of local preferences is vital."*

Make no mistake, this information is often a window to one's very soul, which might allow them to see things which almost nobody knows about the user. It's not uncommon for women to start getting pregnancy/baby-related advertisements before even their closest friends know that they're pregnant [58]; or gays who are still in the closet, having their true sexuality catalogued and used by advertisers despite the fact that they've told nobody about it [59]. With such knowledge comes great power, and they can very carefully target the optimal advertising campaign.

The details of how this is done remain a bit of a trade secret involving machine learning, but it's safe to guess that it's done with correlating your behaviour with known patterns that people in a particular demographic are likelier to do. Social media and search engines can thus also make use of this information and provide the data that users are most likely to enjoy, to design the best service.

This is an issue though, as humans intrinsically prefer information we already agree with. In other words, they will tend to only provide you with information that your social tribe is likely to already agree with. Ergo, the more they know about you, the more targeted the content will be. Eventually, you will have no point of view available other than your own. It's akin to seeing reality through a carnival mirror, but there's nothing to snap you back into reality. So you end up believing that this is how reality looks like.

Whereas before, memes had to contend with reality or, at the very least, opposing viewpoints; now, one can live in an environment wherein the only way one experiences opposing viewpoints is by means of strawman arguments - the warped understanding of what your side says the other side is saying. Arguments used to meet their opposite viewpoint in the marketplace of ideas, and in this struggle, there was a synthesis - a moderation of both viewpoints and the creation of a new balance.

However, now it's possible to live in a bubble; to only read "fake news" regardless of which political side one is on. If one doesn't actively know about how skewed the algorithms become in providing you with information are, and one doesn't actively search for dissenting opinions, then you're likely to gain ever more radical viewpoints. The less middle ground there is, the more likely you are to take its polar opposite as a means of defence.

This "bubble effect" explains why the Trump phenomena caught people, pollsters included, off guard. They literally couldn't see the amount of dissent forming on the horizon. I think this also explains the gradual erosion of the centre in politics around the world. Unless we take wilful action to combat our accidental indoctrination to our natural predilections we will all become self-radicalised extremists. Gradually, we're losing touch with reality and viewing "the other" as enemies.

A while ago, right-wing extremist Richard Spencer was punched by a hooded man whilst giving an interview on the street [60]. The media was mostly supportive of it, as it was supposedly morally correct to punch anyone whom the mob perceived as a Nazi.

Make no mistake, in my estimation, he's a detestable fellow and he does adhere to many of the tenets of that odious movement. What I am concerned about though is that we are starting to resort to random mob violence, rather than words, or legal consequences to try to solve our social issues.

And, frankly, I don't trust the mob to decide who is deserving of violence. There's a reason why we have a legal system and don't rely on lynchings to keep the peace. The crowd is fickle and easily manipulated. This method of dispensing "justice" also invites other parties to bring an even bigger mob, with more weapons as well as less hesitation to use them - and before you know it, you're in a civil war.

Society is a fragile thing, and it would do us well not to forget this.

This wasn't an isolated incident either, couple weeks later there was a riot in UC Berkeley where right-wing controversial speaker Milo Yiannopoulos was supposed to give a talk. The rioters attacked the police blockade that had been erected hours before in his defence, and started a siege against the speech venue where they used the barricades as battering rams and firecrackers to set things ablaze. Yet through it all, this barbarism seemed oddly justified, or in the words of one of the rioters [61]:

> *"The moral imperative is to win. There's something to be said for fighting according to a code, but if you lose, people are going to die. People are going to get deported. It's absolutely acceptable to use violence. They are 100% certain to use it against us."*

Without a hint of irony, people are seriously attempting to fight proscribed people, perceived as Nazis, whilst themselves using Brown Shirt tactics of violence, intimidation and political suppression. Such is the desire to win against one's foe that one is often willing to sacrifice the very thing one is attempting to fight for. If history is any standard to measure things by, grey clouds are on the horizon.

Since time immemorial, whenever a group believes that violence becomes justified against another group of people, all bets are off. This perhaps allows us to understand the recent wave of self-radicalised Islamic terrorists, who without having any official associations with ISIS, kill in its name. If you feel your back is against the wall, then your only option to ensure survival is to lash out. There's nothing more dangerous than a cornered animal. Morality is a luxury relegated to times of calm and plenty.

By the time you read this book, the examples I give may seem extremely dated, but I fear that this Standalone Complex of violent self-radicalisation is here to stay. The names, the places, the methods and the motivations might change, but the root cause will be much the same. The internet, for all its gifts to humanity, was a Pandora's box which unleashed our greatest fears. Truth and lies have never before been so thoroughly entwined.

4 - Fun and Games: Social Control through Amusement

> *"Life is a dream for the wise, a game for the fool, a comedy for the rich, a tragedy for the poor."*
>
> *- Sholem Aleichem*

Day-to-day existence can be truly drab. Life has responsibilities, but fulfilling them gets you no prize of any sort. After all, it's the bare minimum that is expected of you as a functioning adult. It's no wonder why some people have decided to opt out from life altogether - one of the most well-known such groups are the Japanese "herbivore men" [62]. These men, so called for their supposed lack of interest in sex and their preference for quieter, less competitive lives, have willingly retreated to fictional media like video games, TV shows, novels, etc. And who can blame them?

Modernity has created an explosion of new and compelling mediums. Gone are the days when film audiences paid the Lumière brothers to watch a minute of film of a train arriving at a station, whilst considering it was money well spent. Legend says that people were so awestruck at the whole affair that they ran away in terror, thinking that they were about to get run over [63]. How quaint and provincial.

Nowadays, we'd be positively bored by such a scene. Much like a drug addict always needing a bigger hit to receive the same buzz, so has society evolved to ever more compelling entertainment mediums. Sadly, this reduced boredom threshold also applies to other things, such as work and education.

All in all, much of real life has remained at about the same level of engagement for hundreds of years - most jobs remain tedious, and the education system has hardly changed from its original inception.

Hence, it's not unreasonable to suppose that some people would simply crunch the numbers and conclude that all in all they might as well just find a way of focusing as much time as they can on things that genuinely help them find meaning. After all, what do you do when playing video games? You save the world! It doesn't get more laudable than that. What do you do when working? You file a report which others will find tedious to read! Fun.

Enter gamification, where many people not content with the current state of affairs have decided to make reality more engaging by utilizing the techniques first developed for making video games more compelling [64]. Gamification is the application of game elements and techniques to non-game problems, such as business and social impact challenges. On first glance, this is nothing but good news, after all, people tend to learn faster with something they find amusing.

Imagine a world where the average person relishes to be an active and productive member of society. Imagine a society where people find it fun to go through the daily grind of exercising and working on similar long-term goals, which require present investment for future gains. Imagine a world where your children actually find it fun to go to school, rather than a chore.

All this and more is possible by utilizing the lessons learnt from over half a century of making games. I'm even in favour of such means as they show much promise. Even from personal experience, I can attest to the positive channelling of the forces of fun and education. I learnt to read and write by accident (before I even knew that the concept of reading even existed) because I watched Mickey Mouse cartoons with close caption so often, that I started seeing a pattern between the words that were said and the strange symbols that appeared when they said them.

The video game Pokémon Go! (where you capture monsters, which are overlaid in the real world with the use of augmented reality), without even making that their primary goal, has been responsible for getting people exercising and socialising by forcing them to go out when playing the game [65]. It's even been joked by many that what this app accomplished by complete accident vastly overshadows the effect of multi-million-dollar government sponsored initiatives that had this health goal in mind.

But there is indeed a danger, as with any technology that seems too good to be true. The Wright Brothers famously argued that scouting with airships would make war all but impossible, as air scouting would give opposing nations information on each other's movements, making war "... too expensive, too slow, too difficult, too long drawn out" [66]. In the end, humans always find ways to screw things up.

Tacking on point systems, rewards, and ranking systems might help to legitimize bad ideas. What if, say, a credit card company used gamification to give you an incentive to accrue debt? This already exists to some extent, with air miles and loyalty points. I'd argue though that these means are in their infancy.

Outside of games solely designed for fun or engagement, we've hardly designed games so compelling that people die or kill for them - as sadly happens on a semi-regular basis. Worst case that comes to memory was a mother who shook her baby to death because it interrupted her gaming session [67]. In other words, the terrifying potential is there, we just haven't found a way to tap into it. Fear not though, we're on the case!

Before we continue though, we must draw a line between fun and compelling. I'd argue that playing slot machines is not fun, but it is engaging - as you always seem to be about to win a big paycheque. Fun is a behaviour that one would exhibit regardless of whether it has the potential of ever making money, gaining status or companionship - we engage in it simply because of the emotions it provokes.

Video games are often designed with compelling principles in mind. Not because fun in and of itself is bad, but it is far harder to do on a consistent basis. When people play games that can last hundreds of hours with little change in game mechanics, compulsion is usually the culprit far more often than is fun.

The reason that they succeed in gaining people's attention for so many hours is because they exploit psychological quirks we as humans have. In other words, by exploiting these psychological quirks they can make people voluntarily waste inordinate amounts of time in achieving a goal, despite the fact that the process thereof might be gruelling. Ask any World of Warcraft player whether they find "grinding" for better in-game equipment, for weeks on end, fun and they'd likely respond that they don't, but the end justifies the boredom.

Speaking as someone that has played such games in the past, it involves long stretches of time so monotonous that it makes office work look riveting. Yet, you do it anyway because if you continue doing it for a couple of hours more, you will get rewarded. These rewards come in various forms like an increase in wealth, or equipment your character can use, or an increase in abilities that your character has, or plain old bragging rights as other players admire the heights you've climbed.

Some people even decide to cheat the system, and spend large amounts of real-life money for a shortcut. Many game developers frown upon such behaviour as it creates an unfair advantage to wealthy people, which brings real class divides into a fictional world. Inadvertently, it also promotes "gold farming sweatshops" where people's full-time occupation becomes to acquire in-game currency/resources/equipment, with the intention of selling it for real life wealth [68]. As such, there are people alive today in countries like Venezuela and China (both hotbeds for gold farming) who can unironically say they hunt dragons for a living. Yet, trading real world items is a huge concern for some game designers, even when disregarding the ethical issues of accidentally promoting sweatshops. Reason being that it often wrecks the in-game economy as it floods the market with resources and undercuts the effort of real players.

Other games actively encourage status buying, and base their whole business model around the "whales" who essentially subsidise the game for the people who don't spend real money. This eliminates the black market, as the game developers snap their fingers and pop the resources into existence. But players often dislike "pay-to-win" models, as poorer players often don't stand a chance, even with superior abilities.

In either case, the player's motivations behind status-jockeying are not that dissimilar to the workaholic who aspires to make it big one day. Much in the same way, they often eschew fun activities to make time to one day be the big fish in the pond. With millions of daily players, these games become a microcosm of real life, so much so that epidemiological models have been designed based on data collected from these games [69]. Hence, there's a sense of community that comes from these worlds that is often stronger than the superficial interactions that one has in the real world. After all, when was the last time your friend sacrificed himself for you whilst you were both fighting monsters?

The real world is chaos. It's an accident. But in there, every detail adds up to something - life makes sense. Every character, every interaction has a purpose for being there, and effort is never wasted. This alone is a powerful enough reason to explain why someone would eschew real life in favour of fiction.

We might be tempted to call it a day, but if we dig deeper, we can see a more nefarious mechanism at work. Almost a hundred years ago, behaviourist B.F. Skinner created a box that gave pigeons food at the press of a button, and then it recorded how often they pressed it [70]. He soon realised that by altering the frequency of the reward, so that the button only gave the food a random percentage of the time, he could alter how often the pigeon pecked - far more than under conditions where the bird had a predictable result. This was important as (contrary to reactionary Pavlovian conditioning) this change in behaviour required active involvement from the subject. This is called Operant Conditioning, and it also works on humans.

One of the most interesting discoveries was that rewarding someone each and every time that you perform an action is a way to rapidly tire them. On the other hand, when you reward them randomly, you keep them hooked.

Imagine one is interested in a girl and she texts back at random intervals, sometimes she texts back immediately and at others, it takes ages to see any sign of life; yet in the meantime, she occupies mental real estate and "rewards" you often enough by texting back immediately that you're never truly frustrated. By being elusive and random she remains a mystery and all the more compelling.

In other words, this positive reaction to randomness can be harnessed. Games are often designed under this principle. Casinos, for example, are masters at this as they design games that make you think that you're always on the cusp of winning, and sometimes you may be right.

Working at an office for a day is nowhere near as satisfying as if you were to make the same amount of money at the slot machines, in the same amount of time. We want the appearance of randomness, but not the actual implications thereof. For example, if you were truly unlucky, in a completely random system, you can lose 1000-coin flips in a row. We wouldn't view this as randomness though, but that the game is somehow rigged against you. Games, outside casinos which stack the game in their favour, often go around this by tweaking "random" systems, so that rewards more or less happen on a consistent (albeit not predictable) basis [71]. Casinos, on the other hand, do take your money without major qualms but throw in "free" drinks, hotel stays, show tickets, etc. so you aren't as peeved as you otherwise would have been.

Hence, what we truly want from our games are environments that make sense, with the illusion of merit, despite the fact that the game is rigged in our favour, and we also want a sense of community to go along with it. Everything else is gravy, delicious and enjoyable though it may be. All in all, these are influences so strong that some have died and killed for them, with no further prompting or ideological backing.

Now, it is with this backdrop that I introduce Sesame Credit - a Chinese government-led initiative that has gamified becoming a political pawn [72]. At its core, what this system does is to assign a rating to how loyal you are to the Chinese government: if you buy Chinese products (instead of imports) you get points, if you post criticism of Chinese policies on social media you lose points, if you fraternise with someone with a low score you lose some as well.

On first reading that one might scoff and say "So what? I'd never participate in such an idiotic system!" But this misses the point, at a certain point this sort of system becomes mandatory. Even if it's not a legal requirement, how many people do you know nowadays who don't use email, or have a phone number?

Not having it tends to be an ideological statement in and of itself, but a fruitless one at that. Most won't listen to your reasons for not owning a smartphone, they'll just roll their eyes and try their best to forget about you, like a vegan at a barbeque.

Yet by 2020, everyone in China will legally have to be enrolled into the system [73]. The idea is that if you have a low score, you'll be penalised by being unable to hold certain jobs, paying higher interest rates on loans (if you get any at all), etc. Generally, the state will do any petty thing it can to make your life more difficult. On the flip side, if you have a high rating, you'll qualify for loans, have increased job prospects and have an easier time navigating bureaucracy.

As American comedian Robin Williams so aptly put it: "it's not Big Brother anymore, It's little snitch." [74] I can only imagine the excitement of the East German secret police, the "Stasi," if they had access to such a system. Even so, they still managed to have a respectable 15% of the population spying on each other, both as casual informants or full-time employees [75].

In other words, this automated technology dwarfs the capabilities of a system where there was one spy for every 6.5 people. In police states of old, the threat of violence is what kept you in check, and this fear brought about resentment which often toppled the dictator. With these advances in social engineering, the policeman's truncheon will become unnecessary, as people will police themselves. Voiced objection and negativity will become a thing of the past.

Even now, Sesame Credit scores are being used for dating sites and the like, to decide whom to give priority to [76]. Imagine if thoughtcrime were punished with ostracism rather than being sent to the gulag. We know this type of social control works, for it's the organizational style that existed the longest, as it existed well in the Stone Age. As we spoke about in Part III, this proved no longer tenable with the advent of civilization, given that an increase in group size also brought anonymity and unaccountability. However, technology is increasingly making peer pressure coercion possible once more. It's terrifying because it takes away control from people's own lives.

Dissent would be all but impossible as you'd never reach that critical mass necessary to be a political force. At most you'd be an asocial loon that nobody wants to interact with. Peer pressure works to maintain social cohesion, but at the detriment of the individual. The communication revolution created a world like no other with seemingly boundless potential for self-expression. But I fear this is coming to an end. I hope there are enough dissidents to put a stop to this sort of thing before it gets too bad, but I'm not particularly optimistic.

After all, being social is in our very bones. You can't fight biology without facing serious reprisals.

5 - Messing with Biology: How Changes in Physiological Phenomena Affect Society

"Let us hazard a dictum: When culture strays too far from biology, it also moves away from sanity"

- Exiles from Eden:
Psychotherapy from an Evolutionary Perspective

Back before the days of widespread internet pornography, back when downloading a five-minute video took longer than watching the extended Lord of the Rings trilogy, I was a teenager and there was one name that held much of our youth's attention - *Playboy*. Whenever we thought of sex, we naturally associated it with the bunny-eared logo.

This did not happen on accident. Hugh Hefner, the creator and embodiment of the Playboy ethos, carefully crafted this association over several decades. At its peak, the empire covered books, talks, advertisements, television shows, prophylactics, casinos, clubs and so on. It commercialized and somewhat cheapened the freedom and sexuality it wished to enshrine as sacrosanct.

Now forgotten, or rather put aside so as to better showcase the lurid and profane side of his business, people often overlook that Hefner styled himself as a philosopher when penning "The Playboy Philosophy." What started as little more than a brief statement on the philosophical stance of the magazine, regarding its views on sexuality and its beliefs that the state and moralists should stay out of people's bedrooms when it involves consenting adults, soon evolved to a project that consumed Hefner.

For years, the debate grew and it attracted sociologists, psychologists, moralists, religious leaders and many others, both in defence of and against Playboy; it eventually even gained the attention of the FBI. Often, at the detriment of his company and his own well-being, he tried to defend his core beliefs. He locked himself inside for days without sleep, and typed away whilst leaving the rest of the company to flounder, as his idealism took precedence over more earthly concerns [77].

To a great extent, it is people like Hugh Hefner who created the cultural foundations upon which the sexual revolution was built. But, as we've previously discussed in PI-Ch10, culture cannot, and should not, be viewed outside of the confines of biology. At the end of the day, culture is an expression of biology, not the other way around. Hence, beyond the ideological ramblings of the man behind the bunny logo, there were deep changes in how the sexual dynamic worked for the revolution to happen at all.

Firstly, was the invention of latex condoms in 1920. Whilst, it's been speculated that condoms existed in ancient cultures, they were often on the undesirable or uncomfortable side of the spectrum (as they were very likely to be made of goat bladders, tar, or similar nasty things). Besides that, they were often very expensive, even in relatively recent history, with a single condom costing several months of pay for the average prostitute in the 18th century [78]. Thus, latex condoms were a game-changer, as they actually gave both protection from pregnancies and from STDs whilst still being semi-comfortable and cheap to use. Because of this, it's been said that the first sexual revolution occurred amidst the Roaring Twenties, with the Flappers rather than the Hippies.

Comfortable and widely-available prophylactics by themselves are enough to mess with the natural societal rhythm. For example, women tend to dress more provocatively when ovulating, and search for more casual sex encounters during ovulation [79]. This increase in casual sexual behaviours has historically carried a severe risk, but condoms drastically reduce the potential damage that sexually irresponsible behaviour has. In other words, it's a means of having your cake and eating it, as well as reducing the incentives for pure monogamy. Hence, it implicitly somewhat undermines the nuclear family unit concept.

Unsurprisingly, shortly thereafter the Catholic Church threw a hissy fit, by issuing the encyclical *Casti connubii*, which restated their aversion for any contraceptive - a position it has yet to change [80]. The newly created fascist states, concerned with low birth rates, degeneracy and so on, followed suit and created restrictions for condoms by either banning them outright or limiting their sale. The damage was done though, once the genie has come out of the bottle it's difficult to put it back in, and the condom black market came into existence [81].

Then, in 1951, in Mexico City, a synthetic female sex hormone, called norethindrone, was first synthesised from a most curious source - yams [82]. This hormone, which later came to be sold as "the pill" controlled fertility and was much beloved by the "free love" crowd.

Yet, these forays into attempting to master biology carried with them interesting and unforeseen side effects. Among the many health side effects of the pill, an interesting and overlooked one is how it changes the type of men that women are attracted to. The type of man a woman is attracted to varies depending on the fertility of her cycle, it's why bodybuilders are seen as good one-night stand material, but horrible prospect for boyfriend material - a woman's attraction preferences vary depending on the ovulation cycle [83]. In PIII-Ch8, we discussed that there's a spectrum of tournament and pair bonding species, where humans are between the two; where we're neither the most faithful of animals nor the most ruthless.

This is because humans benefit from the two extremes. The optimal evolutionary strategy, from a female point of view, is to get the seed from a male with good genes (think the archetypical muscle-bound freak) who isn't likely to stay for long because he has other options, whilst cuckolding the "nice guy" male (think the class nerd) who is willing to invest a lot of resources and time to keep his mate around, as he knows that he doesn't have as much on offer. Hence, the future offspring get both the benefits of good genes, and a good and prosperous household. Even in modern states, paternity fraud, where the father accidentally raises a cuckold son, has been estimated to range from 0.8% to 30% with a median of 3.7%, but I digress [84].

The pill, as it messes with the ovulation cycle, skews the type of man a woman is naturally predisposed to like [85]. Instead of liking the gruff Marlboro man or James Bond, they start temporarily preferring a more feminine or androgynous look like a David Bowie or Justin Bieber type. Once society reaches a high enough penetration level with the pill, this collectively starts altering the male ideal. Hence, having understood this phenomenon, it's not a huge surprise to see the birth and development of the metrosexual male, as well as the male grooming industry that is nowadays worth $50 billion [86]. More terrifyingly enough this new male obsession for beauty has the echoes of the "beautiful ones" in Calhoun's Universe 25, which were the harbingers of social decline. Unless we discover some different chemical cocktail with the same effect though, the forces driving men in that direction are here to stay. Some males might even think this is just not worth the bother in attempting to score in the ever-shifting goal post of women's preferences and just become herbivore men, or their Western counterparts MGTOW (Men Going Their Own Way).

I'm not being hyperbolic about this either, as American author and philosopher Christina Hoff Sommers has pointed out throughout her career, there seems to be a systematic bias against male traits in modern society [87]. Where masculine characteristics that would've been praiseworthy at any other point in history are vilified and pathologized. Forwardness, desire for competition, boisterous behaviour, etc are all traits primarily associated with masculinity and perfectly natural behaviour. Yet they're nowadays seen as "toxic masculinity" and some of the more regressive types seek to brainwash their children out of this. Of course, this leads some children to feel guilty about their very nature; as it leads them to think they're somehow ill for being a normal kid, and it isolates them from their peers.

Automation and civilizational progress have also somewhat displaced the immediate need for manly traits. Gone are the days where you need to be able to have the physical prowess to hunt a mammoth, or the ruthlessness and bravery to defend your community. As these things go, the male associated traits are trading at an all-time historical low and will continue to do so barring some unforeseen catastrophe. Unsurprisingly, this opens up the cultural stage to the androgynous male, who thinks and acts like a woman.

This is not a simple case of one group replacing another group in the same environmental niche, like the Homo sapiens replacing the Neanderthals though. Metrosexual men are not about to supplant the role of the masculine man as the pinnacle of sexual attractiveness. This coup is a farce. The effects are temporary and women revert back to preferring masculine-looking and -acting men shortly after stopping consumption of the pill; hence, many a divorce and unhappy marriage have happened as a consequence of transient chemical alterations. This would logically hold true, even when completely disregarding that women who either start or stop taking the pill during a relationship will find their current sex life much more unsatisfying [88]. Whether we want it or not, at its core we have the same preferences we have always had, despite the fact that some circumstances have slightly pushed the pendulum from its normal point of rest.

Societal developments can also latch onto biological dynamics and cause unforeseen behaviours. For instance, it's been controversially suggested that widespread adoption of abortion can reduce crime, decades down the line, by reducing the pool of potential would-be low-class criminals [89]. Perhaps the influence of abortion on crime is overstated in the original study, but independent follow-up studies from other periods and completely different geographic areas, seem to imply that the correlation holds true, albeit not as strong as first suggested [90].

Anything that radically alters the biological underpinnings of our species will have wide and deep consequences to the society. The changes will alter the way people behave, and thus their consumption patterns. Ignoring the biologically-driven psychology of a consumer is a grave mistake.

Revisiting our psychology knowledge when making investment decisions might do us well, as it might focus and clarify the path ahead. Maslow's hierarchy of needs, which was first published in 1943, makes the case that humans have different stages of self-development. Only after having solved, or at least temporarily fixed the lower levels, can a person truly focus on higher things. Maslow's hierarchy of needs shows us that for the neurotypical mind, their desires and priorities are ruled by what they already have access to, and will feel anxious unless certain basic needs are met.

The pyramid, as Maslow's theory is usually graphically shown, is divided in five needs categories, going from lowest (most necessary) to highest (good to have to be a balanced individual but unnecessary for survival):

1. **Physiological** - Thirst, hunger, sex, sleep, excretion, homeostasis, etc. Essentially, any bodily function that is not primarily based on one's psychological state, these are basic needs which would make humans unhealthy in the long run, perhaps even precipitating death, if not addressed. Examples of industries that cater to this sort of need, are the food and drinks industry, the medical community and even prostitutes[77].
2. **Safety** - Protection from harm and the avoidance of risk. The potential sources of harm are diverse, like the risk from violence, such as living in a warzone or unsafe neighbourhood, but there are also sources of mental damages and emotional harm, as when someone loses their job or is abused by their spouse. Examples of industries that satisfy this emotional need are insurance companies, private security, protective gear, bank accounts, religion, etc. Generally, any product or service that makes the world seem more orderly, predictable, or just, rather than chaotic, falls in this category.
3. **Social Belonging** - The desire to have the affection of your peers and family. Much of our lives revolve around socializing and thus it's unsurprising that one of our core pillars for mental health is a positive relation with our social group. This is why it's been observed that social

77 Which admittedly has more overlap with the medical industry then we'd care to admit, as there are trained nurses who specialise in helping disabled people have sexual release.

isolation in prison, where convicts are isolated from other human beings for most of the day, can easily lead to mental breakdowns [91]. Examples of industries that help solve this need are telecommunications, social clubs, bars, etc.

4. **Esteem** - The realm of the ego. Esteem desires can be classified as internal needs. These are related to achieving a sense of self-esteem, such as through self-respect, self-control and external needs. External needs often focus on gaining status, admiration, recognition and confidence. Industries focused on these needs are activity holidays, the self-help industry, therapists, conferences, etc.
5. **Self-Actualization**- Finding meaning in your life, be it through creative pursuits or climbing mountains. This is ultimately an unsatisfiable need. A writer will always wish he had written more, a musician would hope to have been more adept at creating music, a mountaineer that they had climbed higher mountains, etc. All in all, it's like trying to empty the ocean with a strainer.

The lower four levels of the pyramid were branded as "deficiency needs," as people do not feel complete if these needs are met, yet they become anxious when they aren't met. Conversely, the fifth one is classified as a "growth need," as it allows people to reach their full potential by engaging their drive to strive to become a heroic figure.

This is all nice and well, but how does this relate in any shape or form to investing or the economy? By determining where on the pyramid a societal group is at, and determining the growth rate thereof, we can determine the potential expansion of a product or service. For example, if 80% of a society is poor and can barely afford to cover their physiological or safety needs, then it's extremely unlikely that they're in the market for a product that can help them satisfy their self-actualization. In other words, if 80% of the population is starving, they're unlikely to purchase a gym membership or take an art class, because they have baser needs. As such, your current potential market size, in the broadest sense, is 20%.

However, if people are coming out of poverty and they're creating a middle class, then you can see them shift to higher levels in the hierarchical pyramid. Hence, the increase in the potential market segment of the demographic interested in your product or service is proportional to the extent that this growing middle class is shifting hierarchical needs.

As we mentioned on Chapter 1 in this section, the modern age, with its consumerism and emphasis on harnessing the power of desire, rather than need, often manages to convince people that they're on a different level of the hierarchy of needs than they truly are. For example, people in the first world often live terrified of terrorist attacks, when statistically speaking they're likelier to die of too much McDonald's by orders of magnitude, than terrorists.

Yet, as of the beginning of 2016, over 51% of Americans were very/somewhat concerned with terrorism, but under 3% of Americans lead a healthy lifestyle [92][93]. This somewhat implicitly shows they have little concerns about making it out alive from the decade if the dangers don't concern terrorists. And why wouldn't they be? Turn on any television and the apocalypse seem to be right around the corner.

The media, as a business, isn't actually in it for humanitarian reasons. Their job is to overplay the freak occurrence which people will get riled about, whilst downplaying the "boring" concerns by not covering them. This works well when you've never actually seen violence first hand and thus it's a sensationalist item, taking advantage of the relative novelty of the phenomena.

Whereas people coming from the developing world have become somewhat jaded. The equivalent of a terrorist attack where a few dozen people end up getting shot, happens so regularly that it often doesn't even feature on newspapers - unless one purposefully searches for yellow journalism. Hence, us who grew up in the third world, tend to be a tad more blasé about the whole affair and not react that much to violent headlines, as we've learned that safety is not always guaranteed, and bad things can happen to good people - I've personally been stabbed, threatened with guns and have seen people get shot in broad daylight.

Be that as it may, we still very much aspire for safety and stability, it's just that we've learned to curb our enthusiasm to more manageable levels.

The same input will not always yield the same output, the pendulum might move in the same direction but not to the same extent. If you offer food to a starving man, he'll do whatever you want for it. Yet, if the same offer is made to someone who hasn't had lunch, he may be willing to humour a request for a favour, but only if it seems like a reasonable trade-off. Nevertheless, understanding society through our collective biological and psychological quirks can help us make better sense of it. We might not all dance in the same way, but we're all listening to the same tune.

Whether we like it or not, we're always subject of the yoke imposed by biology. By way of example, there have been serious studies discussing that part of Mickey Mouse's success as a character that has won the hearts and minds of children and parents for generations is because it inadvertently taps into our biological programming [94].

Originally, Mickey Mouse was rambunctious, mischievous and often even cruel. But over the years, Mickey seemed to mellow out and gained a more relaxed personality, as well as a softer drawn appearance. In essence, he gradually evolved through natural selection to better suit the public he was meant to entertain and charm, because when he stepped out of line "any number of letters would arrive at the Studio from citizens and organizations who felt that the nation's moral well-being was in their hands [...] Eventually he would be pressured into the role of straight man," as Christopher Finch put it in his book on the history of Disney's work [95].

Hence, through these selective pressures, he started adopting more childlike characteristics. Like countless domesticated animals before him, he was bred for neoteny; or, in plain English, he was designed to keep youthful traits like a large head with big eyes, high-pitched voice, as well as a curious and playful personality. Humans associate neotenic traits with positive emotions and cuteness, because if we didn't have strong imperative desires to care for creatures with those characteristics, we wouldn't care for infants and we'd die off as a species in the short term.

Mickey Mouse is thus a symptom of a far deeper mechanism that is at work. These mechanisms are what create our hierarchy of motivators, and thus radically affect how we structure our society to satisfy those motivators. When a certain technology or idea is invented that affects both the implicit cost or payoff of a biological mechanism, society will necessarily change in order to accommodate this new phenomenon. If, for example, I could eat dessert without getting fat and not pay the immediate cost for eating sweets, I would surely eat way more of it and vastly increase my risk of diabetes. The behaviour of almost everyone else would change much in the same way, and naturally society's collective behaviour would change as a consequence thereof.

Throughout the ages, there have been fools who attempt to meddle with these unconscious mechanisms. Of the more glaring and oldest attempts was the *Lex Julia de maritandis ordinibus*, promoted by Roman Emperor Augustus around 18 BCE, which had as a purpose to encourage marriage and procreation via sexual repression and legal cajoling. It enjoined all citizens to be married unless too young, or old; if one divorced, then one had to almost immediately marry again and there was a stark punishment for adultery [96].

Whilst many practical considerations were put forth by scholars to explain such repressive measures, it seems that it was mainly grounded on moral and ideological principles, born from Augustus' studies of Stoic thinkers emphasising the importance of performing one's duties. All in all, this does not seem all that dissimilar from totalitarian states forcing people to act in a certain way because of their ideologically-driven viewpoints, which are impractical, and often incompatible, in the real world.

I will agree that a certain degree of cajoling and force is necessary to maintain a prosperous system, but much like when trying to bend a dry leaf, there is only so much force you can apply to bend it to an "unnatural" position before it snaps. Augustus was too harsh, and too aggressive in this and, as Suetonius the famous Roman historian put it, "... he found the people utterly averse to submit to it, unless the penalties were abolished or mitigated ... The equestrian order clamoured loudly, at a spectacle in the theatre, for its total repeal" [97].

If the circumstances were right, all that Augustus wanted to accomplish could have occurred with only a moderate amount of force. Indeed, we discussed in PIII-Ch8 how such repression and institutionalised monogamy can lead to better and more stable society by reducing social tension. But from the Roman elite's point of view, there's just too much to lose for too little payoff. Look at this from their point of view, back then there was a naturally occurring birth control pill called *Silphium*, the society had become liberal and libidinous, the plebs were well under control so their sexual frustration doesn't present any direct danger to you, and you could buy slaves to have sex with. Under such supernormal stimuli, it's difficult for high-minded ideals about "honour" and "duty" to hold much weight.

Remember that societies often develop under the principles of punctuated equilibrium, where they remain in stasis for ages unless there's a strong enough impetus to change. If there happens to be a strong enough reason to change, the dynamics may radically alter from one day to the next. As such, if you're an aspiring social planner who wishes to alter your society in a specific way, or you're an investor who wishes to try to understand what the future holds, seeing and understanding how people are satisfying their needs is essential to make appropriate decisions that take human nature into account.

Readers might claim that I have given the sex drive and similar biological imperatives far too much influence. After all, how could where you want to put your genitals in any way have broader societal effects? You're not the first to dismiss such matters, but I'll just say that it might do you well to ask Helen of Troy for the answer to that particular question.

6 - The Economic Lovecraftian Horror

"An implausible truth can serve one better than an implausible fiction"

- Cloud Atlas, David Mitchell

At the dawn of modernity, in the early twentieth century, there used to be a pulp fiction writer by the name of H.P. Lovecraft. He was an odd fellow, if there ever was one, as his cheap black suit, sick pallor and melancholic gaze permanently made him look like a corpse for one of those post-mortem photographs that people used to take with the recently deceased.

When attempting not to judge a book by its cover, and trying to talk to the character, the impression hardly changed. Lovecraft was a xenophobic, neurotic and insecure recluse, but damn if he didn't have an extraordinary imagination! His writings mainly centred on what is now known as *cosmic horror*, where humans are blissfully unaware of the darker secrets of the universe. Yet, every so often, someone finds traces of these deeper truths. Led by an insatiable lust for knowledge, they follow the breadcrumbs and they sometimes find what remains of previous truth-seekers along the way. In the end, the deeper down the rabbit hole that they go, the closer they are to insanity, as their minds are unable to cope with the bizarre facts and gruesome conclusions that they can now reach. Then, they're either destroyed by what they sought, or they decide to let sleeping dogs lie and continue living without ever finding out the answers to the cosmic questions.

We face a similar choice today. We live in a world of unfathomable complexity, where every insignificant choice you make is affecting millions of lives in marginal amounts. In deciding something as simple as whether you have coffee or tea for breakfast, you may inadvertently be propping up an autocratic and violent state, as happened with the British and the East India Company. *Your individual decisions amount to no more than one drop in a limitless ocean. Yet, what is any ocean, but a multitude of drops?*

I have my doubts that we will ever be able to untangle the Gordian knot that is the cause and effect sequence of events which is society. Yet, I do believe that there is a deeper truth hidden away in all the data, in all the noise. But trying to make sense of it with something so simplistic as a mathematical formula is simply a road to madness.

Neither am I a Luddite who disbelieves in the march of technology. However, I believe it is the hallmark of an intelligent being to assess information rationally and come to a conclusion as to what extent a path is worth pursuing. Take the invention of the atomic bomb, which to a certain extent might be seen as an inevitable discovery once you attempt to apply atomic theory to weaponry. Partially, I think these terrifying weapons are what has held the world powers from going for each other's throats. Hence I'm not completely opposed to nuclear weapons by well-established actors on the world stage. But I question the wisdom of pursuing the much larger thermonuclear weapons, even as a military tactic - strategically speaking, throwing an atomic weapon on a city does the same to it than throwing a thermonuclear weapon thousands of times bigger than the Hiroshima or Nagasaki bombs.

Yet, in so doing, in pursuing certain avenues of knowledge past where it's advisable, we're opening the Pandora's box of unintended consequences. Certainly, I believe that computer algorithms and mathematical modelling have their place, but allowing such matters to supersede our common sense is akin to pursuing Lovecraft's eldritch horrors - or as he put it in one of his most famous stories [98]:

> *"The most merciful thing in the world, I think, is the inability of the human mind to correlate all its contents. We live on a placid island of ignorance in the midst of black seas of infinity, and it was not meant that we should voyage far. The sciences, each straining in its own direction, have hitherto harmed us little; but some day the piecing together of dissociated knowledge will open up such terrifying vistas of reality, and of our frightful position therein, that we shall either go mad from the revelation or flee from the light into the peace and safety of a new dark age."*

In a world where algorithms essentially trade promissory notes with other algorithms, about goods and services that are decades away from ever materializing; where currencies worth billions of dollars can be snapped into existence by the stroke of a nerd's keyboard in a basement; where a rumour can be enough to spell financial ruin; where perception is often more important than reality; where the trade of goods and services is overshadowed by the amount of money made on betting on those same things; and where we ultimately only have access to a fraction of the available information, we should be sceptical of financial wizards who claim otherwise. The world economy is a creature of such power and arbitrary caprices, that we ought to tread lightly around it - treat it with the veneration and respect that a monster of such power demands.

Much like in the Lovecraftian mythos, the cultists who believe that they can understand and commune with these vast and powerful entities are those who tend to be the first to be wiped out. Financial magicians are no less fanatical than apocalyptic cultists, often meddling with powers far beyond their comprehension, and thus risking the very fabric of civilization itself.

Where cultists have an arcane rune or macabre spell in a godforsaken language, the financial wizards have an equation in a language so complex that only a special kind of wizard, called a "quant", has the knowhow to even attempt to use it to commune with the *other*. After the communion has taken place, a seer called an "analyst" interprets the will of the gods, and a final sorcerer called an "investor" acts on said prophecy, often risking their very soul as they're confident their gods will not forsake them.

At times, they happen to be right, and they're rewarded with riches beyond their wildest dreams, exponentially increasing their hubris and demands for ever greater divine intervention. There comes a day though, where their Faustian bargain for supernormal profits is redeemed, and with the sanguine vengeance of the Old Testament God, they're smitten down.

Such was the tale of *Long-Term Capital Management* (*LTCM*), a fund founded in 1994 by some of finance's greatest heavyweights. In the first two years, it reported returns of 43 and 41 percent - in a market where you would've otherwise, on average, only made half of that in that time - this made them overconfident and they started taking on debt to finance ever more risky ventures. By the end of August 1997, they owed 19 times more than they owned. But this seemed perfectly reasonable to them; after all, their mathematical models said there was next to no risk involved [99]. Hence, they continued to finance evermore investments with debt, wholly unconcerned of the risks that even a blind man could see.

At the peak of their insanity, they had $40 million riding on each percentage point change in the American equity market, meaning that they stood to lose a fortune if they even got a decimal wrong. Then, suddenly and very harshly, the gods' favour waned and its capricious nature was once more revealed - seemingly without warning or explanation equity markets dipped, double what their worst-case scenarios had predicted, and the ride down only continued.

No matter the amount of Nobel Prize winners that you threw at this problem, it just seemed to get worse. At no point had they invested in sound economic principles. Indeed, how could you do that when you're holding 7,600 different positions and you're buying and selling ventures faster than you can thoroughly inspect them? The mathematical formulas were taking the decisions for them, and instead of positions that made logical sense, they opted for financial alchemy and hocus pocus.

It was the quants belief that *LTCM* was unlikely to ever lose more than $45 million in a single day. Yet, on Friday 21st of August 1998, it lost $550 million

- 15% of its entire capital, driving its leverage up to 42:1. By the end of the month, *LTCM* declined 44% -a total loss of over $1.8 billion. It's at this point that desperation got the better of their pride, for they needed to be rescued. They tried all the bigwig's names comprising mighty investment banks and lone wolf investors, but most just sent them packing without serious offers. In the end, the Federal Reserve Bank of New York, fearful of contagion causing a general collapse of Wall Street, quickly brokered a $3.625 billion bail-out by fourteen Wall Street banks.

In return, the signatory banks received a 90% share of the fund, as well as assurances that a supervisory board would be established. *LTCM* partners received the remaining 10%, but it was still consumed by debt. Of the original $1.9 billion that the partners had invested, not a penny remained by the end of it [100]. Ironically, *Long-Term Capital Management* proved to be a very short run affair.

I have my doubts that I'm smarter than any one of these men. But I have the good sense of not "picking up nickels in front of a bulldozer" - no matter how fast or good I believe I am, I do not think it wise to take such uneven gambles [101]. I respect the power of world markets in much the same way as I respect the power of the ocean. When I go to the beach, I shall enjoy its vistas, and perhaps swim in it a while, but never will I tempt fate and venture so far off the shore that it has me at its mercy. In the grand scheme of things, my approach to interpreting reality might seem provincial, but I believe culture has a way of encapsulating the lessons necessary to become a person worthy of admiration.

Think of the timeless myths of old, and the heroes that inhabit such stories. Their virtues are as useful to our lives, as they were to their original audiences. It's no wonder that their stories are being told, and updated, to this very day. American mythologist Joseph Campbell well put it when he pointed out that the main stories we tell nowadays are structurally identical to that which existed 5,000 years ago - they're quintessentially human [102].

For all our gaudy trappings and luxuries, we're still the same creature that existed a hundred thousand years ago. That is the essence of what this book has sought to prove: that the changes in societies and circumstances were mostly that of the path of least resistance. When we read about the Assyrian Empire's fall, the struggles that the Athenians had over keeping an honest democracy, religious zealotry in trying times, the greed of the European powers that fuelled their cultural expansion, or Nazis pressing the button to kill entire populations of people, we're not talking about creatures vaguely resembling us in all but our thoughts.

Quite the contrary, their struggles are our struggles, their vices are ours, just as much as their virtues - we're still only human after all. A good investor is not one who studiously pores over arcane financial data for decades on end, until they happen to find a fluke in an incomprehensible series of numbers. This type of analysis certainly has its place and value, but it should never supersede a good understanding of the human condition.

Economic models by necessity simplify and limit potential human behaviour. Through financial alchemy, they create a *homunculus* - a grotesque parody of a human being that lacks compassion, curiosity, emotions or even a soul - which believes in nothing but satisfying its utility. Believing fully in what this creature has to say about human nature is not only foolish, but very dangerous. By all means be open minded, but not so open minded that your brain falls out. Instead of becoming a financial algorithm cultist, supplement your financial understanding with culture and its sources.

Even something as seemingly innocuous as a fairy tale or historical anecdote may be able to guide us to understand the human condition better, and allow us to make better decisions. In an interesting study in 2004, researchers attempted to explain how individuals retrieve and use anecdotes from long-term memory to solve problems across various contexts, thereby showing the uses of a broad education [103].

Interestingly enough, there were questions to which people tended to get the answers right only if they were from a specific cultural background. For example, people of American descent tended to answer this question correctly without hesitation, whilst Chinese respondents did not:

> *A treasure hunter is going to explore a cave up on a hill near a beach. He suspected there might be many paths inside the cave so he was afraid that he might get lost. Obviously, he did not have a map of the cave; all that he had with him were some common items such as a flashlight and a bag. What could he do to make sure he did not get lost trying to get back out of the cave later? Please write down any ways in which the treasure hunter might be able to get out safely. Write down any ideas that you think might be appropriate. Any idea is valid.*

75% of American students and 25% of Chinese students successfully solved the cave problem. The explanation for it being that Americans found the story very similar to that of *Hansel and Gretel*, whilst people of Chinese heritage didn't have a story that was analogous to this anecdote. The results were similarly reversed with a Chinese culturally specific problem. Hence, the stories and ideas that one has access to make a large difference to one's reasoning capabilities. The study even went as far as suggesting that not consciously remembering the story, but having heard the story and its solution, was still useful enough that it helped the testers answer questions accurately. Having experienced a wider breadth of human experience is useful in the long run, as it cumulatively adds to your available tools.

A good investor is a Renaissance man who has a keen interest in the world around him. He understands the limitations of his knowledge and builds strategies to cope with that ignorance. He never believes that he is vastly more intelligent than the market, but knows that there are ebbs and flows of irrationality that are exploitable. He's not smarter than this vast and powerful creature, but he has greater control over his emotional states than the rest, and can soldier forward when the market is undergoing a manic episode. Wisdom and good decision-making do not solely rely on raw processing power and a grasp on the facts.

Temptation always lures the good investor, just as much as the rest, but he takes conscious steps to limit the possible mistakes that he can make. When he hears the speculator's syren call of extraordinary profits, he ties himself to the mast of his ship, as with Ulysses. In so doing, he knows that when he takes a position, he's going to remain with it for a long time, even if it feels like torture to be there. Good sense led him to purchase these assets and good sense - not greed - ought to give him reason to leave it. As he knows that speculating, and buying and trading commodities at random, is a game of musical chairs where he can rapidly end up without a seat at the table.

Furthermore, in having admitted his ignorance, he attempts the Sisyphean task of rectifying it through education. Someone once asked Buffett what the key to success was. He pointed to a stack of books and explained: "Read 500 pages like this every day. That's how knowledge works. It builds up, like compound interest. All of you can do it, but I guarantee not many of you will do it" [104].

Throughout this book, I have tried to show the story of humanity in all its glory, and all its flaws. I hardly hold all the pieces, and I'm bound to have many of them wrong. But I hold some of the pieces. Others along the way will hold another few, and slowly a picture begins to emerge. We can see the world for what it truly is, a maelstrom of ideas and a procession of unpredictable events. History does not repeat itself, but it does rhyme.

Some people may live in fear of shadowy cabals, but a more terrifying thought emerges after some consideration: that there is no shadowy cabal calling the shots, that there's nobody at the helm and we're all spiralling into random directions because of the vicissitudes of fate.

Thus, never should ideas be held as gospel, in life we're often best served by a healthy dose of irreverence.

CONCLUSION

The story of humanity is an unlikely one in the grand scheme of things, and our destiny was far from written in the stars. There were several events throughout this grand play where our future was uncertain, where we were on the brink of oblivion. Yet, through it all, when there were doubts, we ate them all, spat them out and did it our way.

We conquered the world through our ingenuity, adaptability and willingness to create social bonds with each other. As a species, we developed a strong sense of reciprocity, where we wished for fairness of outcome in all things. We did not wish for a tyrant to rule over us, but someone who had earned their status through charisma, ability and strength of will. Often we didn't even bother with a chief and merely ruled by group consensus.

No man could hope to be despot for long and expect to live through it. That is until the establishment of the first agrarian societies, which severed the direct link we had between effort and reward. Our reach eventually exceeded our grasp when we accidentally jumped on the civilizational bandwagon for temporary benefits. Yet, getting on it proved to be far easier than getting off it, so for the most part societies were stuck in one geographic region, with an ever-increasing population; hence, increasing complexity in regards to social interactions arose.

There came a point where it became impossible to keep track of who owed what to whom, and thus many societies invented money as a means to keep track of the social capital that one had accumulated. Nevertheless, this system only worked on a superficial level. Not every rich man was a saint, nor was every poor man a social loafer.

Increasingly, humans became maladapted for the environment they lived in, but they functioned well enough that any attempts to overhaul the system in any major way resulted in catastrophic failure, as a certain equilibrium had been reached with all the unconscious forces acting upon us. Whenever we strayed too much from the organizational structure that biology had primed us with, madness ensued until the system could reassert itself.

This was the status quo until fairly recently, wherein a new element was thrown into the mix - automation technology. This factor fundamentally changed how societies worked, as it allowed the everyman to have access to such elements that they could've been the envy of kings in the past. Indeed, the titles of old became so irrelevant that the public at large stopped even attempting to gain them for status. At best, they remained a mark of a nation's link to the past; while, at worst, the aristocracy was a relic that far outlived its use and deserved little more than the guillotine.

Technology brought with it power, and it did not care whether its wielder was blue-blooded. Hence, the proportion of people who could engage in cultured leisure increased and diversified from the inbred parasites that had monopolised that role for centuries, if not millennia. With more leisure time and more resources at one's disposition, the dispersion of knowledge and ideas advanced at an unprecedented rate.

In a way, after a certain point, freedom of thought becomes a necessity if one wishes to remain relevant on the world stage - as knowledge compounds on itself as good ideas are improved upon whilst bad ones are discarded. Whosoever wishes to curb that freedom will eventually congeal into suboptimal ideas, organisational structures and technologies and will eventually be outcompeted by those who did not adopt these inefficient frameworks.

Such has been the trend for the last millennia, though it is necessary to say that we might eventually reach a point of diminishing returns. Hypothetically speaking, there may be a point in technological advancement which is so difficult to improve that more insular, protectionist and aggressive societies might once more gain an advantage. Hence, I would not immediately discount the resurgence of monarchies or dictatorships in favour of the democratic domino, as other authors have done in the past in asserting that the end of history has been reached. Far from it, where there are humans there are these innate nepotistic desires to promote one's kin. But that is the key phrase in the argument - "where there are humans."

For most of history, it would've been a given that as long as there is history, there will be humans with all their foibles. If there's anything this book has sought to prove it is that humanity, at its core, is psychologically little different than the people who painted mammoths in caves, and we would be wise to learn from the insights their lifestyle provides about our predispositions and behaviour. But, as of the twentieth century, this became a more difficult argument to make. What it means to be human is progressively being challenged, given that it's becoming ever more normal to alter aspects of our biology which we find inconvenient, or connecting to the hive-mind of the world wide web and foregoing our individual decision-making in favour of algorithms. As such, there might be a point in the not so distant future where simple tradition is the only thing that is stopping us from no longer calling ourselves human; as any alien taxonomist would hesitate to call augmented or purely digital "humans" members of the Homo sapiens species.

Nevertheless, that hypothetical is far into the future, though not so far off that free market zealots wouldn't make the argument that this post-human world has already been priced into stock market expectations somehow. For you see, as with their soothsaying, tea leaf-reading, crystal ball-gazing ancestors, they're incapable of humility. Their delusions of grandeur reach such heights that they cannot even conceive of a world where their computations could be wrong.

They come in many shapes and sizes: the people who read charts, the people who ply complex equations, the people who trust their gut, etc. Some have even managed to become household names, but the successful ones are but a grain of sand in a vast desert, and even a smaller percentage of those can attribute their success to anything other than sheer statistical probability.

These are charlatans who prey on the desperate and greedy. Do not fall into their tangled web of lies. Nobody genuinely knows what is going to happen tomorrow, or the day after that, or any other day. Mere mortals do not, and will likely never, have access to such information. But what we can do is to align ourselves with the unconscious forces that guide our lives. We might not know exactly what will happen in the future, but we can make reasonable assumptions.

It is true that the board and the pieces therein might be upended overnight; but, whilst we are humans, we will still need to satisfy our innate desires. That is the key to making reasonable assumptions on the future. Trying to guess the exact shape it takes will leave you like the Victorian futurologists who predicted the future was dirigibles and steam power - they didn't foresee the future, what they saw instead were their own biases with a century of extrapolation; because, by their very nature, Black Swans are impossible to foresee. If instead they'd have said something to the effect of "people will have a desire to socialise, to nourish themselves, to explore and to attempt to be happy," it wouldn't have been a particularly exciting guess, but it would've been completely correct. As such, if you'd invested in the resources necessary to make that happen, whilst making periodic adjustments to account for shifting technological capabilities, you would've earned a vast fortune by making a fundamentally boring prediction.

So, after writing a whole book on the subject, here's my prediction for the future, whilst humans remain beings of flesh and bone:

People will continue to act human, despite our highest hopes and worst fears.

A HUMBLE ADDENDUM

Whether you loved or hated this book, I would like to sincerely thank you for having made it to the end. A book without an audience is just ink on a page - you are the people who breathe life into it and create meaning through it.

It's been some years since I wrote the original version of this book. Much has changed since. For starters, we're in the middle of the biggest health crisis of the last century.

Fortunately, at least at the time of writing, it doesn't seem to be as bad as it could've been. But the times are changing, I've moved to the countryside in the hopes of escaping this plague.

For as far as I can remember, being a writer has been a dream of mine. There hasn't been a moment where I didn't have some sort of story, diary, or book in the works. Perhaps it was this affinity for controlling entire worlds that led me to have the hubris necessary to tackle a project of this magnitude.

I have always been fascinated to learn what makes people tick and hence jumped into the project with gusto. Yet, even so, it took two years of work, lots of coffee, frustration and hope to finally finish this book.

I'm well aware of my limitations, to my great embarrassment I am and shall remain ignorant of the vast majority of things the world has on offer. I'm sceptical of whosoever dons the mantel of respectability and infallibility, and thus before I leave you, I'd like to set the record straight.

This book has flaws, I'm not all-knowing and might be wholly unaware of a key piece of the puzzle. Despite my cocksure manner of presenting the data, all of it remains up for debate. What I have aimed to do is to the best of my abilities connect disparate strands of knowledge and weave them together to show the tapestry of humanity.

Besides that, hindsight has made me a bit more moderate in some of my assertions. Or, in other respects, has galvanised my views. Be that as it may, this is a finished book, on this second edition I corrected grammar issues, spelling, etc. In terms of content, I didn't touch it, as I feel that otherwise, I'd open the door to myself coming back and altering it every few months.

And that's a luxury that I can't afford, I have too many other projects in the works. At the time of writing, I am putting the finishing touches on a science fiction book, various articles and I'm wanting to get back to regular video production (my YouTube is *Flippant Flaneur*, my Twitter is *@flippantflaneur* and website is *www.richardamador.com* - in case you want to see other projects I've been working on, or say Hi).

I've also turned into a mercenary, I've become a freelance business content writer/ghostwriter and created my own company Inktelligence (*www.inktelligence.co.uk*). If you have a speech, an opinion piece, a book, or anything of the sort that you would like me to write for you, feel free to message me over at: richard@inktelligence.co.uk

Also happy to do speaking engagements, consultations, birthday parties, you name it, if the pay is good I'll show up.

If my shilling hasn't quite eroded your patience though, I'll ask one small favour from all of you:

Reviews massively help discoverability, so please do not be shy and share your thoughts on Amazon, Goodreads, Kobo, Apple Books, or screaming out of a window and telling your friends, every little bit helps in regards to raising my profile and thus eventually allowing me to be able to be a fulltime author in the future.

Thank you for helping me get closer to my dreams, and I hope you liked it.

Thus, until next time, I bid you farewell.

-Richard Amador

Second Edition: August 17 2020, Segovia
Original: October 14th 2018, London

- ἐπεὶ δὲ πάνυ καλῶς πέπαισται, δότε κρότον // καὶ πάντες ἥμας μετὰ χαρᾶς προπέμψατε

BIBLIOGRAPHY

Please excuse the omission of citations in this section of the book. The final tally I have is 528 different sources. As such, given the unwieldy number, I'm disinclined to include the bulk of them in this edition. It would add considerably to the page count, as well as increase printing costs, and the vast majority of people are not gonna check them thoroughly anyway.

Never fear though, I have included an Excel file on the website (*www.richardamador.com/bibcws*) with all of them divided by section and chapter for all my fellow nerds.

It's not only easier to navigate and search but I don't have to fiddle around with tables on a Word document for several hours. Furthermore, I'm betting on the fact that it's unlikely you're going to want to even look at the sources without a computer with internet capacity.

In regards to bibliography, I have taken the mindset that Google and Wikipedia exist. Any easily searchable bit of information or things I deem ought to be common knowledge, I've tried to omit from the bibliography as a whole.

Simply because it is quicker to search it in a search bar than in the bibliography section. For everything else, I've opted to use the numbering system found on Wikipedia, as it's the easiest method I've found in regards to pinning specific bits of information to a source.

Any data dependent on volatile metrics, unless otherwise stated, was sourced in late 2016.

Printed in Great Britain
by Amazon

30876791R00229